THE PASTOR'S PEN

The Pastor's Pen

Larry Albanese

Xulon Press

Xulon Press
2301 Lucien Way #415
Maitland, FL 32751
407.339.4217
www.xulonpress.com

© 2018 by Larry Albanese

All rights reserved solely by the author. The author guarantees all contents are original and do not infringe upon the legal rights of any other person or work. No part of this book may be reproduced in any form without the permission of the author. The views expressed in this book are not necessarily those of the publisher.

Scripture quotations taken from the Amplified Bible (AMP). Copyright © 1954, 1958, 1962, 1964, 1965, 1987 by The Lockman Foundation. Used by permission. All rights reserved.

Scripture quotations taken from the King James Version (KJV) – *public domain*.

Scripture quotations taken from the Holy Bible, New International Version (NIV). Copyright © 1973, 1978, 1984, 2011 by Biblica, Inc.™. Used by permission. All rights reserved.

Printed in the United States of America.

ISBN-13: 9781545632994

*"I am the root and the offspring of David,
and the bright and morning star."*
"And the Spirit and the bride say, Come."
"Surely I come quickly."
"Even so, come, Lord Jesus."
Revelation 22:16, 17, 20

Acknowledgements

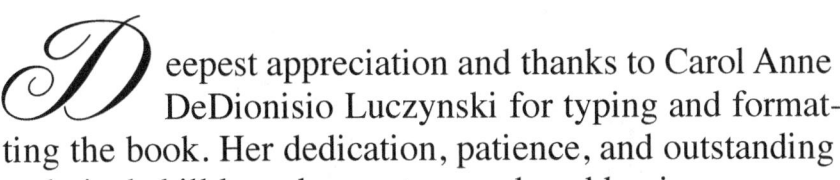

*D*eepest appreciation and thanks to Carol Anne DeDionisio Luczynski for typing and formatting the book. Her dedication, patience, and outstanding technical skill have been a tremendous blessing.

Deepest appreciation and thanks to Jennafer K. Davis for her excellent technical assistance.

The lovely white dove pictured on the cover page was handcrafted by artist Richard M. Rumball (7oilpainter@gmail.com).

1938—2016

*"I have fought a good fight, I have finished my course,
I have kept the faith."*
2 Timothy 4:7

Larry Albanese was born to Italian immigrant parents in Aliquippa, Pennsylvania where his father worked in the local steel mill. He was the fourth of five siblings and the first to be born in America.

At the age of fourteen, a friend invited him to a little Italian Pentecostal Church where revival had broken out. He was saved, baptized in the Holy Spirit, and his life was forever changed.

He was called into the ministry and attended Eastern Bible Institute outside of Philadelphia. He and his wife had two daughters, Linda Marie and Joyce Ann.

He was an Assembly of God pastor for almost fifty years. He pastored Full Gospel Tabernacle in Roxborough, Pennsylvania, First Assembly of God in Erie, Pennsylvania, Assembly of God in Santa Barbara, Calif., and First Assembly of God in Warren, Ohio. He travelled internationally preaching and teaching.

The first two sections of the book are a collection of monthly articles he wrote to his Church while he was pastoring. The first section includes topics like The Resurrection, The Baptism in the Holy Spirit, Servanthood, Knowing God, and many more. The second section teaches on The Bride of Christ. The final section of the book includes articles he wrote specifically to minister to Pastors.

Table of Contents

1. The Vision 1
2. The Resurrection—Our Foundation. 3
3. The Blessing of Pentecost is the Baptism
   of the Holy Spirit 6
4. God and Changing Times. 9
5. How Are You Treating Jesus? 12
6. Commitment Without Legalism. 15
7. Revive Us Again 18
8. I am a Disciple 20
9. The Baptism of the Holy Spirit and Witnessing ... 23
10. The Spirit of Christianity-Servanthood 26
11. The "Make Me Feel Good" Mentality 29
12. Jesus Wept—Then and Now!. 32
13. Saved But Disqualified. 36
14. At Ease in Zion 40
15. Neutralizing the Cost of the Cross 43
16. Being or Doing? That is the Question 48
17. The Day of Pentecost and the Coming
    of the Holy Spirit 52
18. The Unfading Glory. 56
19. Going Back or Going Forward. 59
20. The Church is a Prophetic Body 63

21. He Shall Baptize you with the Holy Ghost,
    and with Fire 69
22. A Tale of Two Churches.....................73
23. Loving the Lord and the Sufferings of Christ ...77
24. God's Two Processes in Making Us: Part 1.....82
25. God's Two Processes in Making Us: Part 2.....85
26. Depending on the Spirit or on Goals 88
27. Men and Women of the Spirit 92
28. Deep Calls Unto Deep or Reality
    Responding to Reality 96
29. He Shall Not Fail Nor Be Discouraged
    (Jesus Never Fails).........................100
30. Servanthood—The Key to Eternal Greatness ..104
31. Within and Without 108
32. Pentecost, God's New Thing 111
33. Two Areas of Truth 115
34. The Power of His Resurrection 118
35. Knowing God.............................121
36. The Glorious Baptism With the Holy Spirit....124
37. Separation and Detachment 127
38. Followers of Christ, Then and Now: Part 1 130
39. Followers of Christ, Then and Now: Part 2 135
40. The Church Under Attack 139
41. The Lost Vision 143
42. The Privileged Christian and His Inheritance....146
43. The Wonder of it All......................149
44. How do you See Jesus? (Going Beyond
    Christ's Humanity)........................152
45. Pentecost, Pearl of Great Price...............155
46. The Church in the Midst of an
    Ungodly World...........................159
47. Losing Appreciation for the Sacred:
    Lamentations 2:5–9 Part 1 162

48. Losing Appreciation for the Sacred:
    Lamentations 2:5–9 Part 2 167
49. Sleeping Through the Rapture 171
50. Salvation, Entry into the Spiritual Life:
    John 3:5 175
51. What God Blesses He Breaks 178
52. The Agony and Sufferings of the God Head ...182
53. In the Fulness of Time 187
54. The Hidden Christ 190
55. The Name of Jesus 193
56. The Unsearchable Riches of Christ 196
57. The Two Great Deliverances 199
58. It Happened on Pentecost Sunday 203

THE BRIDE OF CHRIST

59. The Most Important Book of the Bible 209
60. The Spirit and the Bride: Part 1 213
61. The Spirit and the Bride: Part 2 217
62. The Spirit and the Bride: Part 3 222
63. The Spirit and the Bride: Part 4 226

ESPECIALLY FOR PASTORS

64. The Will of God and the Ministry 233
65. The Role of the Pastor as Shepherd 238
66. The Need for Preachers 241
67. God's Principle for Preparation:
    Galatians 4:1–5 244
68. From Common to Hallowed 249
69. Taught of God 253
70. Honoring God 257
71. The Snare of the Fowler...................261

72. Corrupt What Cannot be Cursed 264
73. From Deception to Corruption...............268
74. The Two Contrasts in the Church...........273
75. The Burden of the Lord 278
76. The Job Principle 282
77. Losing Jesus...............................285
78. The Curse of the Thorns and the Fir Tree 288
79. An Unforgettable Christmas Season Service 294
80. Ministering to the Lord 298
81. Faithful to the Vision: Part 1 302
82. Faithful to the Vision: Part 2 305
83. The Seventh Church........................309
84. Perilous Times 314
85. Speech, Thought and Motive 317
86. Preparing the Lamb to be the Shepherd.......322
87. The Pastor's Jerusalem....................328

THE VISION

*D*ear friends, today you are reading the first issue of our new monthly bulletin, The Vision. It is to serve as a call and reminder that we have been called to a higher calling than anything in this world. As Paul said to King Agrippa in **Acts 26:19, "I was not disobedient unto the heavenly vision."** Paul was committed to obeying the vision the Lord gave him by aligning his life with it.

The Lord has given to all of us the same vision. The heart of the vision is **"To know Him in the Spirit and to make Him known in the Spirit."** It is to see the eternal as greater than the temporal. This is the heart of our bulletin. I want to share with you messages that will take you into Christ and words of encouragement to follow Him *"whithersoever He goeth" (Rev. 14:4).*

As we begin a New Year, it is clear that we are nearing the Coming of the Lord. Exactly when that will occur, only the Father knows, but the abounding signs tell us it is very near.

We are of those who live ready for whenever He comes, be it now or in the future. It is not for us to know the day or the hour, but it is for us to be occupied until He comes. Till then let us keep our eyes focused on Jesus, the Author and Finisher of our faith. As we enter the New Year, it behooves us to examine ourselves and see where we are in God.

Though we have a human nature, as does the world, we are not like the world, who live in great fear about the future. Many are turning to materialism in order to "drug" themselves from what they sense is coming. As Christians, we know the Lord is coming. The world doesn't know this nor believe it when told, but they do sense the future is foreboding.

Much fear exists in the world, but *"God hath not given us a spirit of fear; but of power, and of love and of a sound mind" (2 Tim. 1:7).* There isn't anything more sound on planet earth than the Church of the Living God. Consequently, she must show herself steady and strong in the midst of such troubling times. Our stay is Jesus, in spite of world conditions.

Thus, in light of the world situation and the increase of difficult times, what is the Church to do? First, be a light to a darkened world. We have the Spirit of the Living God abiding in our lives. He brings peace and joy and strength to carry on. Then, we must ever keep the Vision of God's glory and purpose before us.

We are a people of eternal purpose. Our lives have a desired end and that is *"that I may know Him, and the power of His resurrection" (Phil. 3:10).* The Vision is always that *"Christ liveth in me" (Gal. 2:20),* which results in my knowing Him in the Spirit. Paul said, henceforth know we Christ no more after the flesh, but we know Him by the Spirit.

Pastor Albanese

THE RESURRECTION — OUR FOUNDATION

As we approach Easter, the world will commemorate it differently than the Church does. To the world, the emphasis will be Easter eggs and bunnies. To the Church, the emphasis is the Power of God manifested in Jesus Christ by raising Him from the dead in a glorified body. Unfortunately, the world has no understanding of the message of Easter.

The Resurrection shows Christ defeated death and the proof of it was that death could not hold Him. When one dies and leaves earth, they don't come back because there is no escape for natural man from death. Death has a right to claim sinful man but not the redeemed man. While the body goes to the grave, the spirit of the redeemed goes to Heaven. Jesus overcame death just as *Isaiah* prophesied in **25:8**: *"He will swallow up death in victory."*

To overcome death, God had to have a hand in it, for only God can destroy death. With the Resurrection, God showed His power is stronger than death's power to hold man. Easter should always remind us that the power of God is the greatest power in the universe. He does what no other can do. While Satan is the god of death, the Lord is the God of life and greater than the evil one.

It's also amazing to see how God uses the things that are formed against us for us. He turns the curse of death into a blessing by using death to destroy the one who had the power of death, who is the devil **(Heb. 2:14).** The Resurrection was the avenue by which God manifested His power over death, the grave, sin and Satan. It is the Resurrection that destroyed the power and authority Satan stole from Adam. The Second Adam, who is Jesus, did not succumb to Satan's temptations, but overcame!

Satan was successful in tempting Adam and then tried everything he could to get Jesus to sin and turn against God, but failed. In **Romans 4:25**, Paul writes Christ was *"delivered for our offenses."* He was not delivered from our offenses, but delivered *for* our offenses.

Delivered here doesn't mean to be freed from something, but means to be given over to someone. He was **given over** to Satan in the last week of His earthly life, known as the Passion Week, for whatever the devil wanted to throw at Him. Satan tested Him in every way, but failed. Christ's victory over Satan guaranteed the Resurrection of Christ and the forgiveness of our *"offenses."* The verse concludes with Christ being, *"raised again for our justification."*

Dying was not enough; He had to resurrect. If Jesus only died for us, He would still be in the grave, and we, hopelessly in our sins. We would be as despondent and empty of hope as were the Disciples on Good Friday. But His Resurrection guarantees our forgiveness, our acceptance, and restoration with the Father.

Consequently, the Resurrection has given man eternal hope he didn't have until the Resurrection. It has blessed all who believed and served God, both in the Old Testament as well as the New Testament, to the present. This Blessed Hope assures man that as Christ arose from the dead, even so will all who believe in Christ rise to eternal life to be forever with the Lord.

This shows why the Resurrection is the foundation of the Church. Everything the Church has rests upon that one Victory. Hallelujah! Jesus is the Victor! Jesus overcame by shedding His Blood for man, and now man overcomes by accepting the Blood of the Lamb. Isaiah was accurate when he said, ***"HE SHALL NOT FAIL!" (Isa. 42:4)* Hallelujah, Jesus did not fail; nor shall we, if we continue to trust Him and live for Him!**

Maranatha! The Lord Cometh!

THE BLESSING OF PENTECOST IS THE BAPTISM OF THE HOLY SPIRIT

*F*ollowing Easter and Christ's Ascension, the next significant event for the Church is the Coming of the Holy Spirit on the Day of Pentecost. This historic happening took placed fifty days after Easter and is recorded in Acts, chapter 2. It was on the day of Pentecost that Christ gave birth to the Pentecostal Church. He empowered her with the Holy Spirit in order for her to continue the work and ministry He began.

Next to salvation, the greatest blessing the Lord Jesus Christ gave His Church was the glorious Baptism of the Holy Ghost and fire. It was also to empower and keep us until He returns. This is the blessing promised to Abraham so that *"we might receive the promise of the Spirit through faith" (Gal. 3:14).* Its importance is especially noticeable in the Old Testament feasts, where the Feast of Weeks or Pentecost, is second after the Passover.

The Holy Spirit is the very life of God that is breathed into the Church. Without the Holy Spirit, the Church is dead and lifeless, operating mechanically rather than in the power of the Sprit.

In this blind and darkened world of sin and hopelessness, people are spiritually dead and long to see life and reality. The Church alone has what the world longs for and desires. If the Church offers method and entertainment in place of the Spirit, she will fail God and her purpose for existence. The Church is to be alive and vibrant in the Sprit and not given to substitutes for the anointing of God.

The pitiful account of the Church at Sardis in Revelation 3, serves as a warning to the Church today. Apparently, she neglected the message of Pentecost and ended up having a name of being alive but was dead *(Rev. 3:1)*. Somewhere along the way, Sardis lost her anointing and vision, for which the Lord calls her to remember what she let slip away.

The Baptism in the Holy Spirit is imperative to live the Spirit-filled life. It isn't a question of whether or not we choose the Baptism of the Holy Spirit; it is a command from the Lord *(Acts 1:4).* We are to wait until we are endued from on high. We cannot overstate the importance of the Baptism in the Holy Spirit because its effects aren't just for now, but also carries eternal implications.

We live in a day when Christians feel that if a Church preaches salvation, that's all that matters. As important as salvation is, it is only part of the Gospel. Pentecost is the provision of Christ and promise of God and completes the full Gospel. The Baptism in the Holy Spirit is a privilege, given to the Church as part of the New Covenant.

It was John the Baptist who not only identified the Lamb of God but also first proclaimed the Baptism in the Holy Ghost. John received this revelation from God that the Messiah, the Son of God, would come after him and Baptize in the Holy Ghost.

Then Jesus came to be baptized by John, at which time He received His enduement of the Spirit following His water baptism. From that moment on He preached this glorious Baptism in *John 7:37–39*. Then, after His Resurrection, He said, *"they shall speak with new tongues" (Mark 16:17).*

The Baptism in the Holy Spirit is part of our inheritance. With it comes a release of God's power to meet the onslaughts of the enemy. *"For we know not what we should pray for as we ought: but the Spirit itself maketh intercession for us with groanings which cannot be uttered" (Rom. 8:26),* which includes speaking in tongues.

The wonderful blessing on the Day of Pentecost is the marvelous Baptism with the Holy Ghost. Let us seek to be filled with the Spirit that we might live the victorious Spirit-filled life.

Maranatha! The Lord Cometh!

GOD AND CHANGING TIMES

"The children of Issachar, which were men that had understanding of the times, to know what Israel ought to do" (1 Chron. 12:32).

The world is in a state of constant change, which will continue until that which is perfect is come; then that which is in part (division of time) shall be done away *(1 Cor. 13:10)*.

Past and present changes in the world challenge the Church in her desire to maintain revival. Over the years, Church historians have studied past revivals to find the reasons why revival comes when it does. Is it purely the sovereignty of God and/or the result of prayer and fasting, or is it related to difficult economic times?

Some have said we need to go back to a given era when economic conditions existed that lent themselves for revival. While it's true that when economic conditions are severe people tend to pray more and trust God, and the world seems open to the Gospel, we can't go back to duplicate an era of history thinking it will bring revival. **We must find God where we are today**.

Revival transcends economic instabilities. God can work with or without such conditions. He is sufficient to meet the challenge of any era. He is the *"I AM"* at any point of history and under all circumstances, and still reveals Himself to those seeking His face.

In light of this, there are several things to be considered. First, we must recognize there is no socio-economic barrier capable of shutting God out. He's still God and always finds a way to meet His children in spite of conditions.

Secondly, each new social and cultural change provides an opportunity for the Lord to give a fresh revelation of Himself and His glory to that particular generation and need. He is greater than social change and shows Himself as such.

Thirdly, we are called to walk before Him in white, in spite of our environment. Noah lived in changing times but refused to allow the times to influence him. He walked with God in faith and obedience while evil prevailed around him. He found God to be faithful. While the world faced judgment, Noah faced spiritual victory and survival, which is really revival, for neither the Church nor the Christian can survive without revival.

So, while times change and we must adapt, our message doesn't. It's *"the same yesterday, today and forever" (Heb. 13:8),* **for our message is Christ the Unchanging One!**

We don't need to yearn for the past, but we need to seek God in the present for a fresh outpouring that reveals His purpose for our times. Only then will we understand the times in which we live. He wants to reveal Himself through us to this present generation in a new and living way.

With hope and anticipation, the Church must look to Jesus to reveal His purpose for our day. **He has**

something special for our times. Our role is to wait upon Him so we can hear what the Spirit is saying to the Church today!

God grant us the sensitivity and openness to the mind of God, that as the children of Issachar, we, too, will have an understanding of the times in which we live and to know what we ought to do!

Maranatha! The Lord Cometh!

"HOW ARE YOU TREATING JESUS?"

*I*n the times we are living, we want to see how Jesus was treated in His life. *Isaiah 53:3 says, "He is despised and rejected of men; a man of sorrows and acquainted with grief: and we hid as it were our faces from him; he was despised and we esteemed him not."*

Of whom is Isaiah speaking, some earthly king or world leader? No, surely not God's Son, the Lord Jesus Christ. But sadly it is Jesus Christ, the Lord of Glory of whom Isaiah speaks. From His birth in Bethlehem to His death thirty-three years later in Jerusalem, and on to the present day, nothing has change in man's treatment of Him.

While angelic choirs sang His praises, look and see what the people of Bethlehem did to Him on the night of His glorious birth. Bethlehem is a city with a remarkable history. Bethlehem was known as the city of bread and hope in the book of Ruth. It was Boaz's city, the great grandfather of King David. It was there that David was born, and it would become the prophetic place of the birth of the Messiah, the honor of all honors.

Yet for all of this, the Bethlehemites closed their doors. Joseph and Mary had no place to lay theirs heads, and Mary had no place to give birth to the long-awaited

Messiah. Interesting that Jesus later would speak of the door as the entrance to the spiritual heart. *"Behold, I stand at the door, and knock: if any man hear my voice, and open the door, I will come in to him, and will sup with him, and he with me" (Rev. 3:20).*

Closed doors speak of closed hearts. Bethlehem was no longer what her history once was. How sad, to have so much and yet fail in the end for the epitaph is to serve all of us. One's beginning isn't as important as one's end, *"Better is the end of a thing than the beginning thereof: and the patient in Spirit is better than the proud in Spirit" (Eccles. 7:8).*

Bethlehem was also a place of the crowded inns. Crowded inns speak of crowded lives. There is great danger of missing the Lord, when we crowd our lives with activity that is self- centered. Bethlehem missed her greatest hour, for Joseph who was to be the guardian of God's Son, stood outside, and the baby Jesus was born in a stable. This was how God's Son was treated at birth!

When Jesus began His ministry, he traveled in Israel, but never did He return to the place of His birth, Bethlehem, the place of closed doors and hearts, the place of crowded inns and crowded lives. The same holds true for many Churches and many Christians today. Jesus just has to walk away from them.

The Church is so busy, taken up with merchandising the Gospel that when He comes near, we don't even recognize He is among us. We keep pushing for money to do the work of God, and take no heed to His word that it is *"Not by might, nor by power but by my Spirit saith the Lord of hosts" (Zech. 4:6).*

How are you treating Jesus? Do you love Him? Are you seeking to know Him or is your life so crowded that you have little time for Him? Are you too busy for Jesus? It behooves us to pause and reflect to see if Jesus is first in our lives or if He is somewhere lost in the list of things that call for our attention. Friend, how are you treating Jesus?

Maranatha! The Lord Cometh!

COMMITMENT WITHOUT LEGALISM

*I*n the Christian community, the word "commitment" is common and used in reference to our relationship with the Lord Jesus Christ, which is the most important part of the Christian life. We must maintain our relationship with Christ above all else.

Once we have made our basic commitment to Christ as our personal Savior, we go on to deepen that relationship by further commitments. It is in this area where the Christian finds himself struggling and often falling into the trap of legalism.

By way of example, a Christian desires to grow in Christ so he feels the need to commit a certain amount of time daily to prayer. The problem is not in the commitment, which is good and necessary, but rather in what happens to the Christian if he isn't always able to keep that daily commitment.

If for some reason he can't pray that set amount of time one day, the enemy may very well use that as an of object of guilt to the child of God. Here he brings condemnation and the sense of "letting the Lord down," which isn't true at all. The end result too often is the Christian feels he has failed God and gives up his commitment to pray.

A lesson to help us here is found in the story of Israel and Pharaoh. Pharaoh *(Exod. 5:7–8)* demanded Israel to not only meet their daily quota of producing bricks, but also required they get their own straw, which before was supplied by the Egyptians.

God doesn't operate that way; He doesn't demand the impossible. He doesn't say, "now I know you have had a busy day but I still require that set time or else" and then beats on you. He wants to spend time with us but He is not a Pharaoh. While He gently encourages us to meet with Him, He will never put us on a guilt trip! That's what legalism does.

There is a vast difference between commitment and legalism. Commitment is based on love; legalism is based on guilt and insecurity. When a couple marries, they make a commitment to each other based on love. They don't need a legal document telling what is required to have a good marriage. Love dictates that *(1 Cor. 13).* Love tolerates faults without condemning a spouse, and our relationship to Jesus is based on love, not law. The law, like Pharaoh, is hard and demanding, whereas God is love and from Him issues an outflow of love to us.

The sum is that we should make commitments to Christ for prayer and reading the Word daily, etc., but if for some reason one day you weren't able to keep it, don't succumb to legalism and allow the devil to bring you into condemnation. Tomorrow is another day and *"the Lord's mercies* (and new beginnings) . . . *are new every morning" (Lam. 3:22, 23).*

Legalism is not part of the Christian's vocabulary; leaning is. We are constantly learning to lean on Jesus in this delightful Christian life of faith.

> *"Come unto Me, all ye that labour and are heavy laden, and I will give you rest. Take MY yoke upon you and learn of Me; for I am meek and lowly in heart: and ye shall find rest unto your souls. For my yoke is easy, and My burden is light" (Matt. 11:28–30).*

Commitments—Yes! Legalism—No!

Maranatha! The Lord Cometh!

REVIVE US AGAIN

As we begin a New Year, it is important to set our focus on wanting to know Him better as Paul states in Philippians, chapter 3. Paul's entire focus on life originated from that base. He wanted to know Christ in every way. His relationship to the Lord was all consuming in his life.

His constant message, in his writings, was to keep life in proper perspective, by focusing on Jesus, who kept His eye on the eternal. While Paul does not use the word revival, nor it is found in the New Testament, yet he lived in a constant state of revival. Likewise, the Church is to live in such a state. This is the purpose of the Fruit and Gifts of the Spirit, to help us maintain a constant state of vigilance for the things of God.

When we look into the Old Testament, it's interesting to note the references to revival, especially in the Minor Prophets. The prophets of God, known also as Seers and Watchmen, clearly saw the realities of the spiritual life. They saw in the Spirit, what the people did not see and warned of any impending spiritual or moral dangers as Watchmen. While people wavered, they did not. They declared truth, which to them was the all-important purpose of life.

Today, because of the lack of the inspiration of revival, the Church has turned, wittingly or unwittingly, to the myriad of ideas surfacing in Christian circles as the "how to do" approach. It began with the emphasis on a "do it yourself" attitude.

Consequently, we have tons of seminars, books, and programs focusing on the "do it yourself" way instead of God doing it. It seems the Church is hurriedly trying to help God get everything done before Jesus returns, otherwise we won't get everyone in who is supposed to get saved before the Rapture. What silly thinking! **The need today is not to do more, but to know Him more.** And this can only come by way of revival.

Our greatest need today, more than anything else, is to know Jesus better. He gives the increase to the Church, not us. All he asks of us is to trust and obey Him.

As we enter this year, let our prayer be for Him to revive us by sending a mighty revival, born in the Holy Spirit. Habakkuk prayed this prayer for Israel, ***"Revive Thy work in the midst of the years; in the midst of the years make known" (Hab. 3:2).*** Make known what? Himself. The Psalmist prayed ***"Wilt thou not revive us again: that thy people may rejoice in thee?" (Ps. 85:6)*** Both of these statements show what revival does, it brings a greater revelation of God and brings great joy!

God longs to send revival and reveal Himself to us and bring great joy to our hearts. May this be the year for these marvelous manifestations of God among us!

Maranatha! The Lord Cometh!

"I AM A DISCIPLE"

*J*esus, our Lord and Master, is revealed in John's Gospel with many **"I Am's,"** but we as disciples have but one—**"I am a disciple!"** The disciple sees himself as a stranger and pilgrim in this world. His values and goals aren't measured by man's standards or values. **His eyes behold Another,** greater than all. His ears listen to *"a still small voice" (1 Kings 19:12).* His heart is aflame with a passion to know the One who has chosen and called him to Himself. His hope burns within his bosom for the eternal. His life becomes a flame, as a sacrifice on the altar. He is constantly reaching out for more of God. He is driven daily with an insatiable desire to *"press toward the mark for the prize of the high calling of God in Christ Jesus" (Phil. 3:14).* Not position, nor fame, nor fortune, attract Him. He is attracted by the vision in His spirit, of **a Figure hanging on a Cross!** So captivated is he by the vision that his life is changed forever and revolves around it. He will not be disobedient to that heavenly vision. **It is REAL and CAPTIVATING!** He isn't ashamed of being called a disciple of the Nazarene. In fact, his Master lives within him and the life he now lives, he lives by faith in the Son of God, who loved him and gave Himself for him *(Gal. 2:20).* Who and what is such a man? **He is a disciple!**

However, not all Christians are disciples. In the day when Christ came on earth to make disciples, He found many that believed in Him but weren't disciples. The disciples were a distinct group who counted the cost and had *"respect unto the recompense of the reward" (Heb. 11:26).* They went further than just believing in Him, they identified with Him and His Cross.

The same holds true today. Many there are that believe in Christ and are faithful Church attenders and consider themselves Christians, yet, in their lives translate the meaning of the cross to suit personal convenience and ideas that fit their lifestyles. They carry a different cross, unidentifiable and foreign to the Scriptures. The cross they carry is one that beautifies instead of crucifies! O yes, they claim to follow Christ but do so from "afar."

The disciple walks with Him and, as Mary of Bethany, **ever seeking the good part that shall not be taken from him *(Luke 10:42).*** Thus, he sits at the Master's feet, eagerly desiring to learn more and more of Him. The disciple has a personal relationship with the Master. Jesus is his Saviour and Lord, but now another relationship surfaces, that of **Master-disciple.** Jesus, the Master, is the Teacher (by the Holy Spirit and the Word) to His disciple of the things of God.

The disciple desires to go deeper into God. He wants to know him in the fellowship of his sufferings *(Phil. 3:10).* He sees sufferings as identifying with Christ's sufferings *(Col. 1:24).* The sufferings of Christ were not disease related, as Jesus was never physically sick, but He was heartbroken many times, so our identity with his sufferings is also spiritually related.

We suffer when we see men carrying on God's work by worldly methods. We suffer when Christ is used to project one's self. We suffer when worship services are crowded with earthly projects. We suffer when we see the end used to justify the means. We suffer when we hear pleas done in His name, yet losing Him in the process, much like Joseph and Mary in Luke, chapter 2. We suffer when the True Christ is presented and His people don't recognize Him. We suffer when those who should know don't know the ways of God. We suffer when we see those who feel threatened by another's walk with God. Yes, the disciple carries the **"burden of the Lord"** and suffers with Christ!

The disciple comes to a place where he is attentive and content just to hear the voice of the Shepherd. The disciple will be hated by the world. He and the world cannot walk together, but walk on opposite sides of the street. And like the Master, he too will be misunderstood and rejected by his own.

Ultimately, he finds the greatest honor that can be bestowed upon him—the Cross, like his Master. And as he approaches the close of the day, he gladly takes up the Cross for the last time and carries it to walk the last mile of the way with the strength only his Master can give. And finally, the moment comes when he and his Master meet and look at each other and he hears these words from the Master's lips, *"Well done, thou good and faithful servant, . . . enter thou into the joy of thy Lord" (Matt. 25:21).* Yes, by His grace—**"I Am a Disciple!"**

Maranatha! The Lord Cometh!

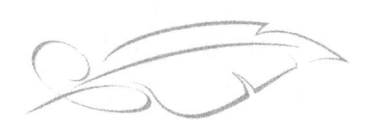

THE BAPTISM OF THE HOLY SPIRIT AND WITNESSING

On the Day of Ascension, the last words of the Lord to His disciples were His command that they should tarry or wait for the Promise of the Father, which is the Baptism of the Holy Spirit. *"Ye shall receive power, after that the Holy Spirit is come upon you: and ye shall be witnesses unto Me" (Acts 1:8).*

They obeyed and waited ten days, when suddenly on the Day of Pentecost, the Lord sent the Holy Spirit from Heaven, as a sound as a rushing mighty wind with tongues of fire. This was to be the birthing of the Church and the beginning of a new era in history.

The word **"witnesses"** in Greek means **"martyrs."**[1] We have mostly interpreted witnesses as bearing witness of the saving grace of our Lord Jesus Christ and this is acceptable. Of course, one can be such a witness without the Baptism in the Holy Spirit. Apparently, there must be a deeper meaning beyond a verbal witness of the sufferings of Christ *(1 Peter 5:1)*. God's call on our lives extends beyond verbal witnessing to being a **"living witness," just as Jesus is the "Living Word."** Obviously, the word "martyr" is associated with the Cross, for there is a definite connection between the Cross and the Baptism in the Holy Spirit.

To understand this, we must see the work of the Spirit in connection to the Cross. First, we must understand the part that the Holy Spirit accomplished in the Lord's work at Calvary; and secondly, understand the meaning of the Cross in the believer's life.

When the Spirit descended on Jesus at His baptism as a dove, it was a sign identifying Him as God's Son and also a sign of enabling Him to overcome the tempter. Later, at the Mountain of Transfiguration, the cloud appears and He discusses His death with Moses and Elijah. The cloud spoke of the Spirit, again enabling Him for this next challenge with the evil one. Because of the Spirit's involvement, victory over Satan was certain!

To understand the Cross, even in a small way, is to know the fury and dread of this challenge that caused even the disciples to flee. For Jesus to bear the Cross required the enablement of the Spirit's Power.

Hebrews 9:14, says He ***"through the eternal Spirit offered Himself without spot to God."*** Anyone who has experienced the Cross in their lives knows we cannot face nor carry it in our own strength. It takes the Power of the Holy Spirit to live the Cross.

"And spake of his decease which he should accomplish at Jerusalem" (Luke 9:31). The word **"accomplish,"** is very significant, for nothing apart from the Holy Spirit will ever accomplish anything for God. Men can accomplish much in their own strength and ingenuity under the guise of the name of God, which will only amount to wood, hay, and stubble.

These same disciples, who fled in fear on that passion night of the sufferings of the Lord, after Pentecost, would boldly proclaim the Name of Jesus and His Resurrection and now had the Power to take up the Cross and follow Jesus.

The sufferings of Christ, with which we identify, are so intense that for them to be accomplished in our lives requires the empowerment of the Baptism in the Holy Ghost. For He enables us to daily take up our Cross and live a victorious life in a world devoid of any spiritual understanding.

This is why Paul connects knowing Christ in the Power of the Resurrection *(Phil. 3:10)* with the sufferings of Christ. Take note that the Power is first mentioned, followed by the sufferings of Christ.

Oh, how important is this wonderful and glorious Baptism in the Holy Spirit. Yes, He will enable us to continue the works and ministry of Christ, *(Acts 1:1; Luke 4:18–19)* but also enables us to take up our Cross and fulfill our identification with this wonderful Saviour, who gave His all for us!

Maranatha! The Lord Cometh!

THE SPIRIT OF CHRISTIANITY-SERVANTHOOD

Living in a world that is given to selfishness and prominence, the teachings of Jesus appear radical. His teachings are not only opposite to what the world teaches, but are in direct conflict with the world. As a result of this new lifestyle that He taught, totally different from anything the people had heard or seen before, they said He was mad *(Mark 3:21)*.

His life was His message, He lived what He taught and living the lifestyle of a servant is the message we get from his life. His entire life permeated His message of servanthood. Even the Prophets prophetically spoke of **the Servanthood of Jesus** and in every place where it is mentioned in Scripture, insight is given into the character of Christ as the true Servant of God.

Isaiah 42:1–2 in particular says, *"Behold my Servant, whom I uphold; mine elect, in whom my soul delighteth ... He shall not cry, nor lift up, nor cause His voice to be heard in the street."* The Father recognizes Jesus as His Servant and notes that Christ is committed to never drawing attention to himself.

Jesus was a servant, not a huckster. He had no wares to sell and no agenda to promote. He came to serve God and man, not promote Himself by abusing His call and office for selfish ambitions. He never misused the power of God for attention. In fact, after healing people He told them not to tell anyone He healed them. **To do otherwise would embarrass God, and Jesus would not in any way do anything that would embarrass His Father.**

Perhaps no greater setting so graphically expresses His servanthood as at the Last Supper, when He shocked the Apostles by taking the basin of water and began washing their feet and wiping them with a towel. It was a scene they would never forget, a scene that would be indelibly imprinted on their hearts for the rest of their lives. Just imagine, God, in the Person of His Son, kneeling before men, whom He created, and washing their feet! Then Jesus says, *"For I have given you an example. If I then, your Lord and Master, have washed your feet; ye also ought to wash one another's feet" (John 13:14, 15).*

To better understand the message of washing one another's feet, we need to know the Eastern custom. When a guest was invited to a home for dinner, the host would arrange to have a servant waiting, with water and towel in hand, to wash the feet of his guest as soon as he arrived in order to refresh the guest from the heat and dust of his journey.

The message remains the same today. As servants, we are to wash our brother's feet from the dirt and grime of this world by encouraging and helping one another. *Phil. 2:3–7* says, *"Let this mind be in you which was also in Christ Jesus ... But made Himself of no reputation, and took upon Him the form of a servant."*

Christ's entire life was one of servanthood and He told us, ***"Verily, verily, I say unto you, the servant is not greater than his lord" (John 13:16).*** Since He lived this lifestyle and He is Lord and we are His servants, He expects us to follow His example and do the same. Servanthood isn't easy but necessary if we are serious in wanting to be like Jesus. The Servanthood of Jesus is the Spirit of Jesus!

Maranatha! The Lord Cometh!

THE "MAKE ME FEEL GOOD" MENTALITY

The Apostle Paul gives some wonderful insights of prophecy concerning the conditions of the world and the Church prior to the Lord's Coming. This is especially seen in his letters to the Thessalonians and to Timothy. His prophetic insights are basically informative as well as warnings. His intentions are to protect and prepare the Church for the falling away of the last days. Paul tells us what to expect, as well as how to respond to those conditions.

In *1 Thessalonians 5:4–5*, he describes the Church as *"children of light,"* or children of understanding. This means the Church should be able to interpret the times as well as discern the deceptive practices of the enemy against the Church prior to the Lord's Coming. Paul knew that in the last days the devil would use the methods of a spiritually dark world and introduce them to a spiritually lukewarm Church.

Paul warns in *2 Timothy 4:3*, of the time (**it's here now!**) when people will have *"itching ears,"* and want them satisfied. In other words, they say, **"tell me what I want to hear, let doctrine wait for another day, right**

now make me feel good and make it fast because I've had a bad day at work." It's just as *Isaiah* said in *30:10:* *"Which say to the seers, See not; and to the prophets, Prophesy not unto us of right things, speak unto us smooth things, prophesy deceits."*

In the world, people are looking for release from the stress of everyday living and turn to the evening happy hour, or some other form of escape. They try anything to make them feel good. To them, immediate relief and being entertained are the major concern, not the end consequences.

This form of thinking, unfortunately, has infiltrated the Church because Christians aren't exempt from life's stresses. One of Satan's enticing devices of the last days will be **"entertainment,"** which has leaped the walls of the world and infected the Church. The difference is the Christian wants his entertainment to be "Christian" oriented. In other words, "since the world is taking care of its own by making them feel good, then Church, why aren't you doing something to make us feel good too?"

Sadly, the Church is accepting this responsibility, which is not her calling. The result is we now have a **"make me feel good"** syndrome existing in the Church. But the Church's calling isn't to make people feel good. The Presence of God does that. **The Church's calling is to present the Living Saviour to a dying world and to spiritually build up the Body of Christ.**

No longer do people turn to the Lord and pray through their problems, they want the Church to laugh them through. This is the prevalent attitude confronting the believer and the Church today. We live in a time when people would rather be entertained than convicted for their sin. **Remember, entertainment will not make you ready for the Rapture, but conviction will!**

Along with this line of thought, entertainment has introduced a "new vocabulary" to the Church. In some areas, the Christians are now calling the Pulpit, the "**stage.**" And the Pulpit lectern has been exchanged for a set of drums or a music board. To complete the scene, people are now bringing a cup of coffee or soft drink and mini-snacks into the sanctuary during service. Then the preacher gets up and gives a short homily and sends the people off with the feeling they have done their duty by attending Church and had "fun."

Some Christians see Church as fun or the place where they will be amused, not where they meet God. The Church is not called to amuse people; it is called to "**amaze**" people. **The Cross is not amusing; it is amazing *(Mark 10:32).*** Calvary wasn't fun. Dying is never fun. The disciples at the foot of the Cross weren't having fun, they were weeping with amazement in seeing the Son of God crucified for the sins of the world.

Certainly, we can have good times and a good laugh together and there's a place for that. The Bible isn't opposed to God's children rejoicing together, but the danger for the child of God is to beware lest he find himself in the grip of the "make me feel good mentality," where all he wants is a good time and becomes blind to spiritual realities.

The Church today needs to exert care lest she takes on the spirit of Esau and exchanges her God given glory for a trite "feel good mentality." The enemy isn't asleep in his quest to weaken the Church. *"Be sober, be vigilant; because your adversary the devil, as a roaring lion, walketh about, seeking whom he may devour" (1 Pet. 5:8).* It isn't just people he wants to devour, but Churches as well.

Maranatha! The Lord Cometh!

JESUS WEPT–THEN AND NOW!

The Word of God is a revelation of God and what He expects of us as we walk with Him. To help us along this Pilgrim Way, He has given us His Word to serve as a mirror in order to teach us His ways. This is to prevent us from missing Him when He comes to meet us.

One of the wonderful blessings of the Word is His promise to be among us when we gather in the Lord's name. We love the Lord and serve Him with a glad heart, but do we realize that the **KING OF KINGS AND LORD OF LORDS** is present in our services? We have the God of the Heavens, the Creator of the universe in our midst and it is His very Presence that makes anything possible.

The Gospels give two accounts where the Lord wanted to manifest His glory. In the first, He wasn't recognized as the Power present to meet their need; and in the second, He was outrightly rejected.

The first story takes place in Bethany, the home of Mary, Martha and their brother Lazarus, who died just four days before the Lord came. God's purpose in allowing Lazarus to die at this time and remain dead these four days, which happened within the last ten days of Jesus' life on earth, was to serve as a sign to the people and the disciples that if the Lord could raise Lazarus after being dead four days, He could raise Jesus after being dead only three days.

When Jesus arrived at Bethany, Martha was the first to meet Him and then a short time later, her sister Mary met Him. He then went to Lazarus' tomb where He saw the people weeping. Here, Jesus Himself wept *(John 11:35)*. While this is the shortest verse in the Bible, it is also one of the most profound. Jesus wept and identified with Mary and Martha's pain, yet He knew He was going to raise Lazarus from the dead, so there had to be a deeper reason for Him to weep.

The reason Jesus wept was because He saw the people were in spiritual darkness and failed to recognize Him as the Resurrection and the Life. As often as He had been to Bethany, visiting Lazarus and his sisters, they failed to see that death had to flee in His Presence. It is like turning on a light switch. When light enters a room, the darkness must go, so when Jesus enters a problem, the problem must go because He is the Answer to all our problems.

Even Martha failed to see Him as the Resurrection and the life **NOW**—not just at the last day *(John 11:24)*. Yes, many of those people believed on Him but their understanding was limited, insomuch that both Martha and Mary didn't fully understand the extent of His power and presence.

There is need today for the Church to see Jesus as the Lord of glory and that nothing is impossible with Him NOW. *Jesus is the NOW God.* He still does miracles today as He did when He walked the shores of Galilee. He has the power to deliver from the bondages of sin, death and sickness. He is the Lord God Almighty! We need to realize who it is that is among us.

The second place where Jesus wept was for Jerusalem *(**Luke 19:41**)*. He didn't weep out of self-pity because of rejection. No, He wept because He knew the consequences of their rejection would lead to the destruction of Jerusalem in AD 70. Israel suffered for her rejection of Christ and her house was left desolate. Anyone who rejects Jesus Christ as Lord opens their life to the devil, who will eventually destroy that man or woman.

Even the Church of Jesus Christ needs to be careful lest she fall into the **"Jerusalem spirit,"** which means accepting Jesus only if He comes on their terms and expectations. The Church and individuals therein, need to ask the question, "Do we want Jesus to come to us His way or our way? Are we open to the moving of His Spirit or do we feel the need to control?" These are some of the reasons why Jesus today is again weeping, but this time it's for the Church.

The Lord saw the Seven Churches of Revelation clearly and sees the modern Church today as He saw each of them. He weeps for today's Church, as He sees she has lost her first love, as did the Church of Ephesus. He sees the Church today as He saw the Church of Smyrna, who had godly people in her midst but also deceivers who claimed to be saved but were of the devil and Jesus weeps. He weeps over the Church today as He sees her following the same path as the Church of Pergamos, who mixed with the world. He sees the Church today as He saw the Church of Thyatira, who allowed false teaching and sin to go unchecked and He weeps. He sees the Church today as the Church of Sardis, whose people once had a true experience but now lived in the past and had become a dead Church, and He weeps. He sees the Church today as the Church of Philadelphia, who were careless about their Crown of Glory and He weeps because He knows the value of the Crown of Glory! He sees the Church today as the Church of Laodicea who became lukewarm and He weeps.

He sees the gradual decline from Ephesus to Laodicea all over again in today's Church, and she has gradually become lukewarm and ineffective. He weeps because the Church has lost her witness. He weeps for the Church today because she has forsaken His ways. He weeps for her today, because the Church wants His miracles but not His Cross. His heart is broken when the Church tries to do God's work by man's methods. **Yes, Jesus wept then and still weeps today because He desires the Church to have God's very best, yet, the Church today is satisfied with less.**

In Bethany and at Jerusalem, He wept because they didn't recognize who He was. May God help the Church today to recognize our Head, the Lord Jesus Christ, and welcome Him with open hearts and make **Him Lord of All. Let us lift Him on high!**

"Who is this king of Glory? <u>The Lord strong and mighty</u>, the Lord mighty in battle. Lift up your heads, O ye gates; even lift them up, ye everlasting doors; and the King of glory shall come in. Who is this King of glory? The Lord of hosts, He is the King of glory!" (Ps. 24:8–10)

"Even so, Come, Lord Jesus!" (Rev. 22:20)

Maranatha! The Lord Cometh!

"SAVED BUT DISQUALIFIED"

As a child of God, we are people of destiny and purpose. The Lord has given us two callings, first, to salvation and the glories of Heaven, and secondly, to the fulfillment of an eternal destiny that begins with the fulfillment of our earthly destiny. *"Thy will be done in earth* (our earthly destiny*) as it is in Heaven"* (our eternal destiny*) (Matt. 6:10)*. How we live our lives here on earth determines our eternal destiny.

However, this pilgrim walk of the child of God is always filled with some danger for one reason or another, which can disqualify the believer in forfeiting his eternal destiny, but not his salvation. Reuben, Jacob's firstborn is an example of this very fact *(1 Chron. 5:1–2)*.

Through one act, Reuben disqualified himself as heir to the blessing for the firstborn. That took place when he defiled his father's bed with his father's concubine *(Gen. 35:22)*. For this reason, he would not "excel," or not achieve God's fullness and destiny for his life *(Gen. 49:4)*. Though not discarded or disinherited, he was degraded.

As a result of his forfeiture of the birthright blessings, Joseph, the next firstborn (from Jacob's second wife, Rachel) was next in line to receive it. As in the Parables of the Pounds and Talents, the Talent was taken from one and given to another. So, here the blessing is taken from Reuben and given to Joseph, who, as the firstborn of Jacob's second marriage, inherited the birthright. The birthright gave dominion and a double portion of the father's inheritance to the firstborn over his other brethren. While Joseph and his sons, Ephraim and Manasseh received the double portion, the dominion went to Judah, as seen when Jacob gave him the Scepter *(Gen. 49:10)* and from Judah would come *"The Chief Ruler" (1 Chron. 5:1–2; Mic. 5:2)* **who is the Messiah**.

The importance of this subject of disqualification is emphasized by the Lord Jesus Christ on several occasions when He told the disciples to "watch and pray." He knew that if the devil can't get a child of God to backslide, he'll do all he can to get him disqualified for God's eternal destiny and purpose for his life.

When it comes to salvation, we all qualify, for the only qualification to be saved is confessing you are a sinner and believe that Jesus is the Son of God. But when it comes to the believer's eternal position in glory, the qualifications are different. On the first (salvation) Jesus paid it all, but on the second (eternal position) we must pay the price by faithfulness in our surrender and obedience under all circumstances. As in the Parable, if we have been faithful, we'll receive the Lord's commendation and made *"ruler over many things" (Matt. 25:21)*. If one fails in this area, he will *not* lose his salvation, but will lose so much that was set apart for him that he could have forever. So great will be the anguish that Jesus said there will be *"weeping and gnashing of teeth" (Luke 13:28)* as it was with Esau.

Hebrews 12:14–25 addresses the danger of disqualification and in particular spotlights Esau, Isaac's firstborn, who took the things of God for granted (the birthright) and sold it for personal reasons and security. This act labeled him as profane and disqualified him in fulfilling his destiny here on earth and in eternity. This is seen when God says, ***"I Am the God of Abraham, the God of Isaac and the God of Jacob" (Matt. 22:32).*** It should have been "I Am the God of Abraham, Isaac and Esau," but Esau disqualified himself. Any other shortcoming probably wouldn't have disqualified him, because Jacob, his brother, was a deceiver, yet because he loved the things of God was accepted in spite of his shortcomings. **This is the heart of the matter. How do we look and treat the things of God, even if they seem insignificant?**

These two brothers, Jacob and Esau, show us that in God's house there are vessels of honor and dishonor *(2 Tim. 2:20–21)*. What makes the difference? It's recorded in *1 Samuel 2:30, "Them that honor Me I will honor"* saith the Lord. That's what makes the difference. Esau dishonored God and became a vessel of dishonor and not *"meet for the Master's use."* Though he's still in God's house, God's plan continues with Jacob, and not Esau, who drifts back into the shadows.

Listen to the words of Jesus, *"what shall it profit a man, if he shall gain the whole world, and lose his own soul?" (Mark 8:36).* While this refers primarily to the unbeliever, there is another aspect that applies to the believer.

Of what profit is it to the Christian if he only lives this life on God's blessing for selfish reasons, as did Israel in the wilderness? Israel saw great miracles in the wilderness when they ate the manna and the quails and saw the Pillar of Fire by night and Cloud by day and much more, yet missed their destiny. They saw and received so much, yet missed out! That can still happen today. That generation disqualified themselves for lack of faith *(Heb. 4:2).* Even Moses disqualified himself from entering the Land of Promise because of disobedience at the Rock.

Dear friends, the spiritual life is not to be taken lightly. Jesus said, *"many are called, but few are chosen" (Matt. 22:14)* **or few qualify!** He has called us to a high calling that goes beyond salvation. Paul refers to it in *Phil. 3:14, "I press towards the mark of the HIGH CALLING of God in Christ Jesus."* He said this many years after he was saved so Paul is referring to a calling beyond salvation, which he kept pressing towards. Paul didn't want to be a castaway. Through Christ he achieved his goal and could rightly say, *"I have finished my course" (2 Tim. 4:7).* May God help us to fight the good fight of faith, so one day we can also say we have finished our course; we have fulfilled our destiny here and look forward in living it there in glory! Like Paul this is our calling too! **HONOR GOD AND THE THINGS OF GOD! RUN THE RACE! AND DON'T STOP UNTIL JESUS COMES! THE OVERCOMER IS THE QUALIFIER!**

Maranatha! The Lord Cometh!

AT EASE IN ZION

It's absolutely amazing how the Word of God is relevant to our times even though it was written many centuries ago. Of particular note is the Book of Amos, which describes the spiritual conditions of his day some 2,800 years ago, and seems as though he is describing the modern-day Church.

Amos was a shepherd tending sheep when God called him to warn Israel of coming judgment. Though not trained to be a prophet, yet he carried a heavy burden for God's people and committed himself to faithfulness to God's call, even under the most severe threats of punishment by Israel's rulers.

He prophesied at a time when both the kingdom of Israel and Judah were enjoying a time of great prosperity. With this prosperity came its fruits of pride, luxury, selfishness, and violence. They felt a false security in their prosperous state, never for a moment believing it could ever end. Yet within a short time, their kingdom would come crashing down for all the nations to see.

The danger was in their lax attitude towards the things of God. They didn't want to be bothered; they were enjoying life. But now God had something to say. At first His Word seemed harsh, but it is His love that moved Him to alert Israel, lest they fall into the same trap as neighboring nations.

In Amos Chapter 6, Amos pronounces a *"woe"* to those in Zion, the household of faith, who are at ease. They are living without any concern of their deplorable spiritual state. They felt secure because of political connections and knowing people of influence in high places (v. 1). But the Lord calls them to look around and see what happened to the other city-states who did the same and no longer exist. **One can't take the same road others have taken and not end up at the same place.**

They never thought reckoning day would come to them so they continued to live the "good life," on beds of ivory and stretched out on their couches and eating well. They enjoyed their music and drinks and wearing expensive colognes. It's the easy casual life. *(Amos 6:1–6)*

We are on the brink of the Coming of the Lord Jesus Christ and the same conditions of Amos' day abound today. Prosperity abounds with its poisonous fruits of pride, luxury and the like. The attitude is to "eat, drink and be merry." This is not the day to be at ease, it is not the time to live the "casual" life and let the spiritual values of our forefathers slip. It's not the time to be spiritually at "ease." It's time to seek the face of God and trim our lamps for **"The Bridegroom Cometh!"** It's time to separate ourselves from the world.

The devil works in very subtle ways, even ways that appear to be innocent so one won't associate these ways with the evil one. We must not forget he is the God of this world and of the "times" in which we live. Satan controls and influences fads, the designing industry, Hollywood (the entertainment capital of the world), television, the gambling industry, etc. He is at work incessantly doing all he can to distract the child of God from making the Rapture.

As in Amos' day, the devil went after Israel and Judah to instill the spirit of ease, so today he has come against the Church with something as innocent as being "casual" to corrupt God's people. The casual scene began just a couple of years ago and now penetrates virtually every strata of society. It's easily seen in the decline of the dress code in banks, schools, the professions, even the ministry and Churches. It brings with it a casual attitude towards morals.

Casual is the "in thing" and indicative of the spirit of ease and false security of the times. What people fail to realize is that what is accepted outwardly today will infiltrate inwardly tomorrow. The devil always attacks from the outward and then works towards the inward. What is going unnoticed by the Church is how you dress outwardly is a telltale of what you are inwardly. It's indicative of a casual attitude towards life in general and spreads throughout one's character. You often hear the words, "Oh, so what? It's ok if no one gets hurt." That's the product of the "at ease mentality."

The "at ease" spirit may appear to be casual but is deadly and can cause the Church to lose her prophetic touch. **It's more than a passing fad; it's part of a subtle trend to break down the Bride's alertness to the Bridegroom's Coming! It's Satan's ploy to weaken the influence and power of the Church, in order to make her lukewarm and non-vigilant of the coming Rapture.**

For the child of God, it's time to re-consecrate our lives to the One who is Faithful and True, and serve Him with a pure heart, so that our lamps are brightly burning when He comes! **Even so, Come Lord Jesus!**

Maranatha! The Lord Cometh!

NEUTRALIZING THE COST OF THE CROSS

St. Paul described the last days as **"perilous,"** meaning hard and difficult days. They will be harsh days abounding with dangers everywhere, especially in the Church. Today, the Church is experiencing a time unparalleled in her history. The forces of secularism have leaped the walls of the Church and found a hiding place in which they can operate almost unhindered.

These forces are anti the Cross and seek to neutralize both the power of the Cross and its glory. Consequently, the Church finds herself struggling on how to reach the world for Christ. Sadly, the Church is moving in a direction she feels necessary to reach the world, but in actuality is nothing more than an accommodation to the world. The world has taken the lead now to dictate to the Church, what is acceptable and what is offensive.

Many Churches see the Cross as offensive to the world, and it is and was ordained to be offensive, but it is also the glory of the Church. Those seeing it as an offense to the world, feel it should be avoided as much as possible in order to not offend the sinner. In fact, some of the leading

Churches today won't allow a Cross in their sanctuaries because it is offensive to the sinner.

Coupled with this treatment of the Cross, some have further decided to change their Church name with a new generic name, as a Worship Center, with the intent of attracting new people to their services. In fact, recently on the West Coast, a Church has changed its name to be called a Worship and Entertainment Center. Can you imagine a Church now as an entertainment center? This is mixing the world with the Church.

It appears that such thinking is motivated in not wanting the unsaved to know they are attending a Church until they get there. One can't help wonder whatever happened to the Church's integrity? Is this the way Jesus meant it to be? Did He not say if we would be ashamed of Him, He would be ashamed of us? We ought to be forthright and let the world know what and who we are without apology or shame.

It seems anything goes for the cause of evangelism even if it means to compromise holiness and separation. The Church doesn't say this but practices it. In many places, the Church appears to have taken the role of an alternative, much like a family club, without cost and offers a program for every member of the family. We have become the new "YMCA" with aerobics, diet programs, dinners, sports, etc. While these in themselves are not wrong, they should not be regarded as priority for evangelism. **Jesus Christ must still be "pre-eminent."**

The truth of the matter is that the state of the Church is in danger today because she has exchanged separation for evangelism. Does this mean one is opposed to evangelism? Of course not, but the convert must take up his

Cross, forsaking his sinful past and follow Jesus Christ and His life style.

In some quarters, the Church has become the new religious corner "convenience store" for all your needs. Her slogan, "Come dressed as you please for a forty-five-minute to an hour service. We offer 'contemporary worship' with loud music, just like the world, to show we care about you and you don't have to stop listening to metal music. We offer the same, except we use Christian lyrics. That's the difference." Yes, the devil is laughing!

With this approach, but in another area, the Church will go to lengths to invent events to offset any worldly holiday, such as Halloween, so the Christian won't feel he missed out on something. **In reality, all the Church is doing is neutralizing the cost of the Cross**. Why do we have to have a pseudo-holiday just because the world has one? Why must we offset what the world does? The answer is NO! We should not have to imitate the world in the fear that we won't draw people. This is not following Jesus; this is following the world. Christ and His message and the power of the Cross are still effective to reach the lost.

Jesus didn't accept a neutralizing of the Cross when He hung on it. They gave him vinegar mixed with gall, which was customary to a crucified victim, to alleviate the pain. But the Lord refused it, in order to pay the full penalty for our sin. He refused to neutralize the cost of the Cross knowing it would nullify His purpose for dying.

The Cross does cost and always demands our all. When one becomes a Christian, a follower of Jesus Christ, he must sit down and count the cost, not find ways to neutralize the cost. **It will cost you to follow Jesus**, just as it cost Him dying for us.

Among many circles of Christian youth today, there is a sense they will miss out on things by following Jesus, so they exchange the wonderful opportunities of saying no to the world, by trying to find ways to serve the Lord and still have the pleasures of the world.

Even parents often give in and allow their children to do what they know is spiritually detrimental, thinking if they don't allow them to do what they want, they will lose them. In seeking to save their children by avoiding the Cross, they will lose them, but if parents are willing to risk admonishing them, even if it offends them, they will save them.

There is no partial or "half-cross." When the Church attempts to lighten the cost of the Cross, it is a neutralization of Christ's call. Neutralization is the same as **"lukewarmness."** The terrible inherent danger of this state is the rejection of the Lord by being spewed out of His mouth *(Rev. 3:16).*

Jesus experienced rejection because His message would not compromise separation. *In John 6*, He did all He could to reach the multitude by feeding them and preaching the message of the Cross of "eating His flesh and drinking His blood" yet they left Him. Did He chase after them saying "Oh, please come back, you misunderstood Me. I didn't mean to offend you; I meant something else. Come, follow Me and we will work out this cost of the Cross, just don't leave." I think not. Jesus meant what He said and stood by His message. If the people rejected His words, then they would have to deal with it. Let us remember, the Church is called out from the world and called to forsake the world, not toy with her. The Church is different, that's why we are called the light of the world, not friend of the world, and it is our separation that will keep our light shining.

The world is doing its ultimate in trying to lure the Church to take her eyes off Jesus and turn to the world for her methods, to proclaim the Gospel. We have one method, which is the same the Prophets of the Old Testament and the Apostles of the early Church used, *"Not by might, nor by power but by My Spirit saith the Lord of hosts" (Zech. 4:6).* **This is still the only way! All others are only imitations!**

Maranatha! The Lord Cometh!

BEING OR DOING? THAT IS THE QUESTION

In the heart of every man and woman is the desire to know God. Innately, we want to have a relationship with Him, as we do with loved ones, yet it seems we find ourselves struggling to achieve a closeness that we desire. Consequently, we set about doing things in the hope of impressing God so He will be pleased with us, to reward us with a revelation or a blessing of some sort showing His pleasure.

This is not only true of human nature, but is accented by the American culture, which is a culture of achievement and result with reward. The truth of the matter is that God is not impressed by our achievements or what we do. He is impressed by what we are. In His sight, the character of a man is more important than his productivity.

The Lord gives gifts and callings to men and will honor His gift, but man must not misuse it for any reason, especially not to magnify self. This is what the Lord Jesus referred to in **Matthew 7:21–23: *"Many will say to me in that day, Lord, Lord, have we not prophesied in thy name? and in thy name have cast out devils? and in thy name done many wonderful works?"*** It is through "wonderful works" man hopes to achieve results and self-aggrandizement.

Results seem to have been the criteria for the approval of God by these individuals, but Jesus said in verse *21* the criteria was not results but *"he that doeth the will of my Father."* It is essentially the same truth that Samuel told Saul, *"to obey is better than sacrifice" (1 Sam. 15:22)* or doing God's will supersedes our efforts. Obedience is doing the will of God and this is what pleases God.

Isaiah 1:10–18 scolds Judah for her dependence on "religious works" while their lives were corrupt. The Lord then calls Judah in verse *18*, to come and reason with Him on the issue of character or being, as more important than all their doings. In the very next verse *(v. 19)* the Lord says, *"If ye be willing and <u>obedient</u>, ye shall eat of the good of the land."* In one word, this is character or being. Obedience shows submission, which is part of character.

God's purpose is to change us and he does this by using circumstances even as Paul says, *"All things work together for good to them that love God, to them who are the called according to His purpose" (Rom. 8:28).* What is that purpose? It is in the very next verse, *"to be conformed to the image of His Son."* In other words, conforming us into the Christ like character.

The image of His Son Jesus, seen in *Hebrews 1:3* and quoted from *Psalm 45:6–7*, is exactly the Image of the Father. Note that the emphasis is on righteousness, which is character. All of God's works are based on righteousness (character). **Again, what we are is more important than what we do.**

Righteousness and character first, then come the works of God through us, all to His glory alone. The righteous man will always give the glory to God, as it is part of His character. Jesus said, *"The Father that dwelleth in me, He doeth the works" (John 14:10).*

When one relies on works or results rather than character, he corrupts himself and will be rejected. Will God still use Him? Yes, because *"the gifts and calling of God are without repentance" (Rom. 11:29).* God will honor His gifts in spite of man's failure (again see *Matthew 7:21–23*) but for one to believe that results are indicative of approval would be most deceiving. Approval is always based on being, not doing.

An example of a man with character but limited ministry was John, the Baptist. This is a man who never performed a miracle *(John 10:41),* but had great character. Jesus attested to this when he said of John, *"Among them that are born of women there hath not risen a greater than John the Baptist" (Matt. 11:11).* This commendation by Jesus is proof that being is more important than doing.

This is not to minimize the importance of miracles, quite to the contrary. It is to show the importance of character to a world that no longer sees its importance but maximizes results. The danger for the believer and Church is that the emphasis on results and works will eclipse the importance of a Christ-like character. This lie is stealthily entering the Church and can become the accepted norm.

In some areas, it has already gained an entrance, where pastors of mega-Churches are often seen and addressed as the "CEO" of the Church. Paul, nor any of the Apostles, would never allow themselves to be identified by the world's corporate lingo. They saw themselves as servants of the Most High, and would never demean the high calling of God by being compared to some corporate mogul.

In closing, let the one who feels discouraged over limited abilities or opportunities to serve the Lord in some great way, remember to love the Lord with all your heart and the words of Micah, *"He hath shown thee, O man, what is good; and what doth the Lord require of thee, but to do justly, and to love mercy, and to walk humbly with thy God?" (Micah 6:8).*

Maranatha! The Lord Cometh!

THE DAY OF PENTECOST AND THE COMING OF THE HOLY SPIRIT

The Lord took forty days with the disciples, establishing the validity of the Resurrection and preparing them for His departure to the Right Hand of the Father. He assured them He would never leave them and the He would send the Holy Spirit in His Place, as their Comforter.

The Lord then led them to the next step, and commanded them to wait for the Promise of the Father *(Acts 1:4),* which is the Holy Spirit, who would endue them with power from on high *(Luke 24:49).*

Accordingly, they obeyed the Lord and returned to Jerusalem with great joy, continuing to praise and bless God *(Luke 24:53).* **Needless to say, they were comforted in hope about the Spirit's coming and excited about what God was going to do for them.**

Many believers are not excited about the Baptism of the Holy Spirit. They don't realize nor understand what the Baptism is all about. Some are even afraid of Him and others embarrassed of Him. The tragedy is the loss suffered forever in the neglect to wait for the Promise of the Father.

There were 500 disciples that went to the Upper Room to tarry for the Coming of the Spirit. However, on the Day of Pentecost, when the Spirit came in fulfillment to the words of the Lord Jesus Christ, and in fulfillment of the prophecy of Joel and the Old Testament types, only 120 remained, or approximately one fourth of the 500.

It's reminiscent of the Parable of the Sower and the Seed, when one out of four brought forth fruit. So here, one out of four remained faithful to receive the Baptism of the Holy Spirit. How sad, that so few believe and receive, when the Promise is for all *(Acts 2:39)*.

On the Day of Pentecost the Spirit fell **_UPON_** them, as He was already **_IN_** them since Easter Sunday evening *(John 20:22)*. Immediately, they began to speak with other tongues as the Spirit gave them utterance *(Acts 2:1–4)*.

The Lord Jesus told the disciples they would receive power and be witnesses unto Him after receiving the Baptism of the Holy Spirit. It's obvious one can be a very effective witness without the Baptism of the Holy Spirit. Apollos is an example of it *(Acts 18:24–25)*. So why would we need the Baptism of the Holy Spirit if you can be effective in witnessing without receiving the Baptism of the Spirit? Also, to what would the disciples and Pentecostals today be witnesses? The answer is that **we are to be witnesses of the Reality of the Power of God, through the Holy Spirit coming upon us, much as were the prophets of the Old Testament.**

The Power is necessary in the spiritual conflict against the forces of Satan. Without the power of the Holy Spirit, Churches can function and grow, but will be ineffective in the casting out of demons and spiritual deliverance. Psychiatry and psychology may have their place but can never take the place of the power of the

Holy Spirt. One never hears of a psychiatrist or psychologist casting out devils; that belongs to the Church endued with the power of the Holy Ghost.

In looking through the Book of Acts, we read how the disciples were able to move aggressively against the forces and strongholds of Satan in a spiritually darkened world, given over to superstition and idolatry. So victorious was the Church that her enemies accused her of ***"turning the world upside down" (Acts 17:6).*** This is what Jesus meant in saying they would be witnesses unto Him after receiving the Baptism of the Holy Spirit.

Being a witness isn't just personal witnessing, but is the dynamic witness of God's power to invade the powers of darkness and establishing the victory of Jesus Christ over the devil, hell, sin and the world. ***"It's not by might*** (man's ingenuity and oratory), ***nor by power*** (man's influence and natural abilities) ***but by My Spirit saith the Lord of hosts" (Zech. 4:6).***

They could now take His power into all the world, fulfilling the Great Commission, for it is linked to the Baptism with the Holy Spirit. Without the Baptism of the Holy Spirit, the Church cannot fulfill the Great Commission because of the influence of evil forces scattered worldwide. We cannot face the devil on our own; we would be defeated every time. We need the same Power Jesus had *(Luke 4:18)* to face the challenges of spiritual conflict the Church has faced since her birth on the Day of Pentecost. Satan is too wise and too strong for the Church, unless we have the power of the Spirit.

Pentecost is a command and a necessity, not an option. **Remember, a believer is a nuisance to the devil, but a Spirit-filled believer is a THREAT to Satan!** This is seen in David's life, how **after he was anointed,** the

Philistines went seeking after him to kill him *(2 Sam. 5:17)*. The devil will do all he can to stop a Spirit-filled Church and believer, because he knows the danger and threat that Church or believer can be to his kingdom.

Thank God for the Baptizer, the Lord Jesus Christ! Thank God for the Baptism in the Holy Spirit! Thank God for Pentecost! Thank God for tongues! And let's not minimize the importance of tongues in spiritual warfare. Satan hates tongues in the Spirit, but God loves it! The enemy fears a Spirit-filled child of God, who prays and speaks in tongues, as he doesn't know what the Holy Spirit is praying through the believer that will hinder his evil work *(Rom. 8:26–27)*.

Now, I ask you the same question Paul asked in *Acts 19:2, "Have ye received the Holy Ghost since ye believed?"* If you haven't, now is the time to seek the Lord to baptize you in the Holy Ghost and fire!"

Maranatha! The Lord Cometh!

THE UNFADING GLORY

*A*s we continue the theme of Pentecost and see God's glory come upon the Church in Acts 2, the glory of God continues in the subsequent chapters of the Book of Acts. Some have suggested the book of the Acts of the Apostles should be called the book of the **"Acts of the Holy Spirit,"** for it is the Spirit of God that is at work, through the Mystical Body of Jesus Christ in Acts.

In order to better understand the glory of Pentecost in the New Testament Church, we need to look closely at the roots of Pentecost seen with Israel in the Old Testament. There we discover parallels with Israel relating to the Church, for Israel is the type of the Church, while the Church is the substance.

Following her Exodus from Egypt, Israel began her wilderness journeys, experiencing the many evidences of God's glory. Her history would be one of miraculous events, which remains unprecedented among the nations of the world. Her lessons are a legacy for the Church's benefit *(1 Cor. 10:11).*

Like Israel, the Church, after the Day of Pentecost, began her spiritual pilgrimage and journeys, under the leadership of the Holy Spirit with a greater glory than that of Israel under the outstanding leadership of Moses.

Were someone to say that a greater day and experience was coming than what Israel experienced under Moses, it would sound unbelievable. How could anything excel Israel and Moses' experiences of the revelation of the glory and power of God? But, *"God having provided some better thing for us" (Heb. 11:40),* did that very thing.

To see this, we want to look at one particular account of Moses coming down from Mount Sinai, with his face shining with the glory of God *(Exod. 34).* The glory of the Lord was so great in the face of Moses, that for the sake of the Israelites, he had to cover his face because of its splendor, and also because he knew it would fade, but didn't want Israel to see it go *(2 Cor. 3:13).*

While Israel saw God's glory in the face of Moses, the Church sees God's glory in the face of Jesus Christ *(2 Cor. 4:6),* which will never fade, but increases as we grow in God. Hence, we go *"from glory to glory" (2 Cor. 3:18)* with the anticipation of receiving our eternal crown of glory that fadeth not away when we are forever with the Lord.

This is the theme of Pentecost, **for Pentecost is the manifestation of God's glory.** The glory of Pentecost is an everlasting glory with increasing magnificence throughout eternity. It is greater than what Israel had, for hers was only an **"an introduction"** of better things to come. But since Pentecost, this Old Testament introduction has now become the **"fullness"** of the Spirit in the Church! And yet, even this is only the **"earnest"** of what is yet to come in eternity!

While the glory of God is as wide as it is broad, in the context of its manifestation in the world today, it is the revelation of the power of God, manifested through His people, in healing the sick and bringing deliverance to a needy world. Jesus, Himself, connected the healing of the sick and raising of the dead with the glory of God in *John 11:4*. In this manner, God's glory is seen throughout the book of Acts in the ministries of the Apostles *(Heb. 2:4),* ministering to the saved and unsaved in the world. The Church today is still the instrument through which God manifests His glory. The only condition is that we believe, if we want to see the glory of God *(John 11:40)*.

Pentecost brought the Kingdom of God to the Church. It shows the reality of the power of the Kingdom to meet every need and onslaught of the enemy for the souls of men. The Lord's Prayer connects these three when Jesus said, *"For thine is the KINGDOM, and the POWER, and the GLORY, forever" (Matt. 6:13).* The Kingdom of God came to the Church at Pentecost with His power and glory through the Holy Spirit and is still with us and will always be with us. He will never leave us nor forsake us. Paul also links the Kingdom of God with the Holy Ghost, *"For the kingdom of God in not meat and drink; but righteousness, and peace, and joy in the Holy Ghost" (Rom. 14:17).*

Jesus began His ministry with the message that the Kingdom of God was at hand *(Matt. 4:17).* His ministry introduced the Kingdom of God to Israel and His disciples. On the Day of Pentecost, not only was the Church birthed, but the Kingdom of God had also come. **When did that happen? at Pentecost.**

If there were no Pentecost, there would be no Church, so let us cherish Pentecost by recognizing its place and role in the Church and the Kingdom for time and eternity.

Maranatha! The Lord Cometh!

GOING BACK OR GOING FORWARD

Once again we find ourselves embarking on a New Year. A New Year has a different meaning for different people. The world sees it as an opportunity to project new goals for their firms and employees, always striving for new markets and greater profits. They view the New Year as a fresh start for greater achievements.

However, the Church has a totally different perspective for a New Year. The Church sees it as another year closer to the coming of the Lord for His saints. She does not march to the beat of the world but is marching to Zion, in step with her Lord and Savior, who spoke of a different kingdom and another world. He forewarns us in Luke, that the things valued by the world are at odds with Him, *"for that which is highly esteemed among men is abomination in the sight of God" (Luke 16:15)*. The world is going in one direction but the Church of Jesus Christ is going in the opposite direction. We live and move and walk in the Spirit, while the world lives and walks *"according to the prince of the power of the air" (Eph. 2:2)*.

The believer pursues a life according to the Will of God as revealed in His Holy Word. The one notable distinction about the Church is that God's Word and Spirit govern her. Our desires and goals are different because we are children of light. Once we were darkness, but now through the Lord Jesus Christ we are light, and have understanding as to the meaning of life and of the life to come.

For this reason, the believer sees a New Year as an opportunity for spiritual growth. Our goals aren't annual but daily as we *"seek for glory and honor and immortality, eternal life" (Rom. 2:7).*

As we look back on the past year, we need to ask the Lord, "Lord, what do You want to do with me in this New Year?" We can't go back to the past but must go on to the future. When God's people move towards Him, He starts a new work in them. The danger is in going back, which will hinder and possibly stop God's work in us. The Lord is constantly challenging us to go on and trust Him.

The choice is ours, to either go on and allow the Lord to build on what He began in you this past year, or go back to the comfort zone and settle there. This was the challenge Israel had in her wilderness journeys. It wasn't easy to break camp, pack up, and go on to the next challenge. Most were afraid to go on and consequently, Israel went in circles for forty years.

God didn't call Israel to waste forty years, by moving in circles and traveling the same terrain again and again. He wanted her to go in and possess the Promised Land of milk and honey, but they choose to stay out. The end result was they died off and the Lord raised up a new generation, who believed Him and marched under Joshua to possess the land promised by God.

Scripture warns of the lurking dangers of going back and not forward. *Ecclesiastes 7:10 says, "Say not thou, What is the cause that the former days were better than these? for thou dost not enquire wisely concerning this."*

This is a warning of saying the past was better than the present. The problem lies in being comfortable with the past, but fearful of the future. It's similar to death. Many Christians fear death because it's an unknown. Dying isn't something one practices and becomes familiar with. It happens and we are forced to take the leap of faith into the unknown and there find the everlasting arms to meet and guide us into bliss. So, it is in walking this life of faith. We may not understand what the Lord is doing but we must follow, otherwise we dishonor Him and like Israel, will spend the next forty years in a wilderness.

Again, Solomon says in the ***Song of Solomon 5:3*** that once you put something off (the old life and ways), don't put it back on. Walk away from it, leave it to rot and disappear. You've outgrown it. It will no longer fit. Have you ever seen people who are determined to wear clothes they outgrew years ago? You need new clothes as you grow; so, spiritually, we need new garments as we grow in Christ. God is always fresh; He isn't stale. He has a plan for each of us and wants to finish it. We must cooperate with Him.

The same thought is carried on in the parable of new wine and old bottles *(Luke 5:36–39)*. The New Testament Church is the New Wine. Interesting, that on the Day of Pentecost, the mockers said, *"These men are full of new wine" (Acts 2:13).* **They spoke prophetically and didn't know it.** Yes, Pentecost was and still is the new wine. Many of the Jewish religious leaders wanted no part of it and preferred to stay with the "old wine," of the Old Testament. They were comfortable with that position. They said as Jesus said would happen, *"The old is better" (Luke 5:39).* **Consequently, they lost out.** The end result was they missed God and lost the blessing. We must not hold on to the past at the expense of losing the present and future. Jesus said, *"Follow Me" (John 1:43),* which we must do if we want to enter the Promised Land.

In this New Year, let us set our hearts to pursue the Lord, even if it means moving out of our comfort zone. In eternity, we will forever be grateful we followed Him. *"He putteth forth his own sheep, he goeth before them" (John 10:4).* Don't be fearful or afraid of what others will think. What each must settle in their heart is, **"What does the Lord require of me?"**

Maranatha! The Lord Cometh!

THE CHURCH IS A PROPHETIC BODY

*F*or many years, ministers and students of the Bible have studied the early Church, searching to discover its "secret" of power. Some, thinking it was their simple form of government tried to imitate it to no avail. Others thought the key was their fellowship, still others thought it was her commune living. Then, in an attempt to be like the early Church, these ideas were tried and eventually became unworkable and ultimately forsaken.

The key is obvious in the words of the Lord Jesus Christ, *"Tarry . . . until ye be endued with power form on high" (Luke 24:49).* This they did and then on the Day of Pentecost received the glorious Baptism of the Holy Ghost. It was from that point, that they saw the power of God manifest with signs and wonders following and went forth propagating the Gospel.

The Church followed the Lord's example, who also was *"anointed with the Holy Ghost and power: who went about doing good, and healing all that were oppressed by the devil; for God was with Him"(Acts 10:38).*

While on earth, Jesus' ministry was that of Prophet, just as Moses prophesied in *Deut. 18:15.* As Prophet, for Him to be effective, He had to be anointed which occurred at Jesus' baptism by John the Baptist, when the Spirit came on Him as a dove as He came up out of Jordan.

After His Ascension, the Church, His Mystical Body, was to fill His role and go forth into all the world making disciples *(Mark 16:15)*. But she could not until she received the same power that the Lord possessed, otherwise she would fail.

Following her anointing on the Day of Pentecost, the Church became a Prophetic Body. Jesus, as an individual was a Prophet. The Church, as a body, has the same anointing as He had, and in His stead here on earth, represents Him in life and ministry as His Prophetic Body. In this calling, the Church is the voice of God in the midst of a darkened world, proclaiming the victory and triumph of Jesus over the devil, the world, sin, death and Hell. To do this you need power, and the Church's power is the same as Jesus'—the power of the Holy Ghost.

God meant for every member of the Body of Christ to be endued with this power in order to be prophetic. For this reason the *"gates of Hell shall not prevail" (Matt. 16:18)*. Paul addresses the prophetic nature of the Church when he speaks of the gifts of the Spirit in *1 Corinthians 14:31–32*.

Once again, let's look at another moment in the ministry of Moses. In *Number 11* we have the account of the Spirit (anointing) being taken or lifted from him and shared with the Seventy Elders *(v. 16–17, 25)*. When they gathered around the Tabernacle, two of the elders were missing *(v. 26)*, yet the Spirit also came on them in the camp *(v. 26)*. Joshua felt this was an affront to Moses and called to forbid them.

Gallantly, Moses responds with a statement to Joshua, which becomes a prayer, *"Enviest thou for my sake? would God that all the LORD's people were prophets, and that the LORD would put His Spirit upon them!" (v. 29).* **Notice the exclamation point.** This prayer was answered on the Day of Pentecost. Today, the people of God have this privilege and right to be anointed with the power of the Holy Ghost, so that we can be the prophetic people of God.

To understand what this means, we need to understand the **call,** the **equipping**, and the **role** of the prophet.

The call of the prophet is not the consequence of anything the prophet himself does. It is the sovereign choice of God *(see Amos 7:14–15)*. The Lord chooses whom He wants, based on His wisdom *(Eph. 1:4).* No man can call himself to be a prophet (although some try) *(Heb. 5:4).* The Lord's call and appointments for positions and ministries are sovereign. The Lord decides who, and where, and what, one is to do.

The equipping of the prophet has to be something from God, who calls the man. God equips the man He calls. Paul says the same in *1 Tim 1:12*, how the Lord called him and *"enabled me"* to the ministry. The equipping is the empowering of the Holy Spirit or infilling of the Spirit, for no man can do the work of God without it being inspired and led by the Holy Spirit.

Now that the prophet has his call and has been equipped, he is ready to fulfill **his role** as prophet and do the Lord's bidding. The prophet continually stands ready to do whatever is required of him by the Lord. He no longer lives for himself. He lives to serve the God who called him and whom he represents. This is exactly the role the Lord means for the Church in order to be prophetic. The Church must not forget her calling and live only for her Lord.

The prophet will face dangers and distractions to deter the fulfilling of his call *(see **1 Kings 13:20–23**)*. He must be resolute in doing the Lord's will. So, the Church will face dangers and distractions but must remain resolute to stand fast in the faith without wavering. As the prophet cannot waver, nor can the Church, for with each waver comes a weakening of his call and purpose.

The prophet was first known as a Seer **(1 Samuel 9:9)**. As See-r, the prophet saw what the average person didn't see. The Lord revealed truth or events to the prophet, by either speaking to him or through a vision, and he was to proclaim what he saw, nothing more nor less **(1 Sam. 3:18)**. John said **(1 John 1:3)** *"That which we have seen and heard declare we unto you."* The "we," refers to the Apostles, who were also prophets **(Eph. 3:5)**. In fact, the Apostles embodied all five ministry gifts as listed in **Eph. 4:11**.

His primary role is to be the oracle or mouthpiece of God, as he speaks in behalf of God to men. He receives a word from the Lord and then speaks it to the people. He must not fear, nor must the Church be afraid, to dispense the message the Lord gives him **(Jer. 1:8)**. If the Lord sends him, the Lord will back him up. The prophet must be clear and direct, and the Church must also be clear and direct **(1 Cor. 14:8)** without any "uncertain sound."

The Church must know God so that the world will know exactly where the Lord and His Church stand on spiritual and moral issues. She must be faithful in discharging the Lord's message for a dying world and to those asleep in her midst. Neither the prophet nor the Church can afford to be "politically correct," they must

THE PASTOR'S PEN

be "message correct" at any price, for the consequence of compromise is too severe.

Then the prophet is a man of signs and wonders. He is a man of deep intercession as was Samuel, who received answers to his prayers. Men like Elijah and Elisha were part of incredible miracles. The Church must be a praying Body to be effective prophetically. When the early Church got together, they always had a prayer meeting that ended with results. They knew how to touch God, with signs and wonders being the norm *(Heb. 2:4).*

Those Spirit-filled prayer meetings are what brought the power of God into action. The early Church was made up of men and women of deep commitment to prayer and fasting (not feasting). As His Church, they understood they were to be His witnesses and represent Him on earth *(Acts 1:8),* while He is away in Heaven. This witness is also called **"the testimony of Jesus IS THE SPIRIT OF PROPHECY" (Rev. 19:10).** This verse thus confirms that the Church is a prophetic body with the Spirit of prophecy of Jesus and the anointing of God.

The message of the prophet was virtually always one of repentance; a call to return to God; to tear their garments or the things they got all wrapped up in; and impending judgment. The Church must not let up on the same message in these last days. The Church is called to and must be prophetic in these closing times of history just before the Lord's Coming.

The world must hear the message that Jesus Christ is coming back and the Church must awaken to righteousness that demands a renewed surrender and consecration to the Lord Jesus Christ. We must not copy the world for results nor view the Church as a corporation with achieved goals. We have one goal and that is to know

Jesus Christ in a personal relationship and represent Him in truth to a dying world. Goal setting is the world's way. Obedience to the Spirit is God's way. God's way is slower and takes longer, but it's sure and the results are eternal.

Maranatha! The Lord Cometh!

"HE SHALL BAPTIZE YOU WITH THE HOLY GHOST, AND WITH FIRE"

The Day of Pentecost is the commemoration of the Coming of the Holy Spirit on the 120 disciples in the Upper Room. In this article we want to look at the blessing of Pentecost and its message to our hearts.

It begins with John the Baptist, the forerunner of the Lord Jesus, who had a three-fold ministry. First, the Lord sent him to prepare the way as Christ's herald. Secondly, he was to identify the Messiah, the Son of God, which he did in *John 1:29–36*. Thirdly, he was to reveal Christ as the Lamb of God, the Savior of the world, and the Baptizer of the Holy Ghost and fire in *Matthew 3:11–12*. Of these, there has always been a question as to what the "fire," meant with the Baptism of the Holy Spirit.

Once again, the Old Testament will interpret the New Testament and when we look there, we have the answer. In *Judges 6*, we read how the Lord called Gideon to deliver Israel from the oppression of the Midianites. An angel appeared to him saying, *"have not I sent thee"* (v. 14) and assured him saying, *"Surely I will be with thee" (v. 16)*. It is comforting to know that whoever the Lord sends, He accompanies.

Gideon then kills and dresses a kid, and with broth and unleavened cakes, is told to put them on a rock *(v. 20)*. The angel then extends his hand with the staff in it and touches the flesh and unleavened cakes and **fire comes out of the rock and consumes the flesh** *(v. 21)*.

The rock speaks of Jesus, our Rock and the fire out of the rock, speaks of the Spirit coming from Jesus. In Moses' day, it was water that came out of the Rock, symbolizing the Holy Spirit, and here it is fire coming out of the Rock. Both water and fire are types of the Holy Spirit. Jesus is the Baptizer of the Holy Spirit, and as John said, *"He shall baptize you with the Holy Ghost and fire" (Matt. 3:11),* showing the Spirit comes from Christ, who sent the Spirit to the Upper Room upon His return to Heaven.

Judges 6:21 shows the purpose of fire associated with the Baptism of the Holy Spirit. It is to **"consume the flesh,"** which means all man's self-efforts, regardless of how well intentioned they may be. God will not accept anything done, even if done in His name, if it is not in the Spirit. *"That which is born of the flesh is flesh; and that which is born of the spirit is spirit" (John 3:6).*

In turning to the next chapter, *Judges 7*, we see the result of the power of the Spirit in delivering Israel from the Midianites. The Lord used a most unlikely method by working through Gideon's three hundred men out of 32,000. In the natural, or the flesh, this seemed not only impossible but also ridiculous, yet in the Spirit, it was mighty. Gideon took the battle without losing a man. God does more in a moment by His Spirit, than men can do with their ingenuity in a lifetime.

The Lord does not depend on the flesh for anything, because it is corrupted and influenced by man's sinful nature. This is exactly what the flesh is—a display of man's sinful nature. We must realize there is enmity between the flesh and the Spirit, as they are contrary to each other *(Gal. 5:17)*.

There are the two forces in us that are in a constant struggle. The one pulls us down to earthly things, while the other pulls us upward to heavenly things. One brings into bondage, and the other into the liberty of the Spirit.

Flesh is the throne of sin in man. It is the natural part of man, with the ability to take on various forms, including a religious form. The enemy uses the religious form, to deceive the child of God into believing it is spiritual. This religious form is subtle and deceptive, and while it is made to look spiritual, it is only an outward "makeup" that appears genuine to impress people.

Anything of the flesh always ends in spiritual death, for it must die in some way. For this reason, we need the power of the Spirit, which comes with the Baptism of the Holy Ghost, to consume flesh, the self-life, making way for the Spirit to be sovereign in and through us.

No flesh can stand in His Presence, as God will not tolerate flesh. This is why we must first be born again, for here is where the spiritual life begins. You can't do anything until you are first born into God's Kingdom. In salvation, we see the first workings of the Spirit in one's life, for it is the Spirit who convicts of sin, and then plants God's seed in our hearts to bring us to salvation. We are born again by the Spirit and accepted by God because we are of the Spirit. Anything other than by His Sprit is rejected *(Heb. 6:8)*.

After we are born again, and have the divine nature of God, we now pray to the Lord to be baptized with the Holy Spirit. The Baptism takes us into God and works within us, to consume all fleshly desires and methods, in living the spiritual life. You don't need the Baptism of the Holy Spirit to live a religious life. Religion is a distortion of truth, but the child of God has been called to the Spirit-filled life. Paul said, ***"Walk in the Spirit, and ye shall not fulfill the lust of the flesh" (Gal. 5:16),*** because the Holy Spirit, as fire, is ever at work burning up the works and influence of flesh in our lives. The Spirit-filled life is the call of God for all His children.

Words are inadequate to express the importance of the baptism of the Holy Spirit for God's children. It is our Inheritance, now in part or earnest, and in eternity forever.

I encourage all who read this article, ***"Have ye received the Holy Ghost since ye believed?" (Acts 19:2)*** If not, then seek the Lord to baptize you in the Holy Ghost and fire!

Maranatha! The Lord Cometh!

A TALE OF TWO CHURCHES

The first three chapters of the Book of Revelation are very important, for in them we see a description of the Church down through the ages as the Lord sees them. These three chapters are relevant to the things John, *"hast seen, and the things which are, and the things which shall be hereafter" (Rev. 1:19).* His message reveals the condition of the Seven Churches, which were contemporary in his day, and the conditions that will exist after John is gone. The revelation given John shows the road the Church will take in history until the Lord returns. The messages to the Churches are warnings to the believer **"he that hath an ear to hear,"** to know how to keep his heart sensitive to the voice of the Spirit. The messages to the Churches were contemporary, prophetic, and historic as documented in Church history, proving the accuracy of this revelation.

In this article, we want to make a comparative overview of the Church at Ephesus, the first Church addressed in Revelation 2, as the paradigm of the early Church, and the Church of Laodicea, as the paradigm of the end-time Church. These two Churches are antithesis to each other.

The early Church (as seen in Ephesus) was a Church with a deep and great love for the Lord. Consequently, she was on fire for God with many wonderful works, and even a standard for judging the authenticity of ministries. She had been faithful and relentless in laboring for the Lord, even in the midst of persecution. The early Church was an active and aggressive Church, who would not allow any impurity in her midst, having learned the lesson from the judgment of Ananias and Saphira, who lied to the Holy Ghost. They preached and lived a separated life from the world and had nothing to do with the idolatry of the times. They protected and preached the Christian faith as delivered by the Apostles.

In the Lord's reproof to the early Church, we see she once had something that now was lost. She had a quality that distinguished her as a standard of what the Lord really expects from every Church and Church period, including the individual believer. That quality was her love for her Lord, which is the principal thing.

The historic accounts of the martyrs of the early Church show the love the early believers had for the One they loved the most in life, counting it a privilege to give their lives for Christ. They loved Him deeply and with all their hearts.

Now, as we look at the end-time Church or the latter day Church as seen in the Church of Laodicea, the last of the seven Churches, we see a totally different picture. She is totally opposite to Ephesus, the early Church paradigm. Though she calls herself the Church, her spiritual state is deplorable. She is the complacent, self-satisfied, lukewarm Church. She has lost all her spiritual attributes and now has a name without a relationship. For all practical purposes she has in essence, divorced herself from her Lord without realizing it. The word love is mentioned once and is from the Lord, expressing His constant love for her *(Rev. 3:19),* in spite of her lost love for Him.

From the conditions of these two Churches, separated by 2,000 years, it's easy to see how through the years, the Church gradually went astray, until today she is almost unrecognizable from what she was born to be on the Day of Pentecost.

She no longer revels in her love for her Lord, but in her "successes." She now has an **increase of material goods**, money, beautiful buildings, and has become independent. She no longer needs faith; she has discovered that she can do God's work with modern day techniques and gimmicks.

Unfortunately, she didn't realize her loss of spiritual vigor and life. Being lukewarm shows mixture with the world has entered her doors and robbed her of her spiritual vision. She had one foot in the world and the other in Church. This neutralized her effectiveness and weakened her testimony.

Her great mistake was in **neglecting the Word of God.** Had she hidden God's Word in her heart, she would have known Jesus' warning about the conditions of the last days, when He said in *Matthew 24:12, "And because iniquity shall abound, the love of many shall wax cold."* This would have alerted her to guard her love only for the Lord.

This overview shows the one major difference between the Early Church and the End-time Church. **The Early Church loved the Lord with all her heart, whereas the End-time Church is in love with herself.**

The greatest need in the Church today is to again fall in love with the Lord Jesus Christ. As the Bride, in Song of Solomon, out of her deep love for the Lord, sought everywhere for Him, so should we search for Him. The Holy Spirit, who is preparing us for Him, will help us love Him again with the first love.

The first commandment is, *"Thou shalt love the Lord thy God with all thine heart, and with all thy soul, and with all they mind" (Matt. 22:37).*

Maranatha! The Lord Cometh!

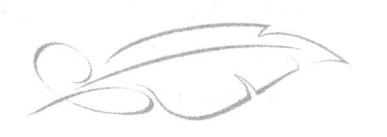

LOVING THE LORD AND THE SUFFERINGS OF CHRIST

This month's article is a follow-up to last month's article "A Tale of Two Churches", in which we saw a difference between the early Church and the present-day Church. The difference was centered in the relationship of each of these two Churches to the Lord. The focus was on the love of the early Church for the Lord, in contrast to the latter day Church, which is in love with herself.

In this article, we want to see what is the one necessary or essential ingredient to bring us to the same loving relationship with the Lord Jesus Christ, as the Beginning and early Church possessed? We want to find the key to loving Him as they did, especially as we are living in the last days of this Dispensation and what is the one abiding truth, that can help us love Him and know Him as never before? It is a truth that is hardly preached today, at least in our affluent society, so essential, and yet so neglected.

To discover this wonderful truth, we need to begin with what I call **The Beginning Church *(1 John 1:1)*.** This includes the Apostles and the believers in Jerusalem, who saw Jesus in the flesh and the events of the Crucifixion, and became Christians after the Resurrection.

What I mean by the Beginning Church, is the nucleus of believers that began with Jesus and remained faithful to Him through His passion. The original is the pristine core of believers, who became the seed and the very heart beat of Christ, from the moment of His Death to His Resurrection. The Beginning Church is the first fruits of the Church, from which comes the early Church, to the existing Church of today.

***Eph. 2:19–20* says,** *"the household of God* (the Church); *And are built upon the foundation of the apostles and prophets, Jesus Christ Himself being the chief corner stone."* In this context, the specific roles of the Apostles and the Prophets appear to this wonderful and amazing body known as the Church. The prophets gave their witness by prophetic word and types, which were fulfilled in the New Testament, whereas the foundation of the Apostles isn't prophetic or by type. The *"foundation of the apostles,"* upon which the Church is built, is their eyewitness account of the sufferings of Christ. Their foundation is their testimony of what they saw, which John refers to in *1 John 1:1–3, "That which was from the beginning, which we have heard, which we have SEEN with our eyes, which we have LOOKED upon, and our hands have handled of the Word of life ... we have seen it, and bear WITNESS ... That which we have seen and heard DECLARE we unto you."*

This sheds light on *Acts 1:8, "ye shall be witnesses unto Me."* Witnesses of what? They are the original eyewitnesses of the sufferings of Christ. It was their message then, and still remains the central message of the Church till He comes again, that the world may know what a Saviour we have in the Lord Jesus Christ.

The Church has one message, which is, Jesus Christ and Him crucified *(1 Cor. 2:2)* and Resurrected.

This is what He meant when He refers to being lifted upon the Cross *(John 3:14).* It is the message of the sufferings Christ that "pricks" the heart of sinners and draws them to Christ *(Acts 2:37).*

The strength of the Church rests in her identity with the sufferings of Christ. The role of Pastors, like that of the Apostles, is by the Spirit, to lead their people to know Christ in the fellowship of His sufferings.

The Apostles and first disciples saw the Lord condemned before Pilate and the jeering mob. They saw Him bleeding from the scourging and carrying the Cross through the streets of Jerusalem. They saw when they nailed His hands and feet to the Cross, and the crown of thorns on His head, with His precious blood flowing down His face. **They never forgot.** From that day, whenever they closed their eyes, they saw those scenes again and again, though they didn't understand what it all meant until after the resurrection. They knew He did it all from a loving heart for them and all mankind.

All who knew Him and believed in Him before the Crucifixion, as Mary, Martha and Lazarus, Mary Magdalene, the Apostles, and others, loved Him even before He died on the Cross. After what they witnessed and saw that day, their love for Him had no limits, insomuch that they were willing to die for Him, for they *"loved not their lives unto the death" (Rev. 12:11).* As the Word says, *"perfect love casteth out fear" (1 John 4:18).* Now, their love for Him cast out all fears they may have had before the Resurrection. They loved Him too much to fear man or devil.

As they thought of those terrible events, they felt a debt they could not pay, and seeing Him suffer such a terrible death for their salvation, could they, or any Christian for that matter, in any Church era, offer Him less than their entire life and being? Words could not express the depth of their gratitude. Living and dying for Him would be the only way.

This takes us back to the original question, **"how could the early Church love Him so much, in comparison to the Last Day Church, and how can we today, though distanced by two thousand years, love Him the same as they did back then?"** The answer is because the Beginning and early Church never forgot His sufferings, which stayed alive forever in their heart and memories. They considered any suffering for His name was an honor, in spite of cost or persecution *(Acts 5:41)*. They loved Him but also felt they owed Him, as do all of us. Their thoughts were, **"He came to identify and die for us, can we do less than identify with Him, by gladly bearing any suffering for His name."**

Here we see a marvelous truth surfacing before us, showing that **one's love for Christ is always predicated upon ones understanding of the sufferings of Jesus Christ.** We must never lose sight of the sufferings of the Lord Jesus Christ! This is why Communion is regularly shared with each other and shows us that His suffering is the catalyst that binds our hearts with love. Communion is the ***REMEMBERANCE*** of His sufferings.

In Greek, the phrase, *"the <u>communion</u> of the Holy Ghost" (2 Cor. 13:14)* is *koinonia*, which means fellowship[2]. The Holy Spirit and Jesus are always in communion, and this phrase, the communion of the Holy Spirit, includes us in fellowship with the Holy Spirit, AND also brings us into the fellowship of His sufferings, so that we will not forget what happened two thousand years ago. The Spirit was there at the Cross and bears witness with our spirit to the veracity of what we read in Holy Writ.

Paul the aged, who would soon face the guillotine, said, *"that I may know Him—and the fellowship of His sufferings" (Phil. 3:10).* He longed to know Christ in the only way we can know Him, in the fellowship of His sufferings! One can know Him as Saviour, but it is not until we partake of His sufferings that we truly identify with Him. The Church today must have a renewed vision of the sufferings of Christ so we, too, can love Him as did those early disciples. The greatest need for the Church of today is to return to the sufferings of Christ and the Cross. **It will humble us, break us, and make us. There is no other way.**

Maranatha! The Lord Cometh!

GOD'S TWO PROCESSES IN MAKING US
Part 1

"But rise, and stand upon they feet: for I have appeared unto thee for this purpose, to MAKE thee a minister and a witness both of these THINGS WHICH THOU HAS SEEN, and of those things in the which I will appear unto thee."
Acts 26:16

As Christians, we must come to see that the Lord has put this entire cosmos and the plan of salvation together with purpose. He has a plan that is well on its way to completion. The completion began when Jesus cried on the Cross, *"It is finished!"* Now, the final touches are being applied until it is unveiled in Heaven.

The plan obviously centers on the Lord Jesus Christ and His believers, who make up His Mystical Body, the Church. The Lord has a purpose for the Church, but the Church must be prepared and ready for that purpose. In order to make her ready, each member must pass through various "classes of learning" or testings to qualify for the eternal purpose. The preparation of the believer is taking place right now, here on earth, through the first process, which is **experience**.

The word "experience" in Romans 5:4 means proof and testing. The process by which the child of God is tested is by Providence. The Lord must set the conditions in such a way that it does not appear to be a test, for it to be a genuine test. The story of Job is a classic example of this procedure.

While Job was going about his business on earth, there was a frank and open discussion going on in the heavenlies between God and Satan, of which Job was totally unaware. To prove the genuineness of Job's commitment to serve the Lord, under any set of circumstances, the Lord had to keep Job from knowing he was being tested and watched under a microscope, or the test would have been invalid and untrue. It would have been much easier for Job, had he known he was being tested. Remember Job did not have a Bible to learn from, nor a comforter or a pastor for encouragement. He was alone and only had his faith and relationship with God to keep him.

God was doing a work in Job that he was unaware of, which would serve as a help to the children of God down through the ages, as well as preparing Job for his role and place throughout eternity. It was his experiences on earth that would make him qualify to fulfill God's role for his place in eternity in Heaven.

God designs all our experiences on earth with this objective in mind. Just as the Lord's Prayer says, *"Thy will be done in earth, as it is in heaven" (Matt. 6:10)*. To paraphrase: "Thy will be done on earth as it is planned and designed for us in heaven."

All the preparation takes place on earth; there is no preparation occurring in heaven. It's much like the stones that were used to build Solomon's Temple: *"And the house, when it was in building, was built of stone MADE READY BEFORE IT WAS BROUGHT THITHER" (1 Kings 6:7).* Solomon's Temple was an earthly temple, but the spiritual temple is the Church, and like Solomon's Temple, it is now being made ready before we are brought to heaven.

When Solomon's Temple was brought together, each stone had been prepared elsewhere and fit right into its place without sound of hammer or ax or any tool. So it is when we get to heaven, we will already have been prepared on earth, and all we do when we get to heaven is fit into the place the Lord has prepared for us. Jesus said, *"I go to prepare a place for you" (John 14:2).* He has gone to prepare the place for us there, while the Spirit is preparing us here, to fit the place there.

It is thus important for us to realize every test in our lives has a distinct purpose of working in us to prepare us for eternity. We know this from God's Word as in the instance with Job. Like Job, by God's grace, we must prove faithful under all circumstances, knowing that *"our light affliction, which is but for a moment, worketh for us a far more exceeding and eternal weight of glory . . . for the things are seen are temporal; but the things which are not seen are eternal" (2 Cor. 4:17–18).*

Experience is one of the tools for this process. The spiritual life is a process with a series of tests of *"hills and valleys" (Deut. 11:11)* or ups and downs in life that work on the inner man.

Next month we will look at the second tool the Lord uses to make us.

Maranatha! The Lord Cometh!

GOD'S TWO PROCESSES IN MAKING US
PART 2

"But rise, and stand upon thy feet: for I have appeared unto thee for this purpose, to MAKE thee a minister and a witness both of these things which thou hast seen, and of THOSE THINGS IN WHICH I WILL APPEAR UNTO THEE."
Acts 26:16

In the article last month, we saw how the Lord uses experience as a tool or process, in making us prepared for heaven. Earth is the preparation place for what awaits us in eternity. We are being made ready, as well as learning much. Then when we get to heaven we will know fully or *"even as also I am known" (1 Cor. 13:12)*.

In looking at the above scripture it ends with the words, *"and of those things in which I will appear unto thee."* The key word in this phrase is the word, "appear," which speaks of a new insight or **revelation**, which is the second process.

Revelation is a wonderful and fulfilling part of the Christian's walk of faith. It is ongoing and takes us from one level of faith to the next level. When Paul used the phrase, from faith to faith in **Romans 1:17**, speaking of righteousness, he used the word revealed with it: ***"For therein is the righteousness of God revealed from faith to faith."***

Our first revelation was the recognition of our sin and hopelessness without Christ, and the realization that He is the Savior and we must call upon Him for salvation. At this point, the Lord began the process of making us by **making** us a new creation in Christ.

The wonderful quality about revelation is that it does not stop at salvation. It is an ongoing part of the believer's life and as such is a powerful tool in God's hands, because it has the power to change us. Spiritual growth is dependent on revelation. This is why it is important to not be absent from the "assembling of ourselves." It is at Church services where the Word of the Lord is revealed through preaching. ***Titus 1:3*** says, ***"But hath . . . manifested His Word through preaching."***

Preaching of the Word is a tool the Lord uses to reveal truth to His people. He said His Word would not return void. If our hearts are open, the Lord always gives us insight into a truth in every sermon we hear.

The prophet Isaiah is a classic example of the power of revelation to change and make a man. In chapter six of his book we read of his revelation when he saw the Lord.

Isaiah was King Uzziah's personal chaplain. The king was a strong-willed man, who began his reign at sixteen years of age and reigned fifty-two years. No doubt his personality had a negative influence on Isaiah, for it's when the king dies that this revelation is given to Isaiah.

This revelation of Isaiah is two-fold. First, it is a revelation of the Lord, who is KING of KINGS and greater than king Uzziah, and then a revelation of Isaiah's spiritual state. When Isaiah saw the Lord, he saw his spiritual lack and said, *"I am a man of unclean lips."* Apparently, Isaiah found himself locked in a political situation that caused him to say things he should not have said and consequently defiled himself.

When king Uzziah died, the obstacle was gone, and the Lord began working on Isaiah, in making him one of the greatest prophets of the Old Testament. Again, the key that made him was revelation. Once he saw the Lord and then himself, he was completely ashamed and cries out to the Lord, *"Woe is me! for I am undone* (incomplete)*; because I am a man of unclean lips"* (Isa. 6:5).

With this confession and breaking, he became pliable in God's hands, enabling the Lord to change him into another man. Isaiah was never the same again following that great vision of revelation. He was a new man, which is obvious by his remarkable inspirational writings. It was this divine revelation that made him a broken man for the rest of his life. Great nuggets of truth poured from his lips and hands into his prophecies as a result.

Then came the purging, when the seraphim took coals of fire from the altar and laying it upon his mouth purged his sin. Now, he was a vessel meet for the Master's use. It was a process, but oh, what results! The Lord could now use him in ways that were before unimaginable. This second part of the process was revelation, confession, purging, and commissioning.

The process has not changed over the years; the Lord is the same yesterday, today, and forever, and so are His ways and His operations. What a privilege to have him "operate" on us!

Maranatha! The Lord Cometh!

DEPENDING ON THE SPIRIT OR ON GOALS

The influence of the world's methods and ways has infiltrated the Church, perhaps none more so than corporate America. At annual business shareholders meetings, CEO's announce past successes and future goals for the coming year and in the future. They in turn are conveyed to the managerial level and passed on to the production departments, where they are encouraged, in a positive way, to meet these projections. Now, there is nothing wrong with this modus operandi (manner of operating) when it comes to industry and corporate America. This is the way the business world operates and it works for them for they know goals stimulate production and production stimulates profits. This is the American way.

The following year they celebrate with the words "We did it!" and set new goals for the next year. It all sounds good, doesn't it? In the corporate world, it's acceptable, but this doesn't work in the believer's walk with God. The world's mode of operating doesn't work in the spiritual realm. It has to be forsaken if we want to move on in God.

How this goal setting has entered the Church is due in large part to the educational opportunities and high skill jobs in today's work force. Many fine Christian people find themselves in good managerial positions with outstanding salaries, and see the positive results of goal setting in their corporation and think it will work in the spirit life. Their reasoning is, since it works at work, why can't it work in the Church and in one's spiritual walk with the Lord? The difference is at work, men perform according to human resources, but in the spiritual life we are to move in the Spirit with His resources. The danger with goal setting for the believer is it breeds self-reliance and independence, with men glorying in the work of their hands and not in the Lord.

The Lord's way of working in the spiritual life, is totally different from man's ingenuity. God's way and man's way have been on opposite sides of the pole since Cain and Abel. The Lord Jesus said man's ways are directly opposite to the Lord's ways in **Luke 16:15,** *"for that which is highly esteemed among men is abomination in the sight of God."*

Paul says in **1 Corinthians 12:3** that no man can acceptably say Jesus is Lord unless the Holy Spirit inspires it. Since the Lord doesn't accept our praise of His name unless it is done by inspiration of the Spirit, how can men expect the Lord to accept their service if it's done by human methods? It's not accepted because it is accomplished in the flesh and not in the Spirit.

We need to understand the spiritual life is exclusively governed by the leading of the Holy Spirit. Our involvement is to render obedience and dependence on Him. As Zechariah wrote it is ***"Not by might*** (human strength),

nor by power (abilities and wealth), ***but by my Spirit saith the Lord" (Zech. 4:6).***

Goal setting in the spiritual life is a guarantee of either failure or bondage in legalism. Let's use Moses as an example. God led Israel through Moses step by step, day by day. Moses never set a goal before the children of Israel and said to them, "Now that we have crossed the Red Sea, we want to be at such and such a place by next week. Then we will have three days' rest and go to such and such a place in another week." Not at all, he quickly learned the key to the spiritual life, **"follow the cloud,"** and let God determine the stops and movements in fulfilling His purposes in our lives.

Some will say our goal is heaven, and that is true in the broad sense, but we had nothing to do with it but respond to the conviction of the Spirit and believe, and the Spirit of the Lord does the rest. After salvation, we have but one purpose in living, and it is exactly what Jesus said, ***"I have come to do thy will, O God" (Heb. 10:9).*** So it is with each of us, we are to do and live the will of God.

It is in doing the will of God that we will then come to know Him and attain to the resurrection of the dead, and find ourselves pressing toward the mark of the high calling of God in Christ Jesus ***(Phil. 3:8–14).*** This is only attainable by counting the things of gain to us in life as loss for Christ, in order to receive the excellency of the knowledge of Christ Jesus our Lord.

Our eternal glory and destiny in eternity will be determined by the degree we are willing to give up the acclaim and values of this world. We must choose to walk the path of the few, who have chosen to follow the Master. The values of the world can never compare with the glories that await us on the other side.

"If any man will come after me, let him deny himself, and take up his cross, and follow me. For whosoever will save his life shall lose it; and whosoever will lose his life for my sake shall find it" (Matt. 16:24–25).

Maranatha! The Lord Cometh!

MEN AND WOMEN OF THE SPIRIT

*I*n this article, we want to see what effect Pentecost is to have in the life of the believer. Pentecost is an experience, not just a day of Church history. We want to discover the meaning of this experience as it relates to the believer and the believer's inheritance.

When the Lord Jesus began His earthly ministry, His message was that the Kingdom of God was at hand *(Mark 1:15)*. It referred to the dawning of a new day in the revelation of God and His glory among His people. It spoke of the coming of the Holy Spirit to anoint and indwell God's people. In looking at the Old Testament, we find accounts of the prophets and a few saints who received a dispensation of the Spirit-filled life that was uncommon to all believers of that era.

Looking at the New Testament, we get a glimpse of what the Kingdom of God would be like, as seen in the lives of two luminaries, who lived in the last days of the Old Testament era, yet are included in the New Testament. Their transition from the Old to the New was by timing and experience. Their lives were meant to be an example of what the Spirit-filled life would mean for the believer. They are Simeon and Anna *(Luke 2:25, 36)*.

By timing, they were both present in the Temple when Mary and Joseph brought Jesus to be dedicated and saw Him in the flesh. By experience, they were impacted by the Spirit's leading in bringing them to the Temple at that precise moment.

As a result of the Spirit resting *"upon Him" (Luke 2:25),* Simeon had heard from the Lord, and was waiting for the fulfillment of Christ's coming. He was a godly man and his devotion was a direct result of the Spirit working in his life. **The Spirit-filled life will always bring one to a new dimension of godliness and devotion to the Lord beyond anything he has known before.**

We are further told it was *"revealed unto him by the Holy Ghost" (Luke 2:26)* that he wouldn't die until he had seen the Lord's Christ. Revelation is the wonderful unfolding of truth, given by the Holy Spirit. The Kingdom of God within us brings with it the wonderful blessing of revelation by the Holy Spirit, who knows the end from the beginning. **Revelation is part of the inheritance of the Spirit-filled life.**

On this particular morning, as Simeon awakened to a new day, he felt the need to go to the Temple though it was not the Sabbath. If it were the Sabbath, his practice was to always be in the Temple for the service and would not need a leading of the Lord to go, but the fact that he felt led to go shows it wasn't Sabbath. He didn't know why he must go but obeyed the Spirit, feeling a strong leading to go. Little did he realize what would happen that day, but the Spirit knew and orchestrated events that would bring fulfillment to his revelation. **This shows the leading of the Spirit is our inheritance as Spirit-filled people.** *Romans 8:14, 17* says the sons (and daughters) of God are led by the Spirit and that it is part of our inheritance.

When Simeon saw Mary and Joseph with the Child Jesus, he knew the consolation of Israel, the long promised and awaited Messiah had come. The Holy Spirit bore witness to Simeon that this was God's Son. ***Romans 8:16*** says, *"The Spirit beareth witness with our spirit."* There are things we can only know by the Spirit and Simeon experienced it here. **The witness of the Spirit is also included in our great inheritance as Spirit-filled believers.**

Then under the inspiration of the Spirit, he spoke a word similar to Mary's Magnificent, and dedicated the Child Jesus. He then prophesied the purpose and fulfillment of Christ's coming. **The Spirit of prophecy is the Spirit of Jesus and also in the inheritance of the Spirit-filled believer.** It is God's will that all His children have the Spirit of prophesy which is the testimony of Jesus Christ *(1 Cor. 14:31; Rev.19:10).* The Church's prophetic anointing reveals itself in many ways including prophecy, for we may all prophecy.

The other person is the godly lady, Anna, who lived a separated life, and was constantly in God's house, serving the Lord day and night with fasting and prayers. She too was led of the Spirit to come into the Temple at that "instant." It wasn't coincidence that she came right at that moment. It was God. She came in and like Simeon thanked the Lord and prophesied of the Redeemer, whom she had just seen.

Thirty-three years later, the time arrived for the revelation of the Kingdom of God. The Nobleman in the Parable of *Luke 19:12*, who went into a far country to receive for himself a kingdom, is the Lord Jesus, who went to Heaven to receive the Kingdom of God. This took place with His ascension to the Father's right hand, as He could not receive the kingdom nor send the Spirit until He was glorified *(John 7:39).*

Then on the Day of Pentecost, the Lord Jesus Christ sent the Holy Spirit to the Church, through whom the Kingdom of God would appear to the world. The message He preached in the beginning of His ministry, that the Kingdom of God was at hand, would now become a reality in the lives of His followers.

The Spirit came to a people who would be more than a people of the Word only, but a people of the Word and of the Spirit, for it is the Spirit that quickens the Word. Jesus did everything by the Spirit and showed the Church this is the way the Church is to operate and function. It's ***"by my spirit, saith the Lord" (Zech. 4:6).*** The Lord has called us to be men and women of the Spirit. Let us ever move in that direction and learn to follow the leading of the Holy Spirit.

Maranatha! The Lord Cometh!

DEEP CALLS UNTO DEEP OR REALITY RESPONDING TO REALITY

The only reality there is in life is in God. He created and made us in His image, consequently, we desire the Lord for He is Reality. Throughout scripture the theme of reality is a reoccurring theme especially in the book of Psalms.

One particular passage in *Psalm 42:7* says, *"deep calleth unto deep."* This call is reality calling out to Reality. The call isn't primarily a call to the ministry but a call to know God. It is the call from the heart of God to the very depth of a man's soul where there exists an insatiable desire for Him alone. It's similar to when the Lord called Moses to come up to the mount to be alone with Him.

It is God calling each of His children, **"Come unto Me,"** for a deeper walk and relationship with Him. When we respond to the Lord's call, which always begins with the Lord seeking to draw us to Himself, then we will find that as we move nearer to Him, He moves nearer to us *(James 4:8).*

Drawing closer to God is always dependent on the way the individual responds to the Lord's appeals to come closer. A person's relationship with the Lord depends on one's responses to God's call to **"run after Him"** (*Song of Sol. 1:4).*

Here, in this deep part of a man's being is where the Lord comes to meet us. The vanities of the self-life can't reach that far because this is a separated place only meant for the Lord. It is the **"hidden man of the heart."** It is man's Holy of Holies. Here lies the real person who finds himself stripped of self, arrogance and the crowd, and desires God and God alone. No demon or usurper is permitted here. The Old Testament High Priest was the only one permitted entry to the Holy of Holies, and it is here that we meet God.

The deep the Psalmist refers to is Reality, who is God, for there is no reality apart from Him. The world system is not reality because the world is spiritually dead and lies in darkness where no reality exists, except the reality of separation from Reality. The heart of man longs for reality, for once you have tasted it you are not satisfied with anything less. Man tasted reality in Eden and lost it. Man lost contact with His Maker and since that time has been searching for it without success because he seeks it apart from God.

When Jesus came, He came in the flesh to reveal the truth of reality for *"God was manifest in the flesh" (1 Tim. 3:16).* As the way, the truth and the life, Jesus' life and message brought hope to man for restoration with Reality. The deep calling unto the deep can be seen in the words of Jesus when He said, *"Come unto me, all ye that labor and are heavy laden" (Matt. 11:28).*

Once we grasp this truth of deep calling the deep then we can better understand the essence of worship. The deep of God is constantly calling to the deep in us to come and worship Him. Some people misunderstand the essence of worship and may see it as God being self-centered. The Lord is not egotistical and egocentric when He calls us to worship Him. He is not selfish or self-centered. So why then is worship so important in the eyes of God that He seeks worshippers *(John 4:23)?*

John chapter four gives insight into the very core of worship where Jesus says to the woman of Samaria, ***"God is a spirit: and they that worship him must worship him in SPIRIT and in TRUTH" (John 4:24).*** He is telling what God looks for in worship. Genuine worship is Spirit-birthed and in truth.

Let's look at the part the **Spirit** has in worship. There is absolutely nothing acceptable to God unless the Sprit inspires it to be acceptable.

Worship has to be birthed by the Spirit. Then it will be genuine worship from the depth of our being with purity of motive and objective, which is always for *" the glory of God" (1 Cor. 10:31).*

Now, we'll look at the **truth** part of worship. The Holy Spirit is the spirit of truth, and continually works in us by weaving truth *"in our inward parts" (Ps. 51:6).* Solomon says, ***"The spirit of man is the candle of the Lord, searching all the inward parts" (Prov. 20:27).*** What is God "seeking" and searching for in the worshipper? It is truth! This is the pure motive of desiring God only.

He seeks for those who worship Him without the intent of impressing Him to gain favor. They worship Him without any mixture of self and selfish objectives or an agenda that says, "if I do this for God, then He will do that for me" *(see **Psalm 49:11**).* Such were the Pharisees in their inward parts; they were men of corrupt motives *(Luke 11:39).*

Whether the Lord does anything for us or not, doesn't matter. All that matters is that we love Him honestly, truthfully and worship Him in Spirit and with a pure motive. Then God will respond to our worship as He did to Noah's burnt offering, after the Flood. It was a sweet savor He smelled. His nostrils were filled with the fragrance of Noah's pure thankful worship, not the fragrance of the meat of the animal sacrifice. We see this purity in the offerings of Israel, for the Lord required them to be of pure gold, pure olive oil and pure frankincense, pointing to the purity of worship *(Exod. 27:20; 30:34–37; 37:29)*.

The Lord takes great pleasure in worship because it comes from His children, who love Him, and it brings Him closer to them. Worship is really the giving of Himself to us rather than us doing for Him. Worship to the Lord is like a son or daughter sitting down with their father at the head of the table and eating together. It is **"supping with the Lord"** *(Rev. 3:20)*. Worship honors God as a son honors his father and is a communion that deepens their relationship.

Deep calling unto deep and reality to reality shows how much the Father longs for fellowship with His children. Jesus died to re-establish this glorious relationship, which was lost in Eden. It is the apex of the spiritual life and should be the pursuit of every seeking heart who longs for more of God.

Maranatha! The Lord Cometh!

HE SHALL NOT FAIL NOR BE DISCOURAGED (JESUS NEVER FAILS)

The prophet Isaiah was given tremendous insight into the life of Christ more than any other Old Testament figure other than David. His message begins with the birth of Christ, born of a virgin and then insight after insight into the life of Christ that is absolutely phenomenal.

"Behold my servant, whom I uphold; mine elect, in whom my soul delighteth; I have put my spirit upon him: ...A bruised reed shall he not break, and smoking flax shall he not quench: He shall bring forth judgment unto truth. He shall not fail nor be discouraged." In this passage of *Isaiah 42:1–4*, the prophet sees the ministry of Christ in the life of the Christian pilgrim, who finds himself in struggle after struggle to a point of discouragement. To such a saint, Isaiah sends an encouraging word regarding the attitude of Christ towards His people in spite of their failure, frustration and seeming defeat.

In this chapter, Christ is presented to the reader as the **Servant of the Lord**, endowed with the Spirit of God to accomplish God's will in bringing justice to the nations and to individuals. Since nations are made up of individuals, the Lord reaches out to the individuals who have been beaten down in life as the result of sin.

Sin is a terrible and merciless master that seeks to continually bind the lives of mankind and ultimately destroy man's soul. Jesus is the only answer to man's predicament. He comes on the scene to do what none other could ever do, deliver and redeem man from the grips of the father of sin, the strong man Satan. Jesus saw the effects of sin in the lives of men and women, to the point of being permanently bruised and crushed with their lives nearly being snuffed out.

The analogy used to depict this truth is that of a reed and flax. Reeds were and still are plentiful in the Near East. To entertain themselves shepherds would pluck them and cut holes into their frame to play songs while tending their sheep. If their reed was inadvertently bumped and bruised, the shepherd would cast it aside and get a fresh one, rather than spend time trying to repair it as they were plentiful. However, what earthly shepherds rejected and cast aside, the Great Shepherd of our soul stakes up the life of a bruised individual and patiently works with it to once again restore a song of hope and joy in their heart.

Many of God's children have carried some deep bruises into their salvation experience. They have tried over and over again to get rid of them, but to no avail. At times they felt unworthy, inept, or of no value to anyone, yet the Lord sees each of us of great value and with a different outlook than what we see in ourselves. He sees what we don't see. He knows things about us that we don't know and **He is not discouraged**.

Then there are those who feel like smoking flax. Flax is the wick of a candle that gives out light. When the wick isn't cared for and is close to burning out, it gives off smoke. The owner would snip the flax off and throw the candle away and take up another fresh candle. The lives of many of God's children have, for one reason or another, become burned out with overwork, worry, and distress. This has resulted with many giving up their ministry, feeling burned out spiritually and unfulfilled. Others have lost hope of ever becoming what they have desired to be for God. But the Lord Jesus hasn't given up on them and knows how to take the smoky wick and transform it into the brightest wick in the house. The Lord won't reject you because you messed up nor will He put out your light or cast you away.

As long as the believer is in human form there will be failure, but the good news is that Jesus isn't through with you. While men may cut you off and cast you away, Jesus never will. He is the God of restoration and hope.

You see, in spite of one's failures and discouragement, **Jesus isn't discouraged and He will not fail in your life** to accomplish all that the Father has ordained for you. He will not fail you in allowing you to end up in failure. He has assured us that He will perfect that which is lacking on our part for His *"strength is made perfect in (our) weakness" (2 Cor. 12:9).*

If ever there was a classic of Christian failure, we would have to say Peter is it. Yet, Jesus didn't give up on him nor was He discouraged over Peter's behavior. The Lord didn't cast him aside as a bruised reed of no value or smoking flax that burned out. Jesus continued to work in Peter's life until he was *"converted"* and then as a result of his failure and restoration was made a strength to the brethren *(Luke 22:31–32).* He became an example to them and to us of the unfailing attitude of Christ towards

His people. Jesus didn't fail Peter nor was He discouraged over Peter's failure.

Child of God, Jesus has not given up on you either. You may have failed and fallen but Jesus isn't going to fail you. He is marching you on to victory just like He did for Peter.

"Being confident of this very thing, that he which hath begun a good work in you will perform it until the day of Jesus Christ" (Phil. 1:6).

Maranatha! The Lord Cometh!

SERVANTHOOD—THE KEY TO ETERNAL GREATNESS

*L*ast month's article on *Isaiah 42:1–4*, introduced us to the lifestyle of the Lord Jesus as the Servant of the Lord, who brought great delight to the Father. It emphasized His workmanship in the lives of His people who find themselves struggling to please God, yet experiencing failure.

This article builds on the same passage but with the emphasis on the term, **"The Servant of the Lord."** If we can get a grasp of this term, it will help the child of God immensely in understanding true servanthood. Once we get a better understanding of servanthood, we will understand what Jesus meant in the Gospels, and in particular in *Matthew 19:30* when He said, *"But many that are first shall be last; and the last shall be first."*

This article is to help one see what must be done in life in preparing for eternity, so we don't end up last in the Kingdom. This is a very critical point. The lower one goes in life, the higher will be his role and place in eternity. Eternal greatness will not be measured by how much one has done for the Kingdom, but by how low one was willing to identify with Christ in His sufferings and humility. **The key to eternal greatness is in servanthood.** This is the eternal issue for the child of God.

We begin with Jesus' example of servanthood. We often quote the title of Jesus as *KING OF KINGS and LORD OF LORDS,* but rarely, if ever, does one hear it said that HE is the Servant of servants. **As a result of being the "Servant of servants," He will be crowned *"KING OF KINGS and LORD OF LORDS! (Rev. 19:16)."*).**

To show the importance of serving, Jesus said He did not come to earth to be ministered unto, but to minister or serve *(Matt. 20:28).* In fact, when He left the Father's right hand to come to earth, He came as a servant *(Phil. 2:5–9).* This passage shows Jesus came to serve, and in that capacity, did the Father's will, which was to die for others. Servants must submit to the will of their masters whatever that may be, even if it includes death. Jesus made a choice to do the Father's will. As it says in *verse 8*: *"He humbled himself, and became obedient unto death, even the death of the cross" (Phil. 2:8).*

He humbled himself and chose to do the Father's will, knowing it would lead to death. This was the reason for His coming. In the spiritual context, as followers of Jesus Christ, we are to follow Him into servanthood so we, too, will please the Father. The father delights when He sees us humbling ourselves in serving others. *"Behold my servant, . . . in whom my soul delighteth" (Isa. 42:1).*

We are to take the *"form"* of a servant. *Phil 2:7 "But made himself of no reputation, and took upon him the form of a servant."* Understanding words helps us unlock hidden truths, as does this word *"form."* In the Greek it is *morphe*,[3] and means the special characteristics of a person. Those characteristics make up the nature of a person and are retained as long as the individual lives.

This helps to understand servanthood. True servanthood isn't being a servant when it pleases one's fancy. It is living the life of a servant at all times and under all circumstances. It is a lifetime commitment of love to one's master and is shown in how we treat each other (see *"love slave"* in ***Exodus 21:1–6***).

Servanthood is a *"good work,"* held before the Lord as an eternal memorial ***(Matt. 26:10–13).*** In other words, Mary's act of servanthood will be kept alive in God's memory forever. This one act shows the importance of servanthood before God.

Selectivity in serving is contrary to ***Matthew 8:9***, which shows the servant cannot be selective as to whom he will serve. When his master says, *"go,"* he is to go; when he is told to *"come,"* he comes; when he is told to *"do this,"* he must do it. There isn't room for disobedience or compromise, there's only room for obedience.

It's also interesting to note the same word—*morphe* (form)[3]—as used in reference to God in ***Philippians 2:6, "who being in <u>the form of God</u>,"*** shows the servanthood SPIRIT OF Deity abiding in the Person of Christ and **founded** in the love of God. Servanthood is **reflected** in all God does and gives in caring for His children and the world. Thus, when we serve one another, we are not only following the example of Jesus but also the example of our Heavenly Father.

Jesus showed the servanthood spirit of deity by being ***"the express image of his*** (the Father's) ***person*** (which includes both character and personality)" ***(Heb. 1:3).*** As He is the reflection of the Father, so we are the reflection of Jesus. Servanthood on our part reflects the spirit of Christ and of the Father. This explains why servanthood is so critically important. It is in servanthood that people will see Jesus and the Father in you. They will glorify the Father in us.

The last visual lesson Jesus left His disciples on servanthood was a domestic washing feet. Here Jesus put everything in proper perspective showing that today is the day of the towel (servitude) and eternity will be the day of the robe (rulership).

One must beware of the dangers to servanthood. The greatest danger is pride. It was the first sin of the universe that first appeared in Lucifer. It is Satan's "weapon of destruction." It is both thief and destroyer of spirituality, empty and full of vanity. It tops the list of the seven sins God hates, *"a proud look* (pride)" *(Prov. 6:16, 17).* Thus, servanthood must be birthed in the heart and expressed in the spirit of love. Otherwise, it will be meaningless.

Remember Jesus closed the lesson of servanthood with the words, *"If you know these things, happy are ye if ye do them" (John 13:17).*

Maranatha! The Lord Cometh!

WITHIN AND WITHOUT

A New Year ought to bring within the heart of every child of God, the desire to press on in the Lord more than ever. It comes full of fresh hope for the Lord's Return, and should He tarry, a longing to continually press into the pursuit of the Lord. Of course, each New Year also brings struggles and distractions to divert the child of God's vision and commitment. But God's Word shows what the Lord expects and how we should live to fulfill His expectations by depending on the Holy Spirit.

A good illustration of this truth is when Moses built the ark. He received instructions from the Lord on how to build the Tabernacle and its furniture, which he oversaw until completion by gifted individuals. ***Exodus 37:1–2*** speaks of the making of the Ark of the Covenant, which would contain the Ten Commandments, also known as the tables of the Covenant; Aaron's rod that budded; and the golden pot of Manna ***(Heb. 9:4)***.

The Ark is a type of the believer's heart, for in our heart we, too, must hide the Word of God, (typified by the Ten Commandments); and feed on Christ, our Manna ***(John 6:50–51)***; and be filled with the Holy Spirit as seen in Aaron's rod that budded. This is the ***"treasure*** *in earthen vessels"* Paul speaks of in *2 Corinthians 4:7*. For this reason, the Lord's command to Moses to build the Ark exactly as shown was because of its great spiritual significance.

The message of the Ark is seen in the wood; it was made of and beautified by the overlay of gold. The wood speaks of man's humanity, and the gold of the divine nature within and without the believer's life. The term "within and without" speaks of man's dual make-up, the inner and outer man, which is our private and public life. The pure gold that overlaid the Ark speaks of the God-nature and its influence in our lives. Gold always speaks of divinity. The challenge everyone faces is to be true in both areas of our lives. For some, they can be kind outwardly but inwardly are in shambles. Others have their inner man in order but outwardly come off looking like anything but Christ-like. Jesus was the same inwardly and outwardly. There was no contradiction in Him.

The Spirit within is working to do the same for each of us, if we are willing to submit to His dealings. He wants to develop the Christ-like nature in us to shine through us, giving spiritual light of being Spirit-filled to a lost world steeped in spiritual death and darkness. The old saying is, "what you see is what you get." In other words, what we are inside is what we are outwardly, for what is in us will come out.

The cry of the human heart is seen in the Greeks who came seeking for Jesus and said, *"Sir, we would see Jesus" (John 12:21)*. The world wants to know if what we profess as Christians is real, and the only way they will believe is if they see the character and ways of Christ emanating from us. They want to see the spirit of Christ demonstrated through us and know it's real. They're looking to see if we are the same inwardly as we are outwardly.

The world will not accept phoniness. They're looking for the real. This is in line with what Paul says in *2 Cor. 3:2–3, "Ye are our epistle written in our hearts, known and read of all men: Forasmuch as you are . . . the epistle of Christ."* If there's a contradiction in one's life between one's life-style and one's profession of being a believer, the world will reject you, not because you are a Christian, but because you are a contradiction.

This New Year offers a wonderful opportunity to seek the face of the Lord and implore Him to help us be the same inwardly as we are outwardly. This is stability, which remains the same inwardly and outwardly when conditions press us to change our behavior in a negative way. We don't want to recede to what we once were, but proceed to what HE is calling us to be, **made in the image and likeness of Jesus Christ!** *(Rom. 8:29).* Then we will receive a "crown of gold" on our heads just as the one put on the Ark *(Exod. 37:2).*

Maranatha! The Lord Cometh!

PENTECOST, GOD'S NEW THING

The Lord Jesus spoke wonderful words about the Holy Spirit, whom He sent in His place, after ascending to the Father's Right Hand. John the Baptist was called to identify Christ as the Son of God and also the One who would baptize in the Holy Ghost and fire *(Matt. 3:11)*.

The Baptism with the Holy Ghost and fire was a new message to the ears of the people, but showed them God was opening a new door and about to do *"a new thing,"* as *Isaiah* prophesied in *43:18–19. "Remember ye not the former things, neither consider the things of old. Behold* (the key word)*, I will do a new thing; now shall it spring forth; shall ye not know it? I will even make a way in the wilderness, and rivers in the desert."* The Baptism with the Holy Spirit is the new thing. While Pentecost was established in the types of the Old Testament, as in the Feast of Weeks, yet its fulfillment was hidden until the Day of Pentecost arrived.

Isaiah's **New Thing** is the **New Wine** Jesus spoke of in *Luke 5:36–39*, and became a **Reality** on the Day of Pentecost. It's noticeable that the mockers on the Day of Pentecost accused them of being drunk with *"new wine."*

They were accurate; however, it was spiritual new wine they were drunk on, not natural wine.

Isaiah 43:18 uses the word ***"Behold"*** in identifying Jesus as the Baptizer in the Holy Ghost. This is the same word John used in identifying Christ in ***John 1:29 "Behold the Lamb of God, which taketh away the sin of the world."*** The new thing God spoke through Isaiah is the Baptism of the Holy Spirit (and fulfilling of the Mystery of Christ) ***(Eph. 3:4).***

The Baptism of the Holy Ghost for Jesus' followers would take place after Christ paid for our salvation and ascended to the Father's right hand. It would come after He cried, ***"It is finished" (John 19:30)*** on the Cross. He finished our redemption and as a result finished the preparation for the coming of the Holy Spirit. The preparation was that no one could receive the Holy Spirit Baptism until he first received salvation. In identifying Jesus first as Savior and then Baptizer, John shows the sequence of salvation and the Baptism in the Spirit. Salvation comes first, followed by the Baptism of the Holy Ghost.

The cleansing of the leper in the Old Testament is a type of the New Testament **experience** of salvation and Spirit Baptism. Leprosy was the most terrible and dreaded disease in the Bible. It was humiliating, debasing, ugly, and deforming. For these reasons, it is a type of sin. When a leper was healed of it, he had to be cleansed by the priest, who would take the blood of the trespass offering ***(Lev. 14:14)*** and sprinkle it on the leper. Following this procedure, the priest would take oil and apply it to the leper, and also **apply it over the blood *(Lev. 14:17).***

Mankind, except Jesus of course, was born a spiritual leper with all its potential of the ugliness of sin inwardly. But one day Jesus found us, and brought us to spiritual inward healing. First came faith to believe and call on His name, then came the blood for our cleansing, then followed the Holy Spirit or the anointing of oil. This speaks of salvation, which is first, and then oil, which is a type of the Baptism of the Holy Spirit poured upon the head of the cleansed leper *(Lev. 14:18)*. On the Day of Pentecost, the Spirit descended upon the 120 in the Upper Room and *"cloven tongues like as of fire, and it sat upon each of them" (Acts 2:3),* meaning, on their heads like the cleansed leper.

We need the blood of Jesus first, followed by the Baptism of the Holy Spirit. On Easter Sunday evening, when Jesus appeared to the disciples locked away in the Upper Room, and He breathed on them and said, *"Receive ye the Holy Ghost,"* they were born again *(John 20:22)*. Then fifty days later, on the Day of Pentecost, they received the oil, which is the Baptism of the Holy Ghost.

On the Day of Pentecost, Peter confirmed this sequence when he said, *"Repent, and be baptized every one of you in the name of Jesus Christ for the remission of sins, and ye shall receive the gift of the Holy Ghost" (Acts 2:38).* The sin issue must always be resolved; the Baptism of the Spirit comes afterward.

Many Christians treat the Baptism of the Holy Spirit as the world treats salvation, which is available to all, yet they refuse it. In principle, the same happens when it comes to the Baptism with the Holy Ghost. The Baptism of the Holy Spirit is for all believers, but not all choose to receive it as they feel they do not need the Baptism in the Spirit. Obviously, this is incorrect for if it was true, Jesus would not have commanded the Disciples to tarry until they received the Baptism of the Spirit, who would endue you with power from on high *(Luke 24:49)*.

Let us seek to be baptized with the Holy Ghost. God wants this for all of His children!

Maranatha! The Lord Cometh!

TWO AREAS OF TRUTH

*I*f there was ever a man who knew God and His ways, it was Moses. He was a **phenomenal man, with a phenomenal understanding of God**, because he had **a phenomenal relationship with Him.** In his closing admonitions to Israel in *Deuteronomy 29:29,* Moses shares an insight on the subject of truth, *"The secret things belong unto the LORD our God: but those things which are revealed belong unto us."*

It is important to understand there are some things God doesn't tell us. For example, the Lord Jesus said, *"But of that day and hour knoweth no man, no, not the angels which are in heaven, neither the Son, but the Father" (Mark 13:32).* No one knows the day or hour when the Lord Jesus will return for the Church, except the Father. He alone knows this secret.

Another secret is the Mystery of the Trinity that God alone knows. There are mysteries that He only knows, but there are other wonderful things He reveals to His children.

He revealed to Paul *(Eph. 3:2–6)* the Mystery of Christ that the Gentiles by faith would become one body with the Jewish believers. This was a secret kept throughout the Old Testament and remained unknown, until the proper time when Christ would come and die for our redemption.

The Book of Revelation is another example of the secrets of God. It was a secret until the Father gave it to the Lord Jesus Christ, following His Ascension to God's right hand *(Rev. 1:1).*

Thankfully, there are things He wants us to know and reveals to us by His Word and the Spirit who will *"guide you into all truth" (John 16:13).* The Word of God is a book of great spiritual truths for this life and eternity. In it God reveals to us truth known as *"principles" (Heb. 6:1).* Principles are the beginning of revelations for the foundation of our "spiritual house," built on the Rock, Christ Jesus.

Then, as one's relationship with the Lord deepens, the Lord reveals Himself to that individual in a personal way *(John 14:21).* This happens first with salvation, when the Lord reveals Himself as Saviour to the individual heart. From there He reveals Himself continually to those wanting to know Him better.

It is necessary to understand that while the Lord has given man freedom, He has also restricted him. Man may be a free moral agent **to a degree**, but is limited by God. This is found in **Genesis 2:16-17** where the Lord told Adam he could eat of every tree in the Garden (freedom) **except** (limitation) for the Tree of the Knowledge of good and evil. This tree was a secret of the Lord.

Adam was told not to eat of the Tree of the Knowledge of Good and Evil for his protection, and was given great latitude to eat any of the other trees. However, if he moved out of the circle he would die.

The example here that will help us see this point is the Ten Commandments. When men violate them and move away from their influence, dire consequences follow. *Isaiah 53:6 says, "All we like sheep have gone astray;*

we have turned every one to his own way." Whether an individual or a nation abandons the Ten Commandments, the end result is the same-judgment. This principle still holds today.

It is dangerous to try to force open a door the Lord has shut. Here also some theologians go astray. They delve into things God has kept for Himself. They cross the line rather than stay within the area of revealed truth, which lead to questioning God's work and judging Him. In the end, the Lord will reject them. *See **Colossians 2:18**.*

Our safety, in these trying times, is to love the Lord our God with all our heart, all our soul and our mind, and all our strength. We are to stay within His Word and not delve into things He has kept secret for Himself, or for the time He has appointed to reveal *(Dan. 12:9).* In closing, we are reminded of the words of Christ, who said, *"If you continue in my word, then are you my disciples indeed" (John 8:31).*

Maranatha! The Lord Cometh!

THE POWER OF HIS RESURRECTION

The quest of Paul's heart was to know Christ in both *"the power of His Resurrection,"* which he mentions first, and *"in the fellowship of His sufferings."* These two extremes speak of life (Resurrection), and suffering, leading to *"being made conformable unto His death" (Phil. 3:10).* Conformed to Christ's death is "liken to His death," with the understanding that this is death to the carnal self in the believer.

The life of Christ is in us by the Spirit, to help us continually increase spiritually within as we walk with Him daily. At the same time, the carnal nature in us is to die daily, that we might become more like Him. John, the Baptist said it succinctly when he said, *"He must increase, but I must decrease" (John 3:30).*

How are we to reconcile the above with the resurrection of Christ mentioned first, and secondly, His sufferings and death? It would seem the order should have been reversed but Paul deliberately put the "power of Christ's resurrection" first, to emphasize Christ's Victory. If Jesus had only died and not resurrected, we could not have been redeemed. In *1 Corinthians 15*, Paul enumerates all the woes that would have befallen mankind if Christ did not resurrect but only died for the sins of the world.

Like Paul, we are to dwell on the Victory of Christ and relate His sufferings and death as necessary, but not the end. **His mission would have been incomplete without the Resurrection.** Certainly, He would *"taste death for every man" (Heb. 2:9)* and die the most horrible of all deaths so we would not have to taste and experience the death He died. What made it so horrible is that it was the death of the damned, as seen by His cry on the Cross. *"My God, My God, why hast Thou forsaken me?"(Matt. 27:46)* This death is still the death of the unregenerate today, but the believer will never experience it as Christ experienced it for all who trust in Him.

When Paul speaks of the fellowship of His sufferings, it means to realize, by understanding the terrible death Christ died. He is asking for revelation to grasp the full extent of the agony of the cross. We enter this understanding by **"IDENTIFYING,"** with his sufferings and death. While Paul knew the value of identifying with the death, burial and resurrection of Christ in water baptism *(Rom. 6:3–8),* which is the first step of our identifying with Christ's death, he wanted to know Him by word, in reminding himself by confessing when tested that he was dead with Christ. As we identify with Christ in His sufferings and death, our understanding will deepen of His agony. Paul wanted to know Him more by word (his confession and reminder that he was in Christ when He was crucified) and deed, which would be in his responses to situations and people when tested by their behavior towards him.

When Paul was tested, he always came back to the truth of the overcoming *"power of His resurrection!"*

He lived in the victory and triumph of Christ over the devil, sin, death and hell. How did he learn this truth? It all began with the process known as ***"reckoning"*** [4] ***(Rom. 6:11),*** which leads to identifying and arriving at a conclusion as to the finished works of Christ. Jesus did it all, and all we have to do is fully accept what He accomplished for us and enter His works by faith.

The Resurrection of Christ is the capstone and foundation of the faith and we are to live in the Power of His Resurrection. He is not on the Cross nor in the Tomb, **He is alive forevermore, seated at the Father's Right Hand!** Now we know Him in the Spirit *(2 Cor. 5:16; Rom. 8:11)* and no more after the flesh since the Resurrection. Hence, we can rejoice in the Power of the Resurrection, which is the moving and power of the Holy Spirit in our lives. By His ignoble death, Jesus protected us from that terrible death by closing its door forever for the believer and in its place, fully opening the door to life eternal and the "abundant life" lived in the Power of His Resurrection. **What a tremendous exchange! Hallelujah!**

Maranatha! The Lord Cometh!

KNOWING GOD

One of the most glaring needs in the Body of Christ today is the lack of the knowledge of God. In many Churches, the emphasis of knowing God has shifted to working for God. One can do great things for God, without knowing God as Jesus said in *Matthew 7:21–23.*

Jesus wanted His disciples and all believers to know God as recorded in *John 17:3, "And this is life eternal, that they might know Thee."* This is the knowledge that goes beyond salvation. *Hosea 6:6* says the Lord is more interested in His people knowing Him, than burnt offerings.

The one man who best exemplifies the pursuit of the knowledge of God is Moses. He is one of the most unique men in history. His life is an amazing account of the designed plan of God in a person's life. He is known as a faithful servant *(Heb. 3:5);* a friend of God, with whom the Lord spake face to face *(Exod. 33:11).*

The fact that the Lord spoke to Moses as a man speaks to his friend *(Deut. 34:10)* shows Moses already had an intimate relationship with the Lord, yet, he wanted more of knowing God, not just theology. He wanted to experience more of God than what he already experienced at the

Burning Bush, the miracles of the Exodus and his times with God on the Mount.

He is the man chosen and called of God to deliver God's people. For such a man the Lord had to prepare him for this call. Divine preparation is always essential and needed if one is to fulfill his destiny. This is why we have trials and tests in life. They prepare us for something greater than our recent state. Moses is a man to whom God revealed Himself. By the time Moses got to Exodus 33, he had already seen much of the miraculous workings of God; yet, at his age of eighty or more he still longed to know more of God. His desire for God did not diminish with age, in fact, the more he knew God the more he wanted of God. His heart panted *(Psalms 42:1)* for the knowledge of God.

Moses' quest for God and God's response to fulfill his prayer, show there is no limit to knowing God if one is willing to seek His face.

His prayer in *Exodus 33:13* is, *"If I have found grace in thy sight, show me now thy way, that I may know thee."* When a man prays such a prayer he always finds grace with the Lord. His prayer isn't a request for an intellectual knowledge of God; it is rather a prayer for a personal experience and acquaintance with God. Today, intellectual knowledge of God can be had in our religious schools, and via books, but a personal acquaintance with God brings experiential knowledge of God.

Knowing God comes by the heart, not the intellect. It is true the intellect plays its part in preaching or reading the word. It goes to the mind first and then to the heart, where it remains and brings change.

Matthew 11:25–26 says, "I thank thee, O Father, Lord of heaven and earth, because thou has hid these things from the wise and prudent, and hast revealed them unto babes." The wise and prudent are the learned and educated and may feel superior to the uneducated. The wise and prudent think they know it all, yet are unteachable in the ways of God. But in God's eyes the humble and meek, the simple in faith and lowly, are the "babes," who have the right spirit and attitude.

This is not a put down of education. We need education in life, but knowing God has nothing to do with it because the knowledge of God comes by revelation by the Spirit of God, not education. If one wants to know God, it doesn't matter if he has attended college or seminary. He needs to pursue the Lord with time in prayer and in the Word.

Jeremiah 9:23–24 says not to glory in one's worldly wisdom (which is position) or riches, but we are to glory in that we know and understand God. God isn't impressed with one's degrees of learning. In fact, Jesus called simple fishermen to give up everything to follow Him and they did. This is the kind of commitment He looks for as His eyes *"run to and fro throughout the earth, to show himself strong in the behalf of them whose heart is perfect toward Him" (2 Chron. 16:9).*

Are you willing to pay the price of separation from the world and leave behind anything that would come between you and your relationship with Him? This is **self-denial** and brings the choice to the individual.

Maranatha! The Lord Cometh!

THE GLORIOUS BAPTISM WITH THE HOLY SPIRIT

The Baptism with the Holy Ghost is a most wonderful and essential gift *(Acts 2:38)* given to the Church, and its importance is far greater than many realize. If we would pause to think of the impact of the Holy Spirit in the life of Christ we would better understand the Spirit's importance and our need to be baptized with the Holy Spirit.

It was the Holy Ghost who performed the miracle of the **Virgin Birth** *(Luke 1:35).* It was the Holy Ghost who led Simeon to **dedicate Jesus** *(Luke 2:26).* It was the Spirit who **revealed to Jesus** that He was the Son of God, for in coming to earth as a man, Jesus divested Himself of the divine attribute of omniscience *(Luke 2:40, 49).* It was the Holy Spirit who **anointed Jesus** with power to do the wonderful works of God *(Luke 3:22, 4:18; Acts 10:38).* Jesus never did a miracle before receiving His baptism with the Holy Ghost. He was and is God and could have done miracles as God, yet to identify with His disciples and man, He did nothing unless **led by the Spirit** on whom He depended for everything.

It was through the Holy Spirit that **Jesus offered Himself** as the Lamb of God, to die for our sins *(Heb. 9:14)*. It was the Holy Spirit that **raised Jesus** from the dead *(Rom. 8:11)* making the Resurrection a reality. It was the Holy Spirit, in the form of a cloud that **lifted Jesus to Heaven at the Ascension** *(Acts 1:9)*. It is the Holy Spirit who is **continuing the ministry of Jesus** through the Church *(Rom. 15:19)*. These verses show how Jesus depended solely on the Holy Spirit in every facet of His life and ministry. If Christ needed the Spirit, how much more must we depend on the Spirit.

Jesus knows the faithfulness of the Spirit and knows we can do nothing without the Spirit. It is for this reason that He sent the Holy Spirit, not only to give birth to the Church, but also to empower us to continue His works. Ten days following His Ascension, the Lord Jesus sent the Spirit to the 120 disciples gathered together in the Upper Room as they waited for His coming. The Spirit came in power, as indicated by the words *"a rushing mighty wind" (Acts 2:2),* for He is the Power of God, and filled the room as the disciples began to speak in other tongues as the Spirit gave them inspiration.

The glorious baptism with the Holy Ghost is essential if the Church is to continue the works of Christ and fulfill the Great Commission. The Baptism of the Spirit will lead all who want more of God into the deeper things of God, for it is impossible to know God beyond salvation without revelation given by the Spirit.

When we were saved, we received the Spirit of God **within** us, as did the disciples on that first Easter evening **(John 20:22)**. The Spirit then came **upon** them at Pentecost, empowering them to continue Christ's ministry of *"all that He began both to do and teach" (Acts*

1:1). Jesus' ministry did not stop with His Ascension, but is continued by the empowered Church with the Baptism of the Holy Spirit.

The glorious Baptism of the Spirit is our inheritance *(Eph. 1:13–14)* that continues throughout eternity. Though the Gifts of the Spirit, as enumerated in *1 Corinthians 12:8–10*, will cease with the Rapture *(1 Cor. 13:8–10),* yet the inheritance of the Spirit will never cease in eternity, as we are eternal *"join theirs with Christ" (Rom. 8:17).* The Baptism of the Spirit is to take us into the Bride of Christ and consequently into the joint-heirship with Christ as His Bride forever. This is why the Baptism of the Holy Spirit is so essential and important.

We must be careful not to see the Baptism of the Spirit as something we can either take or leave. Its importance is seen in the words of Christ when He **commanded** the disciples to tarry until they were baptized with the Spirit *(Acts 1:4).* **His command is still valid today and remains in force until the Rapture.** After salvation, we are commanded to pray and tarry until we also are baptized with the Holy Spirit, as was the early Church.

"Then Peter said unto them, Repent, and be baptized every one of you in the name of Jesus Christ for the remission of sins, and ye shall receive the Gift of the Holy Ghost. For the promise is unto you, and to your children, and to all that are afar off, even as many as the Lord our God shall call" (Acts 2:38–39).

Maranatha! The Lord Cometh!

SEPARATION AND DETACHMENT

*G*od has always sought a people who would willingly separate themselves from the allurements of the world to seek His face and to live for Him. Prior to the Flood, from Abel to Noah *(Gen. 6:9),* there always were a people who remained faithful to the Lord having been taught by Adam of redemption via animal sacrifices *(Gen. 8:20).*

But the establishing of the principle of **"separation,"** really began with the Patriarch Abraham, when the Lord called him to leave his country and friends and relatives *(Gen. 12:1).* God's call to Abraham indicated that if he obeyed God, the Lord would bless him in a great way. He believed and obeyed God and *"departed" (Gen. 12:4)* as the Lord told him. From that time on, God's people have always been called to be separate from the unbelieving world because of its negative influence on the people of God. This was seen in the corruption of Noah's day that influenced the then known world, causing them all to perish except Noah and his family.

Man did not learn from the Flood and as a result built the Tower of Babel in rebellion against the Lord. Here a partial separation began by the judgment of the confusion of tongues. But the Lord knew man would still be rebellious, so He implemented a separation to Himself so His people would not be contaminated or corrupted by the spirit of the world.

From Abraham to Israel, to the New Testament Church, all who choose to follow after the Lord are called to a life of separation. Spiritually, we cannot serve God and be joined with the world *(2 Cor. 6:14–18).* However, in the natural we are in the world but not of the world because He called us out of the world *(John 15:19).*

Separation is the **initial step** that comes with salvation. After separation, the Lord begins to deal with us concerning **"detachment,"** which is a step further than separation. Many Christians live a separated life but still hold on to things, which may not be bad in themselves but are hindrances to one's personal spiritual growth and walk with God.

This too is seen with Abraham, who was told by the Lord to leave his house and his relatives. But Abraham took his father, Terah, with him, along with his nephew Lot. There was partial separation for he *"departed, as the Lord has spoken to him; and Lot went with him" (Gen. 12:4).* Having only partially obeyed God delayed Abraham from entering the land God promised him *(Acts 7:5).* Abraham was delayed because of his father and Lot, and was consequently stuck at Haran until his father died *(Gen. 11:32; Acts 7:4).* Now, only Lot stood in the way.

Lot traveled with Abraham in his own tent *(Gen. 13:5),* but was still a hindrance to Abraham. So the Lord had to **"detach,"** Abraham from Lot. Circumstances caused Abraham and Lot to go in different directions, which brought about the detachment. **Detachment is a complete break.** With Lot leaving, the Lord could work in Abraham fulfilling his destiny in life. He was now free and where the Lord wanted him so he could receive all God had for him, *"And the Lord said unto Abram, **AFTER THAT LOT WAS SEPARATED FROM HIM,** Lift up NOW thine eyes, and look . . . For all the land which thou seest, to thee will I give it" (Gen. 13:14, 15)*. Abraham was **detached** from what would have hindered God's best in his life.

The Lord Jesus gives this principle when He said, *"if thy right hand offend thee, cut it off" (Matt. 5:30).* He is speaking here of detachment. He didn't mean to literally cut off one's hand. What He meant was to cut off anything standing in the way between you and God's best for your life. It may be a good thing, but whatever it is, with God's help, cut it out of your life. Detach yourself from it. It may cost a friendship and misunderstanding, but like Abraham you must follow the Lord's call. Separation and detachment are keys to God's best in one's life for both time and eternity.

Maranatha! The Lord Cometh!

FOLLOWERS OF CHRIST, THEN AND NOW
PART 1

Today, we are witnessing Church growth in an unprecedented manner. Never have we seen so many Mega-Churches whose attendance is running in the thousands. While this appears good, one must stop and ask the question, "How are we to interpret this phenomenon?" Is God in it or is something else going on undetected?

On the Day of Pentecost, the early Church had 3,000 conversions *(Acts 2:41)* and another 5,000 *(Acts 4:4)* the next day. Many see Acts 2 and 4 as the pattern for modern day mega-Churches and see the early Church as the first mega-Church. Now, there isn't anything wrong with a mega-Church, then or today. **The problem is not their existence but their emphasis.**

The difference between today's Church and the early Church, born on the Day of Pentecost, is in the reality of the Baptism in the Holy Spirit. In *Acts 2*, the people in Jerusalem saw and heard the effects of Pentecostal power and recognized its reality, as the result of the 120 that were baptized with the Holy Ghost, speaking in tongues

THE PASTOR'S PEN

as the Spirit gave them utterance. They hurried out to the streets to see the mighty power of God in action.

This was the emphasis and phenomena of that day in the history of the early Church, whereas today the emphasis is no longer Pentecost and herein lies the danger.

It was John the Baptist who first set the tone for the Church's emphasis. He came out of the wilderness proclaiming the coming of the Messiah, and is the first to use the term, Lamb of God, in identifying Christ. **His message declared Jesus to be both Saviour** *("the salvation of God" in Luke 3:6)* **and Baptizer** with *"the Holy Ghost and fire" (Luke 3:16).* Then on the Day of Pentecost, Peter gives the same emphasis by also preaching Jesus as both Savior and Baptizer of the Holy Ghost in *Acts 2:38, "Repent and be baptized . . . in the name of Jesus Christ for remission of sins* (salvation) *and ye shall receive the gift of the Holy Ghost."*

These two titles, **Savior and Baptizer**, were the message and the emphasis of the early Church from its very birth, and must remain the same till Jesus returns. They are *"His legs as pillars of marble, set upon sockets of fine gold" (Song of Sol. 5:15).* What we are seeing in many Churches and denominations today is the preaching of one half of the early Church's message and emphasis. Many are preaching Christ as Savior, which is wonderful, but have dropped the second part, that He is the Baptizer with the Holy Ghost and fire. This is the difference between the early Church's emphasis and today's Church emphasis. **This is tragic in that it is a great loss for the individual believer and the Church.**

As a result, our present-day **culture and corporate** setting has stepped in to set the pace for the operation of the Church. We live in a culture that advocates results and unfortunately, the Church is being influenced by it. Then, there is the corporate setting where the Church is looked upon as a business. Recently, in a Church magazine article, a corporate Christian Executive advises pastors to learn and use corporate techniques to grow a Church. Both, our culture and business methods are secular and carnal means. They work fine in the realm of the corporate, but will not work in the realm of the Spirit. One cannot apply secular methods to meet the needs of a spiritual entity. *Jesus said, "that which is born of the flesh is flesh; and that which is born of the Spirit is Spirit" (John 3:6).*

Secular business is a man-made working machine, but the Church is not a machine, she is a living organism vibrating with the very life of God. Machinery produces inanimate results, while the Spirit gives life, for He is *"the Spirit of life" (Rom. 8:2).* The Church was born by the Holy Spirit and not by technique. The Church did not receive the *"spirit of the world, but the Spirit which is of God" (1 Cor. 2:12).*

For the Church to fulfill her eternal destiny, she must remain under the leadership of the Spirit. If she follows this executive's advice, she will be following the tune of another, and yes, may bring in people, but not have God's Divine approval. If the Church forsakes her roots and takes a different course than the one set on the Day of Pentecost, she will utterly fail.

An analogy of what is happening today in the Church can be seen in comparing the Church activities with those of the YMCA. The national YMCA of America was once the social complex for Christian young people, encompassing a healthy environment with sports and social activities. It did a good work, but now appears

The Pastor's Pen

to have been eclipsed by the Church, and in particular, the mega-Churches. Churches are providing and catering to every imaginable whim and desire of people to keep them coming. The Churches are now **"increased with goods,"** as was the Church of Laodicea. Churches now include such things as a Starbucks coffee shop, exercise programs, bookstores, and conveniently-timed multiple services to fit everyone's schedule.

The services are precise and timed so people can leave through a side door, following a service, enabling the waiting group, to enter by another door. People come and go and feel they've done their duty of attending Church. The problem here is the time restraints that offer no opportunity for altar services or prayer times. Such a tight schedule preempts a move of the Spirit, with preference given to the next service beginning on time. It gives one a feeling that God has to wait His turn until a place is found to fit Him in. Here is where the Church today is different from the New Testament Church who prayed continually. Prayer was the secret of her power. **To them Christ was pre-eminent, not a time schedule.**

The Seven Churches of Revelation give us further insights on the condition of today's Church. It opens with the Lord standing in the center of the Seven Golden Candlesticks, which represent the Seven Churches, and showing Christ as the central figure of the Church. At the close of chapter *3:20,* He is outside the Church, knocking to re-enter its doors.

Each of the Seven Churches represents a Church era until Christ returns. The last Church addressed is the Church of Laodicea, who represents today's Church. In studying the state of the Laodicean Church, we find ourselves looking into a mirror reflecting the present state of the Church as being exactly in the same state as the Laodicean Church.

The Laodicean Church's boast is that she was rich and increased with goods (programs) and lacked nothing. Yet, in the Lord's eyes she was **"wretched, miserable, poor, blind, and naked."** Outwardly, she appeared to be a model Church.

Sadly, she was so taken up with her successes that she was unaware of her true spiritual state. **This shows material success can blind one to reality, and bring with it spiritual deception.**

Jesus warned of the danger in the last days of many being deceived and almost deceiving even the elect, if it were possible *(Matt. 24:11, 24).* The devil's objective for deception against the Church is to corrupt the Church *"from the simplicity that is in Christ" (2 Cor. 11:3).* His goal is to **steal her vision and corrupt her**, by taking up worldly techniques, which will neutralize her power and effectiveness against the kingdom of darkness.

The Church must remain faithful to her Lord by staying within the simplicity of the truth of Christ and *"contend for the faith once delivered to the saints" (Jude 3).* This is the Church's responsibility and hasn't changed since Christ's commission on the Day of the Ascension.

"He that hath an ear, let him hear what the Spirit saith to the Churches" (Rev. 3:22). **May the messages of the Seven Churches resonate in the hearts of all who respond to the Master's knock.**

Maranatha! The Lord Cometh!

FOLLOWERS OF CHRIST, THEN AND NOW
PART 2

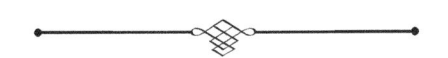

In last month's Vision we addressed the state and condition of today's Church. This month we want to see the state and **condition of the individual followers of Christ.**

What we saw last month in today's Church is a new emphasis to reach individuals, based on corporate efforts and techniques in place of the marvelous move and work of the Holy Ghost. The end result is a shallow conversion based on what Christ can do for "me." It's much like the seed that fell in stony places the Lord Jesus referred to in *Matthew 13*.

In *John 6,* when the Lord fed the five thousand, we see parallels of surface conversions as we do today. Among this group were those who followed the Lord because of His miracles *(v. 2, 14),* and others because He fed them *(v. 26).* To follow the Lord as a result of His miracles is fine, as long as they understood that miracles are a starting point and not an end. Miracles are signs pointing to the Lord and His teachings of the purposes of God.

They followed Jesus all day and now were tired and hungry from the journey. The fact that they stayed with the Lord all day moved Him with compassion to feed them. While He knew many would walk away, He nonetheless was moved that they were with Him all day.

But as it was then, so it is today. Many followed the Lord because He provided them with a meal *(v. 26)*. Many today come to Christ for the same motive, that He will give them what they want. Human nature is such that as long as Jesus keeps providing, people will continue to follow Him. **They were following Him for what He does and not for who He is**. When the Lord began teaching them, the crowd began to realize that following Jesus is more than just seeing needs met.

These are the same ones who chased after Him in verse 24 and enjoyed His presence and fellowship, in so much they wanted to make Him king *(v. 15)*. They were excited about Jesus and even knew the scripture to correctly connect Jesus with Moses' prophecy in ***Deuteronomy 18:18***.

From all outward appearances, they were joyful and excited to be with Jesus and His Disciples. They were zealous to the point of volunteering for ministry so they could do miracles *(v. 28)*. At first this appears to be wonderful that converts are willing to immediately go out and do miracles. Actually, they didn't understand the workings and ways of God, and their desire to do the works of God revealed their motive was the "me" factor. They weren't interested in God's process; they were only interested in the attention of vainglory. We are living in a day of great selfishness and self-interest. Paul warned in ***2 Timothy 3*** that this worldly spirit of selfishness will find its way in the Church.

THE PASTOR'S PEN

Its cover is enthusiasm and misguided zeal. Herein lies the danger of deception. Let us remember, we are in conflict with an extremely cunning and wise enemy with many disguises, including coming as an "angel of light." Not everything that appears outwardly white is necessarily pure.

With such an enthusiastic crowd, it appeared a revival had broken out with the conversion of five thousand men, plus the women and children. But in reality, it was not that way at all. **Crowds and enthusiasm aren't always an indication of revival. Often it's an indication of curiosity. These traits are among us today.**

Jesus now leads them to the first step of the true work of God, which is to believe on Him *(v. 29)*, but instead of believing on Him, they questioned Him and wanted proof *(v. 30)*. What happened to their faith when they said He was the Prophet Moses spoke of?

Jesus then takes them a step further, in revealing Himself to them as the Bread of life. But instead of accepting this revelation, they refuse to believe on Him *(v. 36)*. **Many today want Jesus but not His message.** What happened to all their excitement of just a couple of hours earlier? Well, today, it's the same. Many enjoy going to Church, especially if there's good music to entertain them and short sermons, but if the message calls for a commitment to Christ, they shrink back and begin rationalizing the claims of Christ *(v. 41–42)*.

Many Churches today are aware of these reactions and do all they can to not offend the "new visitors." Jesus is *"a stumbling stone and rock of offence" (Rom. 9:33).* **The Cross is offensive because the precious blood of Jesus was shed on the Cross *(Gal. 5:11)*.** The world doesn't understand the ways of God and that the remission of sins only comes by the shedding of blood. The world doesn't want a "bloody religion," for when they see a Cross they innately know it was their sins that nailed Jesus there.

We cannot separate the blood of Jesus from salvation, for there is no other means of salvation apart from the precious blood of Jesus. Yes, there will be offense if you are serious about taking up your Cross and following Jesus. The offense of the Cross and the Blood of Jesus is with reason, purpose and cause. If people are offended by the Cross and the mention of the precious Blood of Christ, they are as Peter said in *1 Peter 2:7–8*, they are disobedient *"whereunto also they were appointed."*

Many understood His message but could not accept it and left Him **to their own eternal loss** *(v. 65, 66)*. He never accommodated people. Jesus never chased after people who refused to accept His message. **He didn't change His message to accommodate the people because it is truth and complete.** Truth cannot be altered nor mixed with error. It is steadfast. The Gospel message is a two-edged sword. One side is salvation and eternal life, and the one side is perdition and eternal damnation. The choice is up to the individual.

Peter had it right, *"Lord to whom shall we go? Thou hast the words of eternal life. And we believe and are <u>sure</u> that Thou are that Christ, the Son of the living God!" (John 6:68–69)* **There is no other Jesus and there never will be another Jesus!**

Maranatha! The Lord Cometh!

THE CHURCH UNDER ATTACK

As we approach the Second Coming of the Lord, we can expect severe and subtle attacks by the enemy against the Church. Israel's Exodus from Egypt has parallels with the Church's Exodus, which is the Rapture.

When Israel's Exodus from Egypt was near, the Egyptian taskmasters afflicted the people of God, making their lives miserable under Pharaoh's orders *(Exod. 1:8–14)*. Then, when Moses appeared, the time for the Exodus was even nearer and now the leaders of Israel came under attack and were severely beaten *(Exod. 5:14)*. Like Israel in Egypt, which is a type of the world, God's people today are under great duress and stress with the devil doing all possible to make Christians miserable. He doesn't want the Church to leave the world and go up in the Rapture. He knows the Book of Revelation very well and is fully aware of the consequences awaiting him when the Rapture takes place.

As Israel's leaders were targeted and beaten by the taskmasters, so the leaders of the Church today—Pastors, ministers, missionaries, etc. are targeted by the enemy and can expect to be harassed and beaten down in various ways. The Lord sees what is going on and hears groaning and sighing among the people of God and has respect for the Church as He did for Israel *(Exod. 2:23–25)*. This strategy of the enemy to wear out the saints of the Most High is meant to discourage the Church to give up and thus keep the Church from making the Rapture. However, this tactic to wear the out the saints is really a sign to the Church that the Lord is very near in coming. In all the devil's efforts against the Church, he has another strategy that is fraught with danger because of its subtlety

Psalm 83:5 tells how demoniac forces "consult" and discuss their plan of attack and then become "confederate," or join forces to accomplish their goals. What is their goal today? It is none other than to possess or take over the God house of worship and gradually change its identity. *Psalm 83* is a prayer Psalm against those who oppress the Church because of their purposes, which is identified in verse *12: "Let us take to ourselves the houses of God in possession."* **The devil wants to influence and control what goes on in the house of God**. The word possession in Hebrew (*yaresh*) means, **"to occupy by driving out previous tenants and possessing their place: to seize, to rob, to expel, to impoverish, to ruin, to cast out, to make (spiritually) poor."**[5] All these definitions for possession describe the goal of the evil one. What the devil would like to do is shut down Churches and in their place put restaurants and businesses and even a bar as is seen frequently in Europe. He also wants to possess Churches by deviating the Gospel message of Christ and the faith once delivered to the saints. Paul warned in *2 Corinthians 11:14* that the devil can disguise himself and come as an angel of light. This we are seeing today.

Now we need to see some of the ways in which he is attempting to fulfill his objective of possessing God's Houses of worship. The Lord warned and advised the

Church that as it was in the days of Noah so it would be in the days of His coming. Things that happened in Noah's day are happening today as an attack against the Church.

1. Holiness: In Noah's day, the thoughts of that generation were continually evil *(Gen. 6:5)* and verse 4 shows it was basically immoral. Today, the devil is again using immorality, beginning with youth and on up to adults of every age bracket, via the internet and television programming meant to corrupt the minds of believers in order to neutralize the message of holiness.

2. Music: The Church today must be on the alert and beware of wordly music entering our Churches.

3. Modesty: The loss of modesty from the world has now entered the Church. Immodesty and markings of the body are slowly creeping into the Church with acceptance. This, too, is part of Satan's attack against the Church.

4. Marriage and the Home: There is an attack on marriage today, which God ordained for the good of mankind and the family. The devil knows that if he can destroy the family he will produce great havoc on the Church.

The Church is truly living in "perilous times," as warned by the Lord and the Apostles John and Paul. The spirit of Anti-Christ is now already in the world and trying to creep into the Church with the spirit of rebellion and misguided direction as seen in the world. This is telling us Jesus is coming soon! We need to ready ourselves as it says in ***Revelations 19:7, "His wife hath made herself ready."*** Realizing He is coming soon, what we need to do to get ready is to ***"cast off the works of darkness, and let us put on the armor of light" (Rom. 13:12).*** In other words, get rid of the unimportant things that demand so much of your time, and begin, even now as you read this article, recommitting your life to Christ. Renew your consecration to Jesus as a married couple renews their vows of marriage after twenty-five or fifty years of marriage to each other. Remember the following bottom line:

Maranatha! The Lord Cometh!

THE LOST VISION

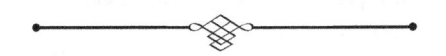

The Church is a prophetic body with a vision of the reality and purpose of life. As the Body of Christ, the Church is to see what the world does not see, and her mission is to proclaim what she sees to a world steeped in darkness and deception. The Church is the embodiment of light in this world as Jesus said, *"Ye are the light of the world" (Matt. 5:14).* The Church is the only Light the world sees and as a result we are their only hope of warning and preparation for future events. If the Church has lost her vision, not only is the world in jeopardy, but so is the Church.

Isaiah 25:7 says all nations have a veil spread over them as a result of rejecting Christ and it will remain on the nations until the Lord returns. The veil is a dark cloud that blinds the world from seeing clearly. Here is where the Church enters the picture. Since she is the only spiritual light in this world, she must be faithful in telling the world that Christ is coming soon, so they can escape the coming judgments of the Tribulation.

Her faithfulness is seen in lifting Christ up as Savior, but also in her message of proclaiming the Second Coming of Christ. It is here where the Church is failing today, and where she has lost her vision. The vision of the Lord's

Return was imparted to the early Church at the Ascension of Christ *(Acts 1:11)* with the angelic announcement, ***"this same Jesus, which is taken up from you into heaven, shall so come in like manner as you have seen him go into heaven."***

The words of the angels burned within their hearts like fire, giving birth to **"the blessed hope,"** which is Christ's Coming. When they saw Jesus ascend they didn't know what it all meant. Was He forsaking them? Would they ever see Him again? These questions rushed through their minds, but when they heard the words of the two angels that He was going to return, they were excited and thrilled. From that moment, they told everyone they met, "Jesus is coming back!" They lived their remaining lives with an inward burning hope of His soon return.

Next came the glorious Baptism of the Holy Spirit on the Day of Pentecost. The Spirit would be with the Church in Christ's stead UNTIL He returns. While the Spirit is still with the Church today, the Church has lost her legacy left to us by the early Church of Christ's return.

They lived the message of His return every moment of the day. Christ's return was the passion of their lives! **Where is that passion today?**

As we look at the Church today, we see Churches closing down Sunday evening services. We see believers taken up with interests other than the interests of the Lord. The early Church met every day for services. Yet, the Church today, who is closer to His Return than in any other generation, instead of having more services is eliminating them by closing down Sunday evening services. We should be adding services, not closing them down. Why is this happening? **Because we have lost the vision and the passion for His Return!**

I daresay the Church today does not believe Jesus is coming back soon, for if she did, every Church would be filled in every service and adding services, so if He should come tonight they would be ready and waiting for Him. The Word says He is coming for those looking for Him *(Heb. 9:28).* They are the ones who still have the vision in their hearts.

Instead, the Church today is changing its message from the Soon Return of Christ to living the good life here on earth now. She is exchanging the prayer life for a pampered life. These are signs that the Church in general has lost her vision and passion for Her Bridegroom. The Spirit is faithful and He is out there looking for those *"whose heart is perfect towards Him" (2 Chron. 16:9),* and He will find a people who have not forsaken the vision of the early Church and are waiting for the Bridegroom to come at any moment.

"And the Spirit and Bride say, Come, Lord Jesus!"

And Jesus' reply is, "Surely I come quickly." Rev. 22:17, 20

Maranatha! The Lord Cometh!

THE PRIVILEGED CHRISTIAN AND HIS INHERITANCE

The inheritance of the Christian Church is far greater than can be imagined. It is a privilege beyond words to have been born in the Church Era, which began with the Day of Pentecost. The words of Jesus in **Matthew's Gospel 11:11,** gives a glimpse of the greatness of our inheritance as well, as the greatness of our privilege to have been born in the New Testament Era. John the Baptist, who is the human bridge between the Old and New Testament, serves as the backdrop to the words of Jesus. He said, ***"Among them that are born of women there hath not risen a greater than John the Baptist: notwithstanding he that is least in the kingdom of heaven is greater than he."***

This is a great statement spoken by the Lord Jesus, that among all the men born since Adam, not one of them was greater than John the Baptist. Of course, one would wonder and question, how can that be? Just think for a moment of the great men of the Old Testament and yet the Lord puts John above all of them. His words about John were a great tribute and testimonial to the greatness of this man.

Yet, the least believer, meaning one small in dignity and estimation, is considered greater than John, the greatest of men who ever lived, except for Christ. As Jesus said, ***"Notwithstanding, he that is least in the Kingdom of Heaven is greater than he** (John)."* This is a phenomenal statement showing the incredible greatness of our inheritance in Christ. We are truly a blessed and favored people!

Now, we want to look at the Kingdom of Heaven and the Kingdom of God, which are synonymous and inter-changeable titles. Neither title is found in the Old Testament. The Kingdom of God or Heaven is a spiritual Kingdom not seen with natural eyes, whereas the physical Kingdom comes at the Millennium.

The term, Kingdom of Heaven, was revealed to John who was the first to preach it was at hand *(Matt. 3:2)*. When Jesus began His ministry, this too was His message *(Matt. 4:17)*. Up to that time, Israel was only familiar with the kingdom of David, which foreshadowed the Kingdom of Heaven.

The preaching of Christ began with the announcement that the Kingdom of Heaven was at hand, but **AFTER** Jesus began His ministry He said the Kingdom of God had come *(Matt. 12:28)*.

With this in mind, we can see how privileged the Church is as compared to the Old Testament saints. What makes the Kingdom of God so special is that **the Kingdom of God is now *IN* the believer *(Luke 17:21)*, which neither prophet, sage or king realized!** This was God's secret *"until Shiloh come,"* who is Christ *(Gen. 49:10)*.

Isaiah prophesied the Lord would do a new thing, which is the New Testament with all its blessings for the believers. This is that New Thing! **This is the privilege we have as New Testament children of God, which the Old Testament believers did not have nor know about!**

Having the Kingdom of God within us makes **the least in the Kingdom of God greater than John the Baptist.**

The Church's inheritance and privileges do not stop here. Another great privilege we have is that we are called the *"children of the resurrection" (Luke 20:36).* The believer will not have to go to Paradise, as did the Old Testament saints upon dying to wait for the Messiah. He has come and resurrected so that when we leave this body, we go directly to Heaven to be with Him forever.

Another privilege is to be in the **Bride of Christ**. This is reserved for the believers who have **made themselves ready for the Marriage Supper of the Lamb *(Rev. 19:7).*** The believers will be married to Christ, while the Old Testament saints will be the wedding guests.

And yet another privilege for the believer is the **Father/child of God, relationship** we can have with the Father, which was prohibited by the veil in the Tabernacle in the Old Testament. There were those in the Old Testament, who had a relationship with God but not as Father, with the exception of David, Isaiah, and Jeremiah who referred to God as Father. But this was rare. The name, Father was reserved for the Church as when we pray, *"Our Father, which art in Heaven" (Matt. 6:9)* **and** *"we cry, Abba, Father" (Rom. 8:15).*

Hopefully, we can see how blessed we are to have been chosen to come into the world at such a time as this. We didn't choose Him, He chose us *(John 15:16).* We are truly privileged and blessed beyond words to be members of the Body of Christ. This is wonderful and incredible, but true! He has made us one with Him by living in each of us. **This is a privilege!**

Maranatha! The Lord Cometh!

THE WONDER OF IT ALL

In 1955, George Beverly Shea, the soloist for Billy Graham, wrote a beautiful song, "The Wonder of it All" that tells how Christians should feel about the Lord and their salvation.

As we look at the state of the Church today, one can't help but feel the Church has lost her "wonder." It seems the Church today is so busy that she has forgotten the real purpose of our salvation, which is to be taken up with Christ, Our Lord, Savior and Bridegroom.

The Biblical Book that best describes this wonder is the **Song of Solomon**. It is a portrayal of the love between Christ and His Bride. Its message is a call to all believers, to return to our first love for Christ and be taken up with wonder for Him. The Bride in **Song of Solomon** speaks of her passion for her Lord, and her pursuit for the Lover of her soul. So constraining is her love for Him that she is unable to sleep or rest. She misses Him so deeply that she rises during the night to traverse the streets of the city, looking for Him whom her soul so dearly loves **(Song of Sol. 3:2).**

Perhaps, we can now understand why the book is called, **"The song of songs,"** or the chief of all the songs. Every book of the Bible is considered a song, but it is obvious from this descriptive phrase, this one is the most important of all the other books. It is a reminder to all believers that our lives, first and foremost, must be taken up with Him. It was so with the Bride in the Song of Solomon and as a result her pursuit of Him, she found Him and held Him, and would not let Him go *(Song of Sol. 3:4).*

It seems today, serving God has become mechanical and dutiful with the loss of the spontaneity of wonder for so many. While the Church appears to be growing in numbers, she also resembles toy soldiers, marching in step without passion or wonder for the Christ.

Sadly today so few seem to care much for seeking after Him. They have a myriad of excuses hidden behind their pet phrase, "God understands." God does not understand why anyone would forfeit the eternal blessings for earthly things that will pass away.

Of the Seven Churches in Revelation, the very first one **lost her first love.** This should serve as a lesson to the entire Church that we must protect our love for Christ first and foremost. Service is secondary. It is just as Jesus said to Martha, *"Martha, Martha, thou art careful and troubled about many things: But one thing is needful: and Mary has chosen that good part, which shall not be taken away from her" (Luke 10:41).*

The busyness of our times is an enemy to the welfare of our spiritual lives. Demands are on every hand, beckoning for our attention. As legitimate as they may seem, they are nothing more than robbers, hiding behind their calls for fulfillment. In these days, we need to recognize what is necessary and what is unnecessary. If we don't distinguish the difference, we will find ourselves with good intentions for the Lord and the things of God, but too tired at the end of the day to give the Lord the attention we owe.

This is why He says in ***Isaiah 55:2: "Wherefore do you spend money*** (time) ***for that which is not bread? and your labor for that which satisfieth not?"*** Why waste our lives for the temporal, when our soul could be delighting itself in fatness (eternal blessings) and the enrichment of our spiritual life *(v. 2–3)*.

Isaiah 9:6 *says,* ***"His name shall be called Wonderful,"* because He is wonderful and deserves our wonder!**

Maranatha! The Lord Cometh!

HOW DO YOU SEE JESUS?

(Going Beyond Christ's Humanity to His Divinity)

Having ministered now for over two years, Jesus was curious to hear what the people were saying about Him and asks the disciples, *"Whom do men say that I the Son of man am?" (Matt. 16:13).*

Their reply indicated there was quite a stir among the people who were buzzing as to what was going on and who is this Jesus. The disciples told Jesus the people were guessing, with some surmising He was John the Baptist, risen from the dead, because of the great following He had, as did John. Others said He was Elijah, because they saw Jesus' miracles and supernatural power; and still others said that He was Jeremiah, the weeping prophet, indicating how obvious it was to see the love and concern Jesus had for God's people. It strongly implies Jesus carried a burden and a broken spirit, and who like Jeremiah, wept over God's people in seeing the spiritual bondage they were under with legalism. These assumptions by the people show they saw Jesus only in His humanity.

After hearing the disciples, Jesus turns to them and asks, *"But whom say ye that I am?" (Matt. 16:15).* Jesus is asking them, "You have been with me now, going on three years, under all circumstances and pressures. You have seen my sitting down and my rising up, and miracles and heard my teachings so tell me, who do you say that I am?"

Peter steps forward and blares out like a trumpet, ***"Thou art the Christ, the Son of the living God"(Matt. 16:16).*** What is different about Peter's pronouncement as contrasted to the peoples' assumptions? The people only saw the humanity of Jesus and missed His divinity, whereas, Peter went beyond Jesus' humanity to His deity.

Yes, Peter and the disciples did see Jesus as a man on a daily basis, but the Father revealed to Peter and to the others, that Jesus was the Messiah, the Christ, and that He was not only the Son of Man, but also the Son of God.

Many today only see Jesus as a man, a teacher, or a prophet. They do not see Him as God. But when a man comes to the point of recognizing Jesus as the Son of God, he recognizes Christ's divinity and finds salvation. Salvation is not based on recognizing Jesus as a man, teacher, or prophet, it comes in recognizing Jesus as the Son of God.

In another passage ***(John 6:68–69),*** Peter adds to this statement, ***"Lord, to whom shall we go? thou hast the words of eternal life. And we believe and are <u>SURE</u> that thou art that Christ, the Son of the living God."***

There was no ambiguity in Peter's tone for he knew from the depths of his heart and soul that Jesus was the Son of God.

It is interesting to follow the steps of Peter to see what brought him to make such a resounding statement, which he spoke on more than one occasion. Peter was brought to the Lord by his brother Andrew ***(John 1:40–42)*** when he met Jesus for the first time. Peter apparently went back to his occupation as fisherman *(Luke 5:3)*. No doubt, he often thought of meeting with Jesus and wondered at the words of his brother Andrew that Jesus was the Messiah. But something happened, causing Peter to finally recognize that Jesus was the Son of God. It happened in Luke 5, when Jesus preached to the crowds from Peter's ship. He told Peter to launch out into the deep and let down his nets for a catch of fish.

Notice, Peter here calls Jesus Master, or commander and teacher, *(Luke 5:5)* and not Lord. This shows Peter saw the Lord as a man, a human with extraordinary gifts. In spite of his feelings, he respected the Lord enough, knowing his brother Andrew was a committed follower of Jesus right from the beginning, to obey His voice. When Jesus told him to launch out into the deep and then let down his nets, Peter thought it was futile as they had worked all night and didn't catch any fish.

Out of courtesy to Jesus and perhaps for his brother Andrew's sake, Peter said to the Lord, ***"we have toiled all night, and have taken nothing: nevertheless at thy word I will let down the net" (Luke 5:5).*** When the net broke with a great intake of fish, Peter was speechless and now saw his spiritual state as *"a sinful man" (v. 8),* and calls Jesus *"Lord."* He saw a miracle that transformed his life. **Here is where Peter went from the humanity of Jesus to the deity of Jesus.** When they got to shore, Peter now forsakes all to follow Jesus *(Luke 5:11)*.

It is in recognizing the Deity of Christ that the miracle of transformation and change becomes a reality.

Maranatha! The Lord Cometh!

PENTECOST, PEARL OF GREAT PRICE

In Matthew 13:45–46, the Lord spoke of the *"one pearl of great price."* While there are several worthy views on this parable, we want to see it in relation to Pentecost.

At His Ascension, the Lord commanded the Apostles *to "tarry ye in the city of Jerusalem, until ye be endued with power from on high" (Luke 24:49).* They went to the Upper Room in Jerusalem to wait on the Lord until the Spirit of God descended on them. They may have had some idea of what to expect since the Lord told them about it during the forty days He was with them, following the Resurrection *(Acts 1:3).*

They waited ten days, *"and suddenly there came a sound from heaven as of a rushing mighty wind, and it filled all the houses where they were sitting. And there appeared unto them cloven tongues like as of fire, and it sat upon each of them. And they were all filled with the Holy Ghost, and began to speak with other tongues, as the Spirit gave them utterance" (Acts 2: 2–4).*

The importance of the Baptism of the Holy Spirit is because it is the manifestation of the power of God, and the work of God cannot be done without the power of the Spirit. Since the Day of Pentecost, the Baptism of the Holy Spirit, which is the power of God, is available for the Church to do the work of God. Anything done in the Body of Christ by man's efforts and programs, in spite of their effectiveness, is unacceptable to God. ***Psalm 127:1, "Except THE LORD build the house, they labor in vain that build it."***

It is possible to get results in God's work by man's ingenuity, but it will show up as vanity on Judgment Day (see ***Matt. 7:21–23***). The work of God must be birthed and quickened by the Holy Spirit, to be acceptable before the Lord. ***Jeremiah 17:5*** warns of he who ***"trusteth in man and maketh flesh*** (methods of man's ingenuity) ***his arm,"*** which will cause one to part from the Lord to depend on carnality. The angel told Zerubbabel, in ***Zechariah 4:6,*** *it is **"Not by might, nor by power, but by MY SPIRIT, saith the LORD of hosts."*** There is no other way.

The parable of the pearl shows why Pentecost is a Pearl of Great Price. A pearl is the result of a foreign object finding its way into the shell of an oyster and painfully irritating it. In response, the oyster releases a secretion that surrounds the foreign body in order to contain it and alleviate the pain. The end result is a beautiful pearl coming out of a suffering oyster.

The Baptism of the Spirit is a pearl of great price because it came out of Christ's sorrow and sufferings. All would have been well on the earth if Adam had not fallen into sin. But sin entered the world because of man's fall and became man's irritant. The pain to mankind was long lasting and severe until the Father sent His Son, the Lord Jesus Christ, as the remedy for sin. In coming to earth as a man, the Lord Jesus entered man's world of sin and sorrow. Though without sin, He was tempted in all points as a man and saw the dire pain and agony that fell on man.

The Lord Jesus knew and understood the answer to man's problem was to die for man, in order to remove the condemnation of sin and then send the Holy Spirit, who would help man to live a life of joy and victory over the power of man's enemy, Satan. God opened the door that would make this possible by giving His Son as a ransom for man *(1 Tim. 2:6)*, and this in turn opened the door for man to receive the Promised Gift of the glorious Baptism of the Holy Spirit.

The blessing of the Baptism of the Holy Spirit is for redeemed man to learn to operate as God operates, and to move in God as God moves in a world filled with sin and evil. Jesus operated as the Father operated and by the Spirit wants us to do the same *(John 14:12),* which is only possible by the Baptism of the Holy Spirit and our total dependence on the Holy Spirit, *(John 16:13–15).*

It is through the Spirit that God accomplishes all His will and purposes in the universe. This is the only way the Church was meant to operate. Any effort by man to operate differently always ends in spiritual death. The Holy Spirit is the Spirit of life and He alone brings life into the Church. He knows the mind and will of God and accomplishes it through yielded vessels. All we are to do is trust and obey God. The pattern is seen through Moses, who obeyed God and by the Rod of God (type of the Holy Spirit) opened the Red Sea and delivered Israel from Egyptian bondage. Samson, though blind, destroyed the house of Dagon by the Spirit and killed over three thousand Philistines. The list of others who through the Spirit did miracles is in *Hebrews 11*.

Back to the parable now. The merchant knew there were pearls of different quality. There are fake pearls that look real, but aren't real. They were not born from a living organism, as in a real pearl. They are manmade and cheap. The real pearl comes from suffering in the oyster.

There is always the danger of deception when dealing with pearls. Here, the Church must be aware of the danger of getting caught up with doing God's work in man's way and not God's way. The Church must also beware of the flesh dictating God's work, instead of dependence on the Spirit's leading.

We find many fake pearls, presenting themselves today as real to the Church. Like the merchant in the parable, the Church must be discerning and needs to **sell out**, by getting rid of man-made ideas and distractions, so she can once again get back to the Pearl of great price—the ministry of the Holy Spirit. It cost Jesus His life for us to receive salvation and the Baptism of the Holy Ghost. He became poor that we might become rich *(2 Cor. 8:9)*. The Holy Spirit is our riches because He is our inheritance *(Eph. 1:13–14)* promised by God, the Father *(Acts 1:4)*. The Baptism of the Holy Spirit is our Pearl of Great Price.

Maranatha! The Lord Cometh!

THE CHURCH IN THE MIDST OF AN UNGODLY WORLD

We are living in a day of great social emphasis. This emphasis has a tendency to blind us to the reality of who we are, and how we are to live in a world that is antagonistic to the Lord Jesus Christ and His Church.

Jesus forewarned the Apostles that the world would hate them as it hated Him *(John 15:18)* and prayed for them and for us in *John 17:15–20.* The reason He gave for the world hating us is because the Lord Jesus chose us to come out of the world *(John 15:14)* and identify with Christ, not with the world system. The world spirit is governed by the *"prince of the power of the air" (Eph. 2:2),* who is the great Rebel-Satan, and Jesus wants us to have nothing to do with this evil power. The world stands for everything that is against God and Christ and is at enmity with God.

James 4:4 says, "Ye adulterers and adulteresses, know you not that the friendship of the world is enmity with God? whosoever therefore will be a friend of the world is the enemy of God."

Enmity means hatred and hostility towards someone, which the world certainly has towards God and Jesus with the worst of hostilities. So, how can the Church and believers be friends with a world that hates the Lord?

This issue is so serious that the Word describes the believer, who is a friend of the world, as an adulterer and adulteress. The Lord even goes a step further to say that whoever is a friend of the world is the enemy of God!

Paul recognized this and warns in *1 Cor. 15:33, "Be not deceived: evil communications corrupt good manners."* His warning further shows that evil company, or mixing and keeping company with unbelievers in their form of fun and games, will not only corrupt the child of God's ethical conduct and morals, but will neutralize the believer's testimony. It will blind the believer to his own spiritual state, and will lead to compromising one's Christian principles.

The world lives for the temporal and not the eternal. Its philosophy is, "Let us eat and drink for tomorrow we die." Meaning, "life is short, so let us indulge in whatever feels good at any cost and live it up." This world-view is based on narcissism and selfishness. The Christian's philosophy is this: Let us serve the Lord and press towards the mark of the high calling of God in Christ Jesus, and be ready for His Return, as Jesus is coming soon to take us to glory. Solomon wrote, *"He that walketh with wise men shall be wise: but a companion of fools shall be destroyed" (Prov. 13:20).* Such communication or interaction with unbelievers corrupts good behavior.

The child of God has too much to lose if he or she becomes spiritually lax, and begins to take up with unbelievers *(Matt. 24:42–51).* At first, it may appear nothing has been lost, but given time the loss will show itself.

Joel, chapter 3, gives an insight in his description of the four stages of the locust. The cankerworm stage is the most dangerous of the four because the cankerworm is the "licker."

He licks his prey to suck out its blood and life. At first, it feels soothing to the flesh of the prey without realizing he is slowly dying. Thus, it can happen to the believer without his being aware of what is happening, until it's too late.

So, how are we to live in a world system that is against God and His children in which we have no part? Living in this world doesn't mean we can't speak or work with the unsaved or shop where they shop, otherwise you would have to leave the earth. But here one must exert care, because the unsaved, as nice as they can be, are in darkness and can have a negative influence on the saved. Remember how Peter was with the unsaved warming his hand and from the influence of their presence denied Christ three times. The Lord warns us to ***"Watch and pray, that you enter not into temptation: the spirit indeed is willing, but the flesh is weak" (Matt. 26:41).***

Actually, there is no relationship with the world. We are pilgrims of another Kingdom the world knows nothing about. Amos said it clearly, ***"Can two walk together, except they be agreed?" (Amos 3:3)*** We cannot walk and agree with a world that crucified our Lord. Paul makes it clear we have no agreement with the temple of the world.

Paul further adds in ***2 Corinthians 6:14–18***, that the Church is not to become a socialite with the world. As pilgrims, **we are called to separation from the world** *(v. 17)* and must remember, this world is not our home; we are just passing through this life to eternal life with Christ.

We must also remember **who we are, to whom we belong, and what the Lord has done for us** in giving us salvation. We owe all that we are to Jesus for without Him we are nothing.

Maranatha! The Lord Cometh!

LOSING APPRECIATION FOR THE SACRED

Lamentations 2:5–9 Part 1

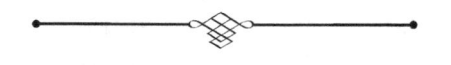

The Biblical story of the relationship between the Lord and Israel is truly filled with deep emotion. How often it is that we fail to realize God is emotional and has deep emotions for His children. This is especially seen with Israel as reflected by the Prophets as this article will show.

The prophet Ezekiel, in chapter 16 of his book, describes the pitiful condition of Israel when the Lord found her. Then verses *6–14* tells us all He did for her and how He gently nourished her and brought her to a place of health. Ezekiel then describes how the Lord brought her to prominence and watched her develop and mature into a beautiful people *(v. 13–14)*. Israel was so beautiful that the Lord married her by covenant *(v. 8)* and made her His possession.

But slowly, her beauty and renown betrayed her *(v. 15)*, causing her to drift away from God to go looking for excitement with her neighboring nations, in particular, the Egyptians. The Lord blessed her greatly with gold and silver, fine clothing, and much more *(v. 16–18)*. But rather than walking by faith, she chose to live by the desires of the flesh *(v. 26)*.

Israel thought she could take the blessings of God and use them personally to buy favor and acceptance with the idolatrous neighboring nations. She was no longer satisfied with the faithful God who had done so much for her; she went seeking idolatrous lovers (v. 33). She wanted flesh! Her crave for flesh was insatiable and she found herself unsatisfied and unfulfilled *(v. 28)*. She left her God for emptiness. *"Hath a nation changed their gods, which are yet no gods? but My people have changed their glory for that which doth not profit" (Jer. 2:11)*.

When a people, a denomination, or an individual loses appreciation for the sacred, they are exchanging the glory of God for "Flesh" (Egypt), *Ezek. 16:26*. Israel did not see nor did they want to see and understand the meaning behind the commands for worship. The meaning behind it all in type was that they pointed to His Son, the Lord Jesus Christ. These commands given through Moses for worship were holy because they came from the Holy Jehovah-God.

The Lord's Prayer says, *"Hallowed be thy name" (Matt. 6:9),* which tells that whatever God touches becomes hallowed or holy. It's like when the Lord called Moses and said to him, *"put off thy shoes from off thy feet, for the place whereon thou standest is holy ground" (Exod. 3:5)*. What made it holy? God's presence. Whenever God sanctions a decree, a person, a place or a thing, it becomes holy. All the Laws and commands of God to Israel were sacred and holy because they came from Him. Sadly, over time, Israel lost the sense of sacredness for these holy things of God and consequently lost the glory of God.

She had so much, yet lost it all. **Why? Because she lost appreciation for the sacred.**

The Lord was deeply upset with Israel for her ingratitude and failing to see the value of what He had done for her. He was angry and grief-stricken over their attitude towards Him and His goodness, showing little regard for all the precious gifts He gave her *(Jer. 2:3)*. The pain of being rejected by His own people was so deep that He determined to put away all the beauty associated with the worship He enjoyed with Israel in a by-gone era.

He violently takes His tabernacle away *(Lam. 2:6)*. He removes the solemn feasts and Sabbaths, and casts off His altar *(Lam. 2:6–7)*. The message here is, "I have made these items sacred and important, but My people have counted them as nothing. I will take them away and their soul shall languish for having lost them. I have no pleasure in them anymore. I will call a people which were not My people *(Rom. 9:25)* who will appreciate all I do for them and I will be their God."

The issue was that Israel lost all respect for the sacred things of God, which the Lord held in high esteem and premium. They lost the sense of sacredness for the tabernacle, the altar, the solemn feasts, and the sacrifices *(Mal. 1:7–8)*. This, along with her idolatry, causes the Lord to divorce Israel *(Isa. 50:1; Jer. 3:8)* and put her away for the Seventy Years of Captivity. Unfortunately, the loss of respect for the sacred things of God is prevalent today, which we discuss more fully next month.

While the Lord tried to do everything possible to forget them, **He couldn't FORGET THEM! He loves them too much!** Here enters the story of Hosea and his unfaithful wife, Gomer. What can separate us from the love of God? *"For I am persuaded, that neither death,* *nor life, nor angels, nor principalities, nor powers, nor things present, nor things to come, Nor height, nor depth, nor any other creature, shall be able to separate us from the LOVE OF GOD, WHICH IS IN CHRIST JESUS OUR LORD!" (Rom. 8:38–39)*

In spite of His love for her, Israel must enter the 70 Years Captivity, and the inception of the times of the Gentiles under Nebuchadnezzar. With this event the Lord now turns from Israel to focus on another people who will appreciate Him for who He is. These are the Gentiles who Israel always disregarded. They will love Him and appreciate all He does for them.

Of Israel, He says, *"I will move them to jealousy with those which are not a people; I will provoke them to anger with a foolish nation" (Deut. 32:21).* We, the Gentiles, are that foolish nation. He further says, *"I will call them my people, which were not my people; and her beloved, which was not beloved. And it shall come to pass, that in the place where it was said unto them, Ye are not my people; there shall they be called the children of the living God" (Rom. 9:25–26).*

Acts 13:48 shows the exuberance of the Gentiles when they learned the door of salvation was now opened wide for them to come in. *"When the Gentiles heard this, they were GLAD!"* The fall of Israel brought salvation to the Gentiles and became the riches of the Gentiles ***(Rom. 11:11, 12).*** But the story doesn't end here. God opens a new chapter in the history of mankind in relationship to Himself, for whom He will make things new ***(2 Cor. 5:17).*** There will be a new covenant for a new people, through whom He will do a completely new thing as revealed by Paul in Ephesians chapter 3. Everything will be new; a new doctrine *(Acts 17:19);* a new testament *(2 Cor. 3:6);* and a new creation *(2 Cor. 5:17).*

Now, the question is, **"Will the Gentiles also fail God and do as did Israel?"** For *Ezekiel (16:44)* said*, "As is the mother, so is her daughter."* Israel is the mother, out of whom came the daughter, who is the Church. Will the Church treat God and His Son as Israel did? We will address this question in the Vision: Part 2.

Maranatha! The Lord Cometh!

LOSING APPRECIATION FOR THE SACRED
Lamentations 2:5–9 Part 2

*I*n last month's issue of the Vision, we saw how Israel took the things of God for granted to the point of hating them and doing despite to them. What God saw as sacred they viewed as unimportant. It's the same spirit that was carried into Jesus' day in the Parable of the Marriage of the King's Son *(Matt. 22:2–10)*. The guests who were invited to the marriage feast of the King's Son **made light** of the invitation. Israel made light of the sacredness of the tabernacle, the solemn feasts, the altar, and the sacrifices Old Testament. As a result, Israel became unworthy as stated in the Parable. It is interesting to note that the same spirit or attitude of Israel in the Old Testament still existed in the times of Christ in Israel.

The king then sends his servants into the highways and to find worthy guests. Those worthy guests were worthy because they accepted the invitation of the king, and appreciated the honor of being invited to the king's son's wedding. Never in a million years did they ever dream they would one day sit at the wedding feast of their king's son. These guests speak of none other than the Gentiles, who would become the nucleus of the Church.

Before the child of God was saved and baptized into the Body of Christ, he never thought nor did he know that he would have part in the Marriage Supper for the King's Son, the Lord Jesus Christ. How precious and meaningful are those promises and blessings of God for those who treasure what the Lord gives to us. Let us appreciate everything the Lord does for us, as a member of the Body of Christ and as an individual believer.

Now the question is, will the Church follow in Israel's footsteps and disdain the things of God, as did Israel? Will the Church take the blessings of God for granted? Will she lose the sense of the sacred too? *Ezekiel 16:44 says, "As is the mother, so is her daughter."* The Church is the daughter of Israel, for the Church was born in the city of Jerusalem on the Day of Pentecost. The Gospel went first to the Jews as God's promised people, then went to the Gentiles as a result of the Jews rejecting it in *Acts 13:46* under the Apostle Paul.

Israel was given objects that were set apart for purposes of worship and thus became sacred, after they were either anointed with holy oil and the blood of the sacrifices sprinkled on it as the Ark of the Covenant. But Israel failed to look beyond the object to the spiritual content the object represented. In the Old Testament era, an object of itself was not holy; it was what the object represented that made it sacred.

An example is the Table of Shew Bread in the Holy Place of the Tabernacle. The Table was made of natural wood and the bread of natural flour, but when that bread became hallowed *(1 Sam. 21:6)* by the prayer of the priest *(Lev. 24:5–9),* it became the **"Bread of His**

Presence," and spoke of Christ as the Bread of Life (*John 6:32–36*).

So, when Israel lost the sacredness of the holy things of the Old Testament, they were literally turning their back on God and His efforts to help them see and understand the things of the Spirit. They chose carnality instead, which became a terrible loss. This is where they erred.

It's like Isaiah said in ***Isa. 6:9–10,*** they heard but didn't understand; they saw but didn't perceive (acknowledge); their hearts were fat with sensuousness and carnality; their ears heavy, meaning God's words were burdensome to them. They wanted lightness or as Paul says in ***2 Tim. 4:3, "itching ears,"*** or scratching their ears to make them feel good. They didn't want to understand or perceive because they liked doing their own thing without condemnation. This is why they didn't like the prophets. They choose to turn aside from God and consequently couldn't understand God and what He wanted to do in blessing them.

This is a serious lesson for the Church today, for Israel, and others in the Old Testament, **are examples to remind the Church today *(1 Cor. 10:11)* of the immeasurable loss that comes to a people or an individual when he or they take the things of God lightly and loses respect for their sacredness.**

Only God knows how very much this very thing is happening in the Church today. As a result of being materially blessed, we think this is a sign of God approving our lives, but the Bible in ***James 2:5*** says He has chosen the poor to be rich in faith.

We saw what the Lord expected from Israel in ***Ezekiel 16*** as far as sacredness was concerned, but what are the things in the New Testament that God holds sacred? **They are: the precious blood of Jesus; Communion; Water**

Baptism; Baptism with the Holy Ghost; the Holy Bible, which is the Word of God; and the Lord's Day.

We cannot preach enough on **the Blood of Jesus.** Peter says it is precious and by *"the blood of the Lamb" (Rev. 12:11),* we overcome Satan **for Jesus' Blood is sacred! Communion is sacred,** but in many circles, it has become a necessary inconvenience, yet God sees it as sacred and holy. Communion is not a tag-on part of a service; Communion and the Word are the main part of any service. **Water Baptism is sacred** as it is an ordinance and command of the Lord. By it we identity with the death, burial and resurrection of the Lord. **The Baptism of the Holy Ghost is sacred** for it the coming of the Holy Spirit on one's life and is the *"earnest of our inheritance!" (Eph. 1:14).* **The Word of God is also sacred** for God puts His word above His name. **The Lord's Day, Sunday, is sacred** and a constant reminder of the greatest event of history, the Resurrection of Christ from the dead and overcoming Satan, death, and Hell! Israel lost the glory of God because they lost the sense of sacredness. May the Church never lose the awe of sacredness as ordained by the Lord!

"Death is swallowed up in victory. O death, where is they sting? O grave, where is thy victory? But thanks be to God, which giveth us the victory through our Lord Jesus Christ" (1 Cor. 15:54–57). **Amen and Amen!**

Maranatha! The Lord Cometh!

SLEEPING THROUGH THE RAPTURE

In Bible days, city walls and watchfulness was very important for a city, as it was a matter of life or death for its citizens. Cities had "watchmen," who served as guards, on the city walls and whose job it was to watch for the possibility of an enemy who would attack the city. Every hour each watchman at his station on the wall would cry out the time and say, "all is well." His fellow watchmen would do the same, and hearing each other's cry put their minds at ease knowing their fellow watchmen were awake and safe.

Jesus repeatedly warned the Church to *"watch and pray,"* because of the dangers of spiritual darkness in the world. He gave the Church Pastors and Prophets, who are called to serve as watchmen of the Church because of the dangers from the evil one. The enemy always seeks for ways to infiltrate the Church in order to corrupt it. The devil, whom Jesus called the wicked one in the Parable of the Tares, does much of his work in the darkness of nightfall *(Matt. 13:25).* His objective is to bring spiritual sleep to the Church so he can successfully plant the spirit of "tares" in the Church. He uses this same scheme to plant tares in the life of a believer. For this reason, Jesus warned the Church and the individual believer to, ***"watch and pray lest you enter into temptation" (Matt 26:41).*** Temptation comes as a result of one's own carelessness and disobedience. The warning to the individual is because he is always a potential prey for our adversary, the devourer *(1 Peter 5:8).*

The tares are weeds, which have no value and resemble wheat. The Jews saw them as degenerate wheat because of their resemblance to real wheat. They are a guise that appears to be something they are not. Botanically, the seeds of the tares are poisonous to man, producing sleepiness that leads to death. Jesus said, ***"the tares are the children of the wicked one" (Matt. 13:38).*** This includes deception and schemes by Satan, including ***"false brethren" (2 Cor. 11:26; Gal. 2:4).*** The devil further looks for opportunities to plant these tares of ideas, in the mind of the believer to confuse him.

This calls for care and diligence on the part of the believer in the light of the promoting of many teachings in the Church today via Christian television, seminars, and radio that may sound good, but are not of God. Here is where the devil enters as an angel of light to deceive, in order to plant tares of attractive but dangerous teachings. Among believers the devil looks for those who are strong-willed and gullible. Such a personality is prime for the devil's purposes because a strong-willed individual will vigorously propagate some new idea, simply because it's new, and draws attention to himself.

Regrettably, the Church today is being flooded and overwhelmed with many new "tares" of good sounding methods and ideas, but they are not of God. The devil is a good copycat and knows how to copy God and how to produce pseudo results to deceive *(2 Thess. 2:9–10)*. He is so subtle with deception that it doesn't appear as deception. It appears natural and the right thing to do, while all the while it is deception so his **"poisonous seeds"** can succeed in bringing sleep to the Church and the believer. His plan is to bring a deep spiritual sleep on the believer and through the believer bring sleep to the Church. Little wonder our days are called **"perilous times."** Danger and peril for the Church lurks everywhere and will worsen as we get closer to the coming of the Lord Jesus.

The emphasis for watchfulness by the Lord Jesus is mostly in the references to His Second Coming. Notice, how often Jesus refers to the false prophets and deception in the last days. In fact, the Word of God puts great stress on the danger in the last days, as a precarious time indeed, because the enemy is working to keep the Church from being ready for the Rapture. He is trying to frustrate and obstruct the plan of God.

Jesus spoke of two in a bed, and one was taken and the other was left behind *(Luke 17:34)*. One was ready and the other was not and slept through the Rapture. When he awakened, it was too late. Jesus said, *"Watch ye therefore: for ye know not when the Master cometh . . . Lest coming suddenly he find you sleeping" (Mark 13:35–36)*. The coming of Christ will be sudden and unexpected even as a thief of the night. The importance of readiness for the Rapture cannot be overstated because of its great importance. Even children need to be aware of Christ's Return and live in its hope.

Prosperity and leisure were the two enemies of the Church of Laodicea, which represents the Church prior to Jesus' Coming. The Lord said, *"He that has an ear, let him hear what the Spirit saith unto the Churches" (Rev. 3:22).*

The message to the individual is beware of these same two enemies in your life as it was in the Church of the Laodiceans. Their spiritual state was mediocre as a result of reveling in their possessions.

A number of years ago, a woman told me of a dream the Lord gave her showing the spiritual state of her Church. In the dream, she saw the congregation of several hundred people, asleep in their pews during a Sunday morning service, and thee ministerial staff was also asleep, slouching in their chairs on the pulpit. **What a message to that Church!**

Paul calls us to *"awake,"* and be alert to the times in which we are living *(Eph. 5:14–17).* Let us take heed and remember the word of *Heb. 9:28, "Unto them that look for Him shall He appear the second time without sin unto salvation."* Jesus said, *"Look up, and lift up your heads; for your redemption draweth nigh" (Luke 21:28).*

Maranatha! The Lord Cometh!

SALVATION, ENTRY INTO THE SPIRITUAL LIFE, JOHN 3:5

The story of Nicodemus coming to Jesus by night is a remarkable story. It shows the spiritual hunger that exists, deep within the heart of man for spiritual reality. Nicodemus heard Jesus speak, for he addresses Him as Master (Teacher). He also saw the miracles Jesus performed and realized Jesus came from God. Having heard Jesus speak and seeing His miracles, he knew the answer to his quest for spiritual reality could only be found in the Lord Jesus.

This realization caused him to seek out Jesus at night rather than in daylight for fear of being seen talking to Jesus and receiving a reprimand from his peers. But Nicodemus's hunger for truth and reality was like Jeremiah's fire in his bones. **He must speak with Jesus!** He approached Jesus alone.

Immediately, Jesus revealed to him the mystery of salvation, which rested on the spiritual truth that man must be born again to enter the Kingdom of God. After this encounter with Jesus, Nicodemus knew truth resided in Jesus alone.

The struggle between truth and deception began with the Fall of man. Since that event, man has been searching for truth to satisfy the inner craving for fellowship with God. However, the Fall released Satan, the father of lies, to lie to man about God and promote a false religion of lies, idolatry and deception which will culminate with the great lie of Anti-Christ in *2 Thessalonians 2:8–12.* Man's fallen and corrupt human nature lends itself to believing the lies of Satan. The Bible says it happens *"because they received not the love of the truth, that they might be saved" (2 Thess. 2:10).*

The truth of salvation that Jesus gave to Nicodemus tells how man today can find spiritual reality that is found only in Jesus. The miracle of the new birth gives man entry into the Kingdom of God, as Jesus said, *"except a man be born again, he cannot see the kingdom of God . . . Except a man be born of water and of the Spirit, he cannot enter into the Kingdom of God" (John 3:3, 5).* This was entirely new and unknown in the Old Testament.

In fact, Jesus gave Nicodemus a glimpse into spiritual theology, kept in the heart of God until Jesus would come and reveal it. This theology of salvation is the greatest gift a person can ever receive through faith in the Living Savior, the Lord Jesus Christ. This wonderful and precious gift of salvation is the door that opens to the believer many more wonderful and precious gifts.

While we are thankful for our salvation and the receiving of eternal life through Christ, salvation is the door that introduces us to the third person of the Trinity, the Holy Spirit *(John 3:5–8).* It is the Holy Spirit, who affects the new birth and it is He that leads us into all truth, for He is the Spirit of truth *(John 16:13).* Salvation opens the door to revelation. In *John 10:9,* where Jesus said He is the door, He also said that we shall enter in, via salvation, *"and shall go in and out, and find pasture."* It is this phrase of *"finding pasture,"* that we want to focus on.

This pasture is the Word of God and in *Heb. 6:1–2,* we read that we are to go on in God's pasture from our point of salvation to perfection, which is completion. Salvation is the entry point and Heaven is the goal or point of completion. So, though we have built on the foundation of repentance and Biblical doctrine, we must go on to higher planes.

As Paul said to the Corinthians, we go *"from glory to glory" (2 Cor. 3:18).* In the Christian life, we continue to grow until the Lord takes us home, but in the natural life, a man grows to a point and then declines by the process of age and the limitation of time. Our spirit is not limited to time because it is eternal by being born again.

Thus, salvation gives us entry to the spiritual life that goes on forever! We take to Heaven the revelation we received here and pick up where we left off on earth. Revelation is an impartation of eternal truth that is in God and given to us now. However, each Christian determines while on earth, their eternal place in Heaven by how far they have grown in God in this life. This has nothing to do with the administrations and politics of Church religion and positions; it has to do with the pursuit of Christ by the individual. So, we go from salvation on earth to eternal revelation of Christ and the Godhead in Heaven. This in itself will be glorious! We as Christians are greatly blessed now in Christ. There will never be an end of the revelation of God in eternity and it will go on and on forever. This is what our blessed salvation through Jesus Christ brings us now and then.

Maranatha! The Lord Cometh!

WHAT GOD BLESSES HE BREAKS

As a steward *"of the mysteries of God" (1 Cor. 4:1),* the Apostle Paul certainly understood what he was saying when he wrote to the Romans, *"O the depth of the riches both of the wisdom and knowledge of God! how unsearchable are his judgments, and his ways past finding out!" (Rom. 11:33)* Even Job expressed the same sentiment in *Job 37:23, "Touching the Almighty, we cannot find Him out."*

When it comes to understanding God's ways of working in the lives of His children, it is difficult to understand just why He chooses a certain road and way to take us through. Certainly, Job was baffled by the events in his life and wondered as to the meaning of it all *(Job 6:24).* Job asks the Lord to tell him why and what is He doing to him *(Job 10:2)?*

So, the hidden purposes of God are developed in the life of a child of God, by the mysterious workings of God that seemingly don't make sense. Since the child of God cannot understand what is going on in his life, he finds himself in a dilemma with questions. The only answer he now has is to trust God, who knows what He is doing and will do the right thing. Our faith must have a foundation to stand on, to keep us from confusion and that foundation is the Word of God.

The servant of God must come to the place of knowing the Lord will work all things for his good, even though it is difficult to understand *(Rom. 8:28).* Peter says, *"Beloved, think it not strange concerning the fiery trial which is to try you, as though some strange thing happened unto you: But rejoice, inasmuch as you are partakers of Christ's sufferings; that, when his glory shall be revealed, ye may be glad also with exceeding joy" (1 Peter 4:12–13).*

Another great verse for direction and encouragement to the one going through the dark night of their soul, is *Isaiah 50:10, "Who is among you that feareth the Lord, that obeyeth the voice of his servant (this is Jesus, see Isaiah 42:1), that walketh in darkness, and hath no light?"* So, as a child of God, you say, "That's me. I do fear and honor the Lord and I obey His voice and do all I know to do to get out of this situation. But I can't get out and it seems things continue to get worse. Tell me what to do because I don't know what to do?"

The answer is to go back to the Word, which is a lamp to our feet and a light for our path. The Word will always have an answer and will give direction for our problem. The answer is in *Isaiah 50:10: "LET HIM TRUST IN THE NAME OF THE LORD, AND STAY UPON HIS GOD!"*

In other words, recognize God is working in you for a purpose for your good, so you can learn to use faith. Remember, faith pleases God and if you act in faith by seeking Him diligently or earnestly with all your heart, He will meet you and reward you.

Now the question is, "Why does God break what He blesses?" The question appears to be incongruous with the nature of God, yet the Lord sees it as harmonious with His nature, knowing what the end result will produce in the life of His children and for God's glory. Definitely, His ways are past finding out.

Our first introduction to this marvelous truth is when Jesus fed the multitude in **Matthew 14:19, 20: "And looking up to heaven, he blessed, and brake . . . And they did all eat, and were filled."** He looked heavenward first, then He blessed, and then he broke.

Looking heavenward speaks of the recognition and dependence on God. Jesus is recognizing that the bread He holds came from God as the supplier of our needs. It is saying that God looks after us in spite of circumstances. He is the faithful God of our lives. This is the first step. Then comes the second step when we bless what we are about to eat. There are many experiences the Lord gives us to eat that are not easy to eat, and after we have eaten and swallowed them are not easy to keep down (as in Ezekiel, the Lord told him to eat the roll).

Many Christians have chosen to live their life on the **"broad way" (Matt. 7:13, 14)** with all its comforts, prestige, popularity, position, and recognition. Sadly, they will not accept this message, but the "few" in the narrow way have accepted it and have found the secret and the reality of the spiritual life. The reason this way is narrow is because few travel it. In fact, few even "find it." With so much that goes on in the Church today, many have turned from the cross to another way and find themselves in the broad way where life is soft and easy. The cross was never meant to be soft and easy. It was meant to bring us to where we die to the world and all its dainties, so we can inherit the light and glory of the Master.

This is why the Lord must break what He blesses, because the breaking process, though painful, makes us *"meet for the Master's use"* and releases us from that *"which is not bread? . . . that which satisfied not?" (Isa. 55:2).* If the Lord has blessed you and then chosen to break you, rejoice, for you are *"a vessel unto honor . . . meet for the Master's use" (2 Tim. 2:21).*

In God's house, there are vessels of honor and dishonor *(2 Tim. 2:20–21).* The difference between the two is that one went through the breaking process, the honorable, and the other, the vessel of dishonor, did not submit to the breaking process. He wanted a shortcut to the ways of God, but there are no shortcuts with God.

It is the broken man that blesses others and becomes *"seed to the sower and bread to the eater" (Isa. 55:10).*

Maranatha! The Lord Cometh!

THE AGONY AND SUFFERINGS OF THE GOD HEAD

Seldom do we take time to think about the sufferings of God and of His Son, the Lord Jesus Christ. We are well aware of the price it cost the Lord to redeem mankind, but have we ever given thought of the sufferings and agony of the Trinity? God the Father paid a great price to bring about the plan of salvation and the fulfillment of His divine purposes in man's behalf. In wanting to identify with His creation, God, for the first time, would suffer immensely. As a result, we can rest assured **God does not ask us to suffer unless He first has suffered. He is the greatest sufferer of the universe.**

It broke the heart of God and caused Him great sorrow at the rebellion of Lucifer and his fallen angels *(Rev. 12:4).* So deep was the anguish of God that He called for a lamentation, which means to beat on the chest and to grieve and mourn *(Ezek. 28:12–19)* over their rebellion. His heart was broken, and for the first time ever, God experienced the pain of His sanctuaries being defiled by the multitude of Lucifer's iniquities *(Ezek. 28:18).* The betrayal of God by Lucifer and his angels caused God great sorrow. It is interesting that as Lucifer betrayed the

THE PASTOR'S PEN

Father, so would Judas betray Jesus. Judas was Lucifer's son of perdition *(John 17:12)*. With this betrayal, Jesus identified with the Father's betrayal.

After, possibly millennia of years, God would start a new creation with a new creature, man, made of flesh and in God's image, and never seen before by angels. But more pain was to come to Him with the fall of man, when Adam chose to follow the voice of the Serpent instead of God's voice.

And then again the Father would suffer, when Israel broke His heart by her idolatrous tendencies. The broken heart of God is vividly seen in the story of Hosea and his wayward wife, Gomer. As Gomer was unfaithful to Hosea in the eyes of all Israel, so was Israel unfaithful to God. The Lamentations of Jeremiah show the anguish of God at Israel's infidelity.

As we turn to the New Testament, we see the Virgin Birth and Incarnation of Christ, which brought great joy to the Father. The life of Christ would continue to bring joy to the Father by Jesus' obedience causing Him to say, **"This is my beloved Son in whom I am WELL pleased" (Matt. 3:17).**

Jesus' mission was to destroy the devil, who is the enemy of God and man, and then **"deliver them who through fear of death were all their lifetime subject to bondage" (Heb. 2:14–15).**

In order to begin His Mission, Jesus had to identify with the agony and sufferings of the Father. As followers of Christ, we are also called to identify with the sufferings of Christ, even as He identified with the sufferings of the Father. In identifying with Jesus' sufferings, we become One with the Father and Jesus.

When we look into the Gospel of St. Luke, we read of Simeon, the aged man who was sensitive to the moving of the Holy Ghost and led by the Spirit to go to the Temple when Joseph and Mary brought Jesus to be dedicated. The Father oversaw every detail in the life of His Son Jesus, from His birth to His Resurrection, and now chose a man who would dedicate His Son. God wanted Jesus to be dedicated by a Spirit filled man, not just some priest. Under the inspiration of the Spirit, Simeon spoke to Mary and Joseph *(Luke 2:30–33),* and then spoke directly to Mary with **very significant words** saying, *"Yea, a sword shall pierce through thy own soul ALSO" (Luke 2:35).* The words of Simeon to Mary show the depth of God's agony over His Son's mistreatment by man that led to His Crucifixion.

Notice between verse 34 and verse 35 is a parenthesis, indicating a separate thought from the preceding words of Simeon. The question now is what is the meaning of the words given to Mary, and who is the *"also"* Simeon spoke of? The *"also"* refers to Mary, and means she *also* would experience the pain of the sword piercing her soul; but the main sufferer here is God, the Father. He watched every move and action from Heaven, of men abusing His Holy Son. God would be the first to feel the pain of a sword piercing His heart, as He watched His Son being nailed to the Cross and He could not do anything about it. Jesus' Heavenly Father and His earthly mother both had a sword pierce their hearts. Simeon's prophecy to Mary was a direct reference to the Father's pain and agony when He sees the sufferings of Jesus at Calvary.

Then Mary, who reflects the anguish of God, will also have a sword pierce her heart. As severe as her pain would be, it would not be like the Father's pain. God's pain was indescribable and is forever scared in His heart. As Jesus forever will have the **wounds in His hands** of the nails of the Cross *(Zech. 13:6)*, so God the Father will forever have the scar of the sword that pierced His heart.

For a moment, we need to look back to the beginning of Jesus' ministry to see how He identifies with the Father's agony. The first persecution of Jesus began in *Luke 4:16–30*, when the people of Nazareth attempted to kill Jesus by throwing Him headlong over a hill. From that day on, Jesus was followed constantly and harassed by the religious leaders. This would be the beginning of Jesus identifying with the Father's agony, which, originally began over His creation millennia years before and is now carried into the life of Jesus. It includes Satan's maligning of Jesus, just as he maligned the Father at his rebellion. Further identity with the Father is seen with the betrayal of Jesus by Judas and reminiscent of the Father's betrayal by Satan.

Jesus submitted to every attack that came to Him so mankind could never say God favored His Son, and protected Him from being tested. By being tested, Jesus showed the angels, man, and creation that He fought the battle and overcame, qualifying Him to be equal with the Father *(Phil. 2:6).*

The sufferings of Jesus identified Him with the sufferings of the Father. **As Jesus identified with the Father's suffering, so must we identify with Jesus' suffering.** Now the believer must also go through testing if he wants to identify with Jesus, and qualify to sit with Him in His glory. As a believer follows Jesus, he will experience the sufferings of Christ by rejection, mistreatment and ridicule by the world.

When Jesus said, "take up thy cross and follow Me" *(Matt. 16:24),* He was telling us, **"Yes, you can get into heaven without paying the price of testing as did the thief on the cross, but you will not qualify to sit with Me in my Throne as I sit with the Father in His Throne *(Rev.3:21),*** unless you are willing to pay the price of testing."

Testing includes sorrows *(*Jesus is called the Man of Sorrows in *Isaiah 53:3),* the fellowship of His sufferings, and being made conformable to His death *(Phil. 3:10).* Scripture constantly calls us to identify with Jesus. Paul identified with Jesus when he wrote, *"I am crucified with Christ: nevertheless I live (*natural life*); yet not I, but Christ liveth in me" (Gal. 2:20).* We will have the *"fellowship of His sufferings"* but also *"the power of His Resurrection" (Phil. 3:10)* to live in His triumph forever!

In closing, we see God the Father was the first sufferer, then Jesus followed the Father's sufferings, and now Jesus calls us to follow in His sufferings even as He followed the Father's sufferings. **If we follow Jesus as over comers, we will sit with Him in His Throne, even as Jesus overcame and sits in His Father's Throne *(Rev. 3:21).***

Maranatha! The Lord Cometh!

"IN THE FULNESS OF TIME"

The Word of God tells us, *"when the fulness of the time was come, God sent forth His Son, made of a woman, made under the law, to redeem them that were under the law, that we might receive the adoption of sons" (Gal. 4:4–5).* God has everything put together in His plan, from creation to the present time. All generations, from the time of Eden to the present are synchronized with creation and move in harmony with God's plan. The Lord has set time as He sees fit.

When we speak of the words, *"the fulness of time,"* we refer to it in a spiritual setting, because it relates directly to the Lord Jesus Christ and Calvary. In fact, the entire earthly process is related to the demonic rebellion against God and His Son. Only God knew back then, that the rebellion would lead to the Cross and would also end at the Cross. God knew deep in His heart the meaning of the Cross, and how it would forever affect Him. Every day, when the Father saw Jesus, He relived the reality of the Cross in His heart.

At the Cross, when Jesus faced the Crucifixion, the Father was there watching His Son, and while the Holy Spirit is not mentioned in *Genesis 22*, yet the Holy Spirit was also there in pain and in tears with the Father. With this in mind, it behooves us as the children of God, to remember the Cross and the sorrow it bore for us by both the Father and the Son.

It is very much like *Genesis 22*, when Abraham heard the voice of God, calling him to offer his son Isaac, whom he loved dearly, for a burnt offering. The Lord watched every move of Abraham and was aware of his anguish during those three dreadful days. God knew He had to find a man in the world, who unknowingly in events, identified with God's agony and the thought of giving up His innocent Son.

God knew if it was possible for Abraham to exchange places with his son Isaac, Abraham would have done it, but it was not possible. It was the same with God the Father, for if it were possible for Him to take Jesus' place, He would have willingly done it. But it was not possible, for He was not human, and a human was required to bring redemption to mankind. There was only One in the universe, who qualified to face and stand up to the evil enemy, who hated both God the Father, and God the Son. Abraham's son was spared death, but not God's Son. Can you imagine the pain in God's heart to hear His Son cry out, **"O my Father, if it be possible, let this cup pass from Me" (Matt. 26:39).** But it was not possible; Jesus had to die for us.

The fulness of time had come and sorrow came with it. There is also an aspect of the fulness of time referring to Jesus and has to do with His appearances in the Old Testament. The appearances of Jesus in the Old Testament have significant meaning regarding His preparation for the upcoming Battle. This is clearly seen when Moses and Elijah came down from Heaven and appeared to Jesus. They spoke with Jesus of His decease, which He was to accomplish at Jerusalem *(Luke 9:30–31)*. Their conversation with Jesus had to do with His preparations and to alert Him of the evil treatment Satan would throw at Him through evil men and soldiers. The preparations were meant to help Him see and understand what to expect.

So, when we speak of the fulness of time, it refers directly to Jesus, even back in the Old Testament. We know Jesus read the Word of God and that He read the prophecies of the Old Testament that referred to Him by the Prophets and the Psalms especially. It is most likely that Jesus' Old Testament appearances were connected to the emphasis of what awaited Him, from His birth and thereafter. In *Isaiah 50:6–8; 53:2–12,* we also see His agony.

Thus the words *"the fulness of time"* refers solely to Jesus and shows Jesus was prepared and ready to confront Satan in order to redeem us *(Gal. 4:4–5)*. Jesus knew the fulness of time had come and the Battle had arrived. But He was ready and made it clear with the words, *"the prince of this world cometh, and hath nothing in Me" (John 14:30). "I have overcome the world" (John 16:33). "Father, the hour is come; glorify thy Son, that thy Son also may glorify thee" (John 17:1).* **AMEN!**

Maranatha! The Lord Cometh!

"THE HIDDEN CHRIST"

In looking at Christ as Divine, we see Him as God and as man. Jesus was divine with the Father before He became human. As God and man, He became the Victorious Son of God, who fought the evil forces of the universe.

His birth led to natural growth as a baby, then to childhood, and then to adulthood. And at the age of twelve *(Luke 2:42),* Jesus was introduced to the religious doctors when he walked into the Temple and spoke to them. As a youth and at this stage of life, they were amazed at His wisdom and spiritual insights. Little did they realize His Heavenly Father was teaching Him *"morning, by morning" (Isa. 50:4–5).* All was well at age twelve, but when He was thirty years of age, those who liked Him as a youth, now rejected Him with threats *(Isa. 50:6–9),* because now Jesus represented truth and righteousness as taught by His Father.

From the day of His birth, to the day of the Ascension, Jesus did not **hide** Himself from the people or religious leaders. He was visible to all, for the Lord's heart was always open to the common people with whom He was comfortable. He would sit and eat and talk with them of the things of God.

After the Resurrection, and for forty days thereafter, the Lord used those days to teach the Apostles the doctrine of Christ as Jesus said, *"My doctrine is not mine, but his that sent me" (John 7:16)*. He told them not to expect to see Him on earth until He returns, *"<u>whom having not seen</u>, ye love; in whom, though <u>now ye see Him not</u>, yet believing, ye rejoice with joy unspeakable and full of glory" (1 Peter 1:8).* The Lord will always be with us and never will forsake us nor leave us, but will be unseen. The Word of God assures us that when a Christian passes away, Jesus will meet us in heaven and then **will be <u>unhidden</u> to us forever!**

After the Ascension, the Lord was hidden from the Church, until the Rapture when Christ will come. During this time of hiddenness, it is the Holy Spirit, who presides for Jesus over *"the goods of his Master" (Gen. 24:10),* just as it was with Eliezer, Abraham's steward, who was the type of the Holy Spirit. The Lord is "hidden" and has limited Himself since the Ascension.

Since the Ascension, Jesus sits on His throne with the Father on His Throne. Jesus is now in heaven, not on earth, where He abides on His throne with the Father until Jesus returns. Jesus is God and is everywhere, but steps aside so the Holy Spirit can do the work of Christ until He comes. The Father said to Jesus, *"Sit on my right hand, until I make thine enemies thy footstool?" (Heb. 1:13).* Stephen also saw the Son of God **standing on the right hand of God,** as he was being stoned.

The Holy Spirit manifests the manifestations of Christ, as Jesus remains with the Father at His right hand and on His throne, so the Holy Spirit is at work fulfilling God's purposes. The workings of the Spirit are seen in *John 16:8–14*. Jesus told the disciples it was necessary for

Him to go away, but if He did not leave, the Comforter wouldn't come *(John 16:7).* During this time of the two thousand years, Jesus waits to hear *"the voice of the seventh angel when he shall begin to sound, the mystery of God should be finished."* The mystery is in the Rapture, which is known only to the Father *(Rev. 10:7).* Shortly thereafter, Armageddon comes following the Rapture.

Jesus also said, *"I will never leave thee, nor forsake thee" (Heb. 13:5),* yet we don't see Him now in the flesh. He remains **unseen** until He comes for the Rapture. Where is He coming from? **He is coming from the Throne of God,** where He has been for two thousand years. The Father said to Jesus, *"Sit thou at my right hand, until I make thine enemies thy footstool" (Ps. 110:1; Matt. 22:44).* The enemies of Christ are those who opposed Christ then, and still oppose Christ to this day.

Paul also refers to Christ as the One who is not seen, *"whom no man hath seen, nor can see" (1 Tim. 6:16).* As Believers we are hid with Christ in God since the Ascension.

Maranatha! The Lord Cometh!

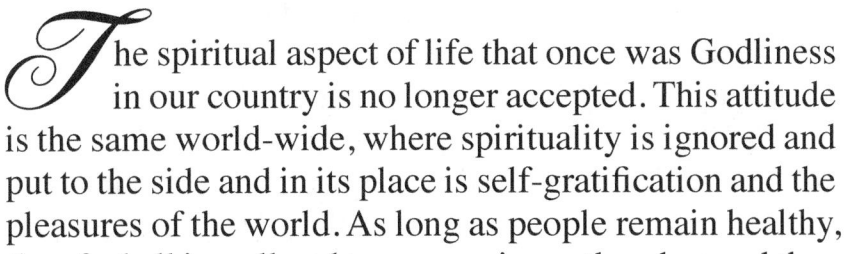

"THE NAME OF JESUS"

The spiritual aspect of life that once was Godliness in our country is no longer accepted. This attitude is the same world-wide, where spirituality is ignored and put to the side and in its place is self-gratification and the pleasures of the world. As long as people remain healthy, they feel all is well and tomorrow is another day, and they go on as if there is no tomorrow. However, when sickness knocks at the door, suddenly reality is awakened for the need for the spiritual.

It's at times like these, that the power of ***"The Name of Jesus"*** awakens the conscience, and brings spiritual light and hope where there once was chaos. The world does not know, nor does it understand the spiritual power that exists when we call on ***"The Name of Jesus."*** Even an unsaved person, man or woman, when they call on Jesus, without realizing it, they experience the power of Christ that is life changing. The power of ***"The Name of Jesus"*** was preached everywhere with the Apostles ***"confirming the word with signs following" (Mark 16:20).***

Jesus gave the first mention and reference of His Name in ***Mark 16:17, 18, "In my name shall they cast our devils; they shall speak with new tongues; . . . they shall lay hands on the sick and they shall recover."*** However, the first public use of *"The Name of Jesus,"* was the first recorded miracle after Jesus resurrected that manifested the power of God. *"The Name of Jesus,"* is the power of Christ that healed the lame man at the temple *(Acts 3:1–9),* when Peter and John called him to believe. It was then that **"his name through faith in his name hath made this man strong" (Acts 3:16).**

The priests, and the Captain of the temple with the Sadducees, were contrary to what God was doing among five thousand believers *(Acts 4:4).* The religious leaders had to acknowledge the man's healing as it was recognized as *"a notable miracle,"* of God's doings *(Acts 4:16).* The religious leaders were afraid of *"The Name of Jesus,"* in so much that they called Peter and John and commanded them not to speak in Jesus' Name. This reveals that a dead religious system in our times is still afraid of a living Spirit-filled Church *(Acts 4:17–20).*

The Apostles were fearless, keen, and sensitive to the Spirit in spite of the threats from the religious leaders *(Acts 4:29–31).* They went forward with signs and wonders that were done by *"The name of thy holy child Jesus" (Acts 4:30).* When they prayed, the place was shaken where they were assembled, and they were all filled with the Holy Ghost, and spoke the word of God with boldness. The Lord confirmed their prayer with miracles through *"The Name of Jesus."* **"By the hands of the Apostles were many signs and wonders wrought among the people" (Acts 5:12–16).** Many multitudes of believers were added to the Lord, both of men and women. The sick were brought into the streets and were on beds and couches hoping Peter's shadow may pass over them *(Acts 5:15).* The multitude also brought the sick and those that *"were vexed with unclean spirits:*

and they were healed everyone" (Acts 5:16). This was the manifestation of the power of God by using, *"The Name of Jesus."*

The Apostles were persecuted, beaten and thrown into the prison *(Acts 5:18–24),* and the Lord sent an angel to free them from the prison. The Church grew under persecution for *"The Name of Jesus" (Acts. 5:40–42). "The Name of Jesus"* is powerful and was held high esteem in the early Church. The devil is aware of the power of God in *"The Name of Jesus"* and does all he can do to stop that name. If the enemy can stop the Church from using *"The Name of Jesus,"* the Church will be robbed of supernatural power.

Paul fought *"The Name of Jesus"* before he was saved, and then suffered much for Christ's name *(Acts 9:16; Acts 26:9). "The Name of Jesus"* has not lost its authority or power; it is ours forever. The early Church understood the power in *"The Name of Jesus,"* and their right to use it for His glory.

We live in a time when people no longer pray or just end a prayer with the word Amen, but it is the power of God in *"The Name of Jesus"* that releases the Lord's power. Jesus taught the disciples to pray with the Lord's Prayer *(Luke 11:1–4),* and then to release faith and power by *"The Name of Jesus" (Acts 3:16, Mark 16:17,18).*

Praying a prayer without *"The Name of Jesus,"* is like sending a letter without an address. The Power of Christ is in *"The Name of Jesus,"* and it befalls upon us to preach *"The Name of Jesus,"* for it is the power of God.

Maranatha! The Lord Cometh!

"THE UNSEARCHABLE RICHES OF CHRIST"

The Apostle Paul makes reference in *Ephesians 3:8*, that he was less than the least of all saints and to him was given grace that he should preach among the Gentiles, **"THE UNSEARCHABLE RICHES OF CHRIST."**

The term, *"the unsearchable riches of Christ,"* was never meant to keep the Church and Believers from the riches of Christ. Absolutely not, instead it is meant to motivate the believer to seek Christ, so they would fulfill the yearning of their heart for Christ. The riches of Christ are Spiritual and eternal, whereas the worldly riches are materialistic and temporal.

Riches and wealth of the world are spoken of as mammon, including opulence. The Lord Jesus said, ***"No man can serve two masters: for either he will hate the one, and love the other; or else he will hold to the one, and despise the other. Ye cannot serve God and mammon" (Matt. 6:24).*** Webster's Lexicon has in interesting definition for mammon as "a personification of wealth as an evil god or influence."[6]

However, the children of God realize the faithfulness of the Holy Spirit to lead us into the unsearchable riches of Christ throughout eternity. The words of Christ and of the prophets, give us encouragement to set aside time regularly, in order to seek the Lord and the riches of Christ in the Word of God. As children of God, and knowing God has taught us, gives us encouragement to press on into the unsearchable riches of Christ, as John wrote, *"It is written in the prophets, And they shall be all taught of God. Every man therefore that hath heard, and hath learned of the Father, cometh unto me" (John 6:45).*

As Son, Jesus also had to learn the ways of God. *Isaiah 50:4* is like a flower that blossomed with insights of how God the Father taught His Son. God the Father would awaken Jesus in the early morning hours, to teach Him as the learned. Obviously, this was during His time on earth. But the lessons Jesus learned from the Father by early rising, prepared Him to face the challenges of the day. Those were times of learning and were the most precious times of waiting on God.

Job was the first to speak of God as *"unsearchable,"* and said, He *"doeth great things and unsearchable; marvelous things without number" (Job 5:9).* David exclaimed God's *"greatness is unsearchable"(Ps. 145:3).* Paul said, *"O the depth of the riches both of the wisdom and knowledge of God! how unsearchable are His judgments, and His ways past finding out!" (Rom. 11:33)*

Like Paul, the riches of Christ enter into our lives upon our salvation and continue with revelations by the Spirit as we grow *"from glory to glory" (2 Cor. 3:18).* The unsearchable ways of God constitute the marvelous works of the Lord, for the unsearchable riches of Christ are inexhaustible, and will never end throughout eternity.

Man cannot exhaust God for God has no end, nor is God limited to anything. When we use the word unsearchable for God, it means man is limited.

The message of the unsearchable riches of Christ is that Christ is inexhaustible, without end. His is the beginning and the end, for He is the Alpha and Omega. Alpha is the first letter of the Greek alphabet, and serves as a title of Christ. It is descriptive of His position as the "beginning." Omega is a title of Christ, signifying "the last," showing Christ is the Beginning and the Ending. The Lord is God and *"which was, and is, and is to come" (Rev. 4:8).* These titles have meanings for mankind, showing man his beginning and dependence on God.

Paul pursued the riches of Christ, leaving us an example of pursuing Christ unto *"the unsearchable riches of Christ."* Thus, when we speak of the *"the unsearchable riches of Christ,"* we see it as the riches of Christ that conform us into the image and likeness of Christ. Like Paul, we say, *"I press toward the mark for the prize of the high calling of God in Christ Jesus" (Phil. 3:14).*

Maranatha! The Lord Cometh!

THE TWO GREAT DELIVERANCES

The harmony of the Old and the New Testament is phenomenal as seen in the Two Great Deliverances of scripture, the one from the Old Testament, and the other, from the New Testament. Events of the Old Testament point to their counterpart and fulfillment in the New Testament.

The first deliverance is Israel's deliverance from Egypt. This miraculous and powerful deliverance manifested to Israel God's unlimited power. It fulfilled God's promise to Abraham of Israel's Exodus from Egyptian bondage, and the hope of possessing all the land God promised to Abraham *(Gen. 15:18)*. The Lord delivered more than two and a half million Israelites, taking them step by step through one of the most formidable and barren deserts on the earth, and for forty years provided them with food, water, clothing and shoes *(Deut. 29:5; Neh. 9:20–21)* in this wilderness.

Up to this time, Israel was under the tyranny of a nation that was hard and brutal. Moses describes Egypt as an *"iron furnace" (Deut. 4:20)*. Joseph experienced its harshness when in prison and *"laid in iron" (Ps. 105:18)*. Pharaoh, Egypt's ruler was a type of Satan, and considered himself divine. Their idol was the cobra serpent, which was worshipped throughout Egypt, and was promoted by the Egyptians by wearing images of the cobra on their headdress. Israel lived under these conditions for over four hundred years.

Eventually, the time arrived and the challenge and battleground took form with Israel as the prize. Pharaoh is determined to keep Israel in servitude, and the God of Israel is determined to free His people from Pharaoh's grip for all these years *(Exod. 3:7–10).*

God had his man ready, as the Lord is never surprised at what the enemy contrives. He always has a man prepared for an appointed time and purpose that will bless and benefit His people. At this time, the man He chose was a man He prepared from birth; that man was Moses. Pharaoh's grip over Israel appeared invincible, until Moses came in the power of God that proved greater and stronger than Pharaoh's kingdom.

Israel's deliverance proved to be a great **physical deliverance** by God's power and would have worldwide implications, including Israel's future and the coming of the Promised Messiah. By physical it means a deliverance that could be seen in the natural and was obvious to neighboring tribes.

The Second Great Deliverance is in the New Testament and is a **spiritual deliverance** that breaks and frees the individual soul from the grip and hold of Satan. It is the greater of the two, as the Messiah is the stronger man than the evil one *(Luke 11:22).* Israel's time had come in the Old Testament with the appearance of the great deliverer, Moses. So now the Kingdom of God's time has also come in the New Testament with the appearance of the Messiah under a set time called the *"fulness of time" (Gal. 4:4).*

This deliverance is not seen with the natural eye as was the Exodus, this deliverance is spiritual and breaks the inner bondage of sin in the souls of men. As Jesus said, the Kingdom of God is not seen but is within the believer, making it the greater of the two deliverances.

This leads us to another parallel of Israel and the Coming of the Messiah proclaiming the Kingdom of God. A year before Israel was to enter the Land of Promise, the Lord directed Moses to make a fiery brazen serpent. This came as a result of Israel's sin in speaking against God and Moses and further resulted in the judgment of fiery serpents *(Num. 21:4–10)*.

The typology here helps us to understand the purpose of this judgment. The fiery brazen serpent represented Satan. Brass (Brazen) speaks of judgment, and since the serpent was nailed to the pole, which speaks of Satan, death and sin were nailed and destroyed at the Cross *(Heb. 2:14)*.

We know Jesus was judged and died on the cross for the sins of the world, but so was Satan judged and destroyed at the Cross for his sin of rebellion. The brazen serpent, in being lifted up and nailed to the pole, **prophetically points to the judgment of Satan at the Cross.** Moses' act of hanging the brazen serpent to a pole was prophetic of Satan's future judgment. Jesus, by virtue of His death, nailed Satan and the defiled ordinances to the Cross *(Col. 2:14–15)*. Jesus exposed Satan's defeat and made a show of him and his cohorts openly. Jesus judged Satan at the Cross, and sentenced him to the Lake of Fire in *Revelations 20:10*, making it unnecessary for him to appear before the Great White Throne on Judgment Day. His judgment is complete for Jesus said, *"Of judgment, because the prince of this world is judged" (John 16:11)*.

Jesus said in *Luke 10:18, "I beheld Satan as lighting fall from heaven."*

This statement by Jesus is prophetic of Satan's fall at the hand of the Lord Jesus Christ. Often this verse is seen as referring to Satan's fall at his initial rebellion *(Isa. 14:12, 15),* but it really refers to Satan's fall in the New Testament as part of Jesus' purpose in coming to earth as recorded in *John 9:39: "For judgment I am come into this world."* What judgment? The judgment of Satan and the world. *John 12:31* says, *"Now is the judgment of this world: now shall the prince of this world be cast out"* of the heavens for the second time. It was at the Cross when *Genesis 3:15* was fulfilled by Jesus, when the seed of the woman would crush the serpent's head. It was also at the cross when the Lord *"condemned sin in the flesh" (Rom. 8:3).*

Words fail to describe the power and greatness of Jesus' victory over Satan. **It certainly will take eternity to unfold the magnitude of His triumph!** How truly blessed we are, knowing Jesus carried our sins to Calvary, and freed us from the rule of Satan, sin and death, through faith in Him. This helps us understand the greatness of the second Deliverance, in the Church era, as Greater than the first Deliverance of Israel. By faith we are the recipients of the grace and mercy of God. Christ and salvation is the greatest gift God could ever give man for which we must be forever thankful.

"Thanks be unto God for His unspeakable gift" (2 Cor. 9:15).

Maranatha! The Lord Cometh!

IT HAPPENED ON PENTECOST SUNDAY

It was Pentecost Sunday, which fell that year on May 17, 1970. I was then Pastor of the Assemblies of God Church known as the Full Gospel Tabernacle at Roxborough, Philadelphia, Pennsylvania.

That particular Pentecost Sunday did not appear to be a day out of the ordinary. It looked like it would be just another spring day. However, it would turn out to be a very unique day in the life of this young Pastor and his wife and their two daughters.

That morning was a bright morning but by noon the weather had changed and was raining. The evening service would be at 7 p.m. That afternoon about 4:30 p.m., I had gone to my office to await our evening guest speaker. The Church was just behind the parsonage so I did not have far to walk. While in my office and sitting at my desk I heard a thumping to which I responded by looking up to locate from where it was coming. To my surprise and dismay, there in my window, was a balloon caught in the Church's rainspout, right at my window of all places. It seemed to be calling me, trying to get my attention.

I gave it a little thought and said to myself, "I'll have to get a ladder tomorrow and get that balloon down from there." Since it was raining rather heavily, I decided to forget about it and just ignore it, hoping that the wind would bring it down in a day or two. Our guest did arrive and I pointed it out to him and made a comment of how strange for a balloon to be stuck in my window! He just smiled and said, "Maybe it's a message from Heaven!"

Having forgotten it, several days later on Thursday, May 21, while mowing the parsonage lawn, I noticed the balloon lying on the ground. As I went to pick it up there I could see a long string attached to it with a letter at its end. I was startled.

As I took it in my hand I saw the return address, which was, "All Saints Church, Wynnewood, Pennsylvania." I proceeded to open the envelope and there discovered a card with a child's handwriting on it. It was a prayer that said, "Dear God, please give me the Holy Spirit from You. Amen."

Needless to say, I felt chills go through me. Was this the message sent from Heaven as our guest said? What was this to mean?

Of course, being Assemblies of God, we believe in the Charismatic movement of the Holy Spirit and the Baptism of the Holy Spirit with the evidence of speaking in tongues. So, I thought to myself why should this letter come to me?

At any rate, I quickly ran into the parsonage and told my wife and then proceeded to find the phone number of the All Saints Church. When I reached the Rector of this Episcopal congregation, I told his the story of how the balloon had gotten stuck in my office window. With

THE PASTOR'S PEN

surprise bordering incredulity, he told me the story of the balloon and the envelope with its contents.

Being it was Pentecost Sunday, that particular morning the Church had the children write any prayer request they may have and attached it to the balloon, sending it skyward as to the Lord. There were varied prayer requests, some asking for help in school, others for closer family ties, etc. None of the children knew what the others were asking. Evidently, one of the children was influenced by the lesson that morning in Sunday School and was asking for the Holy Spirit. Isn't it interesting that this particular prayer came to a Charismatic Pastor and not one of the other prayers?

The miracle of it all was that the two Churches are about 5 miles apart. The balloon had to travel over buildings and trees and over the Schuylkill Valley draft and up over the Manayunk Hills. It must pass over a shopping area and wires and find its way directly to the little Assembly of God Church that sits just a bit lower than the parsonage and to the south side of the building. There would be the problem of missing the Church chimney that arose inches from the Pastor's office and then settling in the spout just at his window. Incidentally, there is only one window at his office and it measured about two feet wide and three feet in length.

The other miracle was that the rain didn't hinder it and that it all happened on Pentecost Sunday and that it went right to the window of a Pentecostal Pastor and not to another Pastor, as there are many Churches in Roxborough, nor was it caught in any thicket or trees as it passed over the A-roof frame of the Church.

This incident spoke to my heart of God's love and care for us. He will go out of His way and do the unusual to show He hears our prayers and especially those of a child! It's as the Lord Jesus said, *"How much more shall your heavenly Father give the Holy Spirit to them that ask him?" (Luke 11:13)*

We Pentecostals have a distinctive legacy to perpetuate the glorious message of Pentecost, the coming of the "other Comforter," whom the Lord Jesus has sent to us.

The importance of receiving the baptism in the Holy Spirit is seen in Jesus' command to the disciples to tarry until they received His promise which is still *"unto you, and to your children, and to all that are afar off, even as many as the Lord our God shall call" (Acts 2:39).*

Maranatha! The Lord Cometh!

The Bride of Christ

THE MOST IMPORTANT BOOK OF THE BIBLE

The Bible is a body of books, made up to minister to the journeying child of God in this evil and sinful world. It is the revelation of God to us.

As the human body has many members with each contributing to it wholeness, so the Word of God is a Body of 66 members (66 Books), each contributing to the Body of Scripture, to minister to the Body of Believers. The most important member of the human body is the head. It is this member that brings function and direction to all the other members of the body.

If we were to ask, "What is the most important book of the Bible?" Most likely, few people would ever think of this one book that even identifies itself as *"The Song of Songs" (Song of Sol. 1:1).* While all the books of the Bible are important and minister in many ways, this one book is the head over all the other books. The reason it is so important is because it reveals the ultimate purpose of God in creating the universe and man.

The entire Bible is comprised of "songs." Each book of the Bible is a song. Sometimes the song is a most wonderful song and at other times it is a song of mixed emotion. At times the Old Testament songs or books are heavier than the New Testament songs due to the Old Testament's dispensational message. The books (songs) of the New Testament are uplifting and encouraging and give great hope to the believer for a great and bright future.

The message of the Song of Songs has great significance for it is none other than the *Song of Solomon.*

The message of the Song of Solomon is about Christ and His Bride. It shows the love that exists between the two. It tells of the pursuit of the Bride *(Song of Sol. 3)* to find Her Lover, the Lord Jesus Christ, and of His desire to feel wanted and loved by her *(ch.5–6)*. The greatest need in the Church today is a loving relationship with Christ. We find ourselves too busy and pre-occupied with the demands of this life that we fail to make and take time to be alone with Him.

The Bride is constantly looking for the coming of Her Bridegroom with the Holy Spirit as ***Revelation 22:17*** says, *"And the Spirit and the bride say, Come."* While she patiently awaits His coming, she is preparing Herself to be ready for the great *"Marriage Supper of the Lamb" (Rev. 19:7–9).* The Bride is cognizant of the price the Bridegroom paid for her hand. It was by His Blood shed on Calvary's Cross that He purchased to Himself a Bride.

We must not confuse the Body of Christ with the Bride of Christ. The Church is not His Bride; the Church is His Body. All believers become members of His Body at salvation, but not all believers will be part of His Bride. Being part of His Bride is not a right; it is an honor and privilege. ***Revelation 19:8***, says, *"to her (the Bride) was granted"* this privilege because she qualified by living a life of devotion and love for Her Bridegroom. As one dear saint said, "Many are called to be in the Bride but few qualify."

Another very important point relative to the Body of Christ and the Bride of Christ is seen with Adam and Eve. The first Adam got his bride out of his body, and so does the second Adam, the Lord Jesus Christ. He will get His Bride out of His Body. Jesus isn't going to marry His Body, but He is going to marry the Bride that comes out of His Body.

For us to see this marvelous truth, the Lord has given us numerous types of the Bride in both the Old and New Testament. One such example of the spirit of the Bride is seen in Mary of Bethany and her deep love for the Lord. When Jesus came to Mary, Martha and Lazarus' home, Mary sat at Jesus' feet listening to Him teach. Martha, her sister, who represents the busy believer was busy working for the Lord in the kitchen, but was shallow on devotion in comparison to her sister Mary. The difference between the two was in their priorities. Mary's priorities were in order but Martha's needed adjustment for Christ is our priority and must always have the pre-eminence in our lives.

For the revelation of the truth of the Bride of Christ, which was hid in the Old Testament, the Song of Solomon becomes the ***"Song of Songs."*** It is the greatest Book of the Bible because it shows the love of Christ for His Bride. It also shows the Father's purpose for the birth of His Son, and His death and resurrection. The Father purposed for His Son to have a Bride throughout eternity. The love between the Bride and the Bridegroom is shown in their commitment to each other. She only has eyes for Him and as a result lives a separated life while waiting

His return, which means that as soon as He returns their wedding will take place.

More than anything in this world, our objective is to pursue the Bridegroom and love Him with all our heart and soul!

Maranatha! The Lord Cometh!

"THE SPIRIT AND THE BRIDE"
PART 1

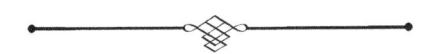

In this article, we want to look further into the beautiful mystery of the Bride of Jesus Christ. The mystery is apparent as one reads the Song of Solomon and finds the many metaphors in the book difficult to understand. While now our understanding is limited, we will experience it in eternity and then fully know the Mystery of the Bride. In the early days of Pentecost, our forefathers put much emphasis on the Bride as they preached on the Marriage Supper of the Lamb and linked it with the message of the Second Coming of Christ.

Unfortunately, over the years the Pentecostal Church has accepted the teachings of the Evangelical Churches that the Church is the Bride. This belief was long held by the Evangelicals until the outpouring of the Holy Spirit at the turn of the 20th century. It was the Pentecostal movement of the nineteen hundreds, and in particular the Assemblies of God, that revived this wonderful truth of the Bride with a deeper understanding as a result of the Baptism of the Holy Ghost.

The Baptism of the Holy Spirit opens doors of marvelous truth. ***John 6:45*** says, ***"they shall be all taught of***

God." How will He teach us? Through the anointing that abides in us *(1 John 2:27)*. Jesus said that *"when he, the Spirit of truth, is come, he will guide you into all truth:* (the Word)" *(John 16:13)*.

However today, the message of the Bride has been set aside. Few there be that preach on it, and many are hesitant to search it out other than saying it's in the Song of Solomon. There is a need today to once again proclaim this wonderful truth of the marriage of Christ and His Bride.

As we look at three of the several marriages in the Word, we will see some wonderful and meaningful lessons. The first is the marriage of Adam and Eve; the second is the wedding at Cana, where Jesus did His first miracle; and thirdly, the Marriage of the Lamb.

Before we go to the marriage of Adam and Eve, it will be worth our while to first look at one of the most significant marriages in the scripture, which relates to the Marriage of the Lamb. This marriage gives insights about Christ and His Bride. It is the marriage of Isaac and Rebekah as recorded in *Genesis 24*. In this account, we will see the most beautiful interaction between the Spirit and the Bride. We begin with the types.

Abraham is a type of God the Father; Sarah is a type of Israel; Isaac is a type of the Lord Jesus Christ; Eliezer, Abraham's servant and steward is a type of the Holy Spirit; and Rebekah, a type of the Bride of Christ.

As a type of the Holy Spirit, Eliezer is mentioned only once in scripture *(Gen. 15:2)*. Like the Holy Spirit, Eliezer *"shall not speak of himself" (John 16:13), but "he shall testify of Me" (John 15:26).* Eliezer speaks of Isaac in *Genesis 24: 36, 38, 48.* Most likely, Eliezer spoke of

Isaac all the way from the city of Nahor in Mesopotamia to Hebron in the land of Canaan, where Abraham resided.

When we look at *Genesis 22–24*, we see Providence harmonizing scripture and people's lives together to bring about the plans and purposes of God. Chapter 22 shows Abraham offering up his son Isaac, who is a type of Christ dying on the Cross at Calvary or Mount Moriah, and points to the sacrifice of Jesus for the purchasing of His Bride *(1 Peter 1:18–19)*. Moriah is where Isaac was offered up and is the same place where Jesus was crucified.

It is also the same Mount where the Temple was built *(2 Chron. 3:1)*.

Chapter 23 of Genesis records the death of Sarah, who is a type of Israel. Her death follows Isaac's being offered up to die and speaks of the Lord setting aside Israel, after the death of Christ, so the Gentiles may enter the blessings of God *(Rom.11)*.

Chapter 24 of Genesis speaks of Eliezer, who is a type of the Holy Spirit, who goes to a Gentile nation searching for a Bride for Abraham's son, Isaac. It is God the Father, of whom Abraham is a type, who sends the Spirit to a Gentile people, to find a Bride for His Son, the Lord Jesus Christ. The ministry of the Holy Spirit, since Pentecost, is to find and prepare a Bride commensurate or made equal for the Lord Jesus Christ.

Eliezer is Abraham's steward even as the Holy Spirit is the Steward of Heaven. As a type of the Holy Spirit, Eliezer gave gifts to Rebekah *(Gen. 24:22, 53),* even as we receive the manifestation of the Spirit seen in the Gifts of the Spirit in *1 Corinthians 12:7–11*.

More interaction between the Spirit and the Bride is seen in *Genesis 24:61*, where it says, she *"followed the man."* It is the Bride's duty to follow the Holy Spirit. We are to be *"led by the Spirit" (Rom. 8:14)* and obey the *"still small voice" (1 Kings 19:12), "a word behind thee, saying, This is the way, walk ye in it" (Isa. 30:21).*

Rebekah is a type of the Bride of Christ. She is a virgin, which speaks of the Bride of Christ, keeping herself only for the Lord Jesus. As Rebekah was beautiful, so the Holy Spirit is now preparing the Bride for Christ and she will be beautiful when Jesus sees her, just as Isaac saw Rebekah afar off and loved her *(Gen. 24:63, 67).*

Rebekah received golden earrings from Eliezer, which speaks of the Bride of Christ having an ear for God. When asked if she would leave immediately to go to Isaac she said "yes" *(Gen. 24:58)* and left her family and loved ones to go to a man she had never seen before but believed the report of Eliezer. The Bride desires to go and be with Christ, though she has not seen Him yet and is willing to leave all for Him!

In Genesis 24:56, Eliezer said, *"Hinder me not."* The Bride must follow the lead of the Spirit and not hinder His work in her life. Rebekah made a choice: *"I will go" (v. 58).* To be in the Bride of Christ is a choice on our part. We must be *"willing" (Gen. 24:5).* Rebekah met Isaac in the field and the Bride will meet Jesus in the air *(1 Thess. 4:17)* to be forever with Him.

"And the Spirit and the Bride say, Come," and Jesus replied, *"Surely I come quickly!" (Rev. 22:17, 20)*

Maranatha! The Lord Cometh!

"THE SPIRIT AND THE BRIDE"
PART 2

*I*n last month's article on *"The Spirit and The Bride,"* we saw the interaction between Eliezer, Abraham's servant, who is a type of the Holy Spirit and Rebekah, who is a type of the Bride of Christ. In this article we want to look at three important marriages and their position in scripture. One is at the beginning of the Bible (Adam and Eve); the second is at the beginning of the New Testament (wedding at Cana, John 2); the third is at the end of the Bible (Marriage Supper of the Lamb).

We begin with Adam and Eve, who are types of Christ and the Bride of Christ. Adam is called the first man Adam and Jesus is called the last Adam or second Adam *(1 Cor. 15:45).* When God created Eve, He put Adam into a deep sleep and from Adam's side took a rib from which He made Eve *(Gen. 2:21–22).* Adam's deep sleep *(Gen. 2:21)* is a type of Christ's death on the Cross. Jesus went into a 3 days "deep sleep" as it were before resurrecting from the dead. Though dead on the cross, the Roman soldier still pierced the side of Jesus with water and blood coming out of His side *(John 19:34).* Both water *(John 3:5)* and blood are linked to salvation *(1 John 5:6)*, and show the shedding of Jesus' blood redeemed His Bride *(1 Peter 1:18–19).*

As Jesus will carry the scars of the nails in His hands from the Cross forever *(Zech. 13:6),* it is very probable He will also carry the sword's piercing scar of His side forever too. The first Adam carried the scar from his side for Eve's creation all his life; even so, the scars of Jesus will forever be a reminder of the price He paid for our redemption.

We now go to the Gospel of St. John in the New Testament, where Jesus' performed His first miracle. We all know the story of Jesus being invited to a wedding in Cana and there turned water into wine. Apparently the governor of the wedding feast, realizing they had run out of wine may have said something to Mary about this problem. She, in turn, tells Jesus, **"They have no wine" *(John 2:3).***

What is noteworthy and significant is Jesus' reply to Mary, **"Woman, what have I to do with thee? mine hour is not yet come" *(John 2:4).*** It is this last phrase that has great meaning. The obvious question is: why does Jesus link His hour (time of death) with wine at a marriage feast? We may also wonder why He choose His first miracle to be changing water into wine, when He could have raised the dead or cleansed a leper, which really would have attracted crowds.

His hour refers to His death *(John 17:1)* and His death to our redemption. By telling Mary at a wedding feast that His hour has not yet come shows a connection between His hour and a marriage. Wine speaks of pressing the life out of a grape to get wine, and refers to Gethsemane, the place of the wine-press where His hour began and where He sweat great drops of blood *(Luke 22:44).*

THE PASTOR'S PEN

Jesus knew His purpose in coming to die on earth, which certainly included salvation for mankind, but went beyond salvation to His ultimate goal, which was to redeem a bride. This message is contained in the Book of Ruth, which shows the redeeming of Ruth, a bride to be, by her Kinsman-Redeemer, Boaz. Boaz is a type of Christ, who also redeemed us by purchasing us to Himself. These types in the Old Testament are filled with spiritual truth meant to open our understanding to the purposes of God.

We now turn to the last of the three important marriages as given above and in particular to the ultimate goal of God for His Son. As Abraham's ultimate goal for his son Isaac *(Gen.24),* was to find him a bride, so the Father's goal for His Son Jesus, is also to find Him a bride who qualifies to be worthy of being Christ's Bride. This brings us to **Revelation 19:1–9** at the close of the Bible, with the prominence on the Marriage Supper of the Lamb.

As pointed out in one of the past articles, the Song of Solomon opens as the *"song of songs,"* because of its emphasis on Christ and His Bride. All the other "songs" or books of the Bible, mostly have a message that deals with the correction of the people of God. The **Song of Solomon** does not deal with correction; it deals with an eternal love between the Bridegroom and His Bride that began on earth but finds its fulfillment throughout eternity.

Salvation, the Baptism with the Holy Ghost and healing are all gifts. Anything after that will cost us because anything after that deals with our spiritual growth and development predicated on choices. To be in the Bride of Christ is not a right we have as Christians. It is a privilege. **Revelation 19:8 says, *"To her was GRANTED that she should be arrayed in fine linen, clean and white."*** It is granted to us and bestowed on us because we qualify by the life we lived on earth in relationship to Christ. **It has nothing to do with "doing," it has to do with "being," made in His likeness** *(Rom. 8:29).*

Let's look back at the time when the mother of James and John brought her two sons to Christ and requested that they may both sit, one on the right and the other on the left hand of Jesus in *Matthew 20:21, 22.* She asked Jesus to "grant," this request. There is more to receiving a grant than just a request. One must qualify. Jesus' reply was, *"are ye able to drink of the cup that I shall drink of, and to be baptized with the baptism that I am baptized with?"* What Jesus was saying to them, and to all Christendom, is that a cost is involved for such a privilege, to be in the Bride. As James and John had to qualify, so must we qualify if we wish to be in the Bride of Christ.

Many Christians think that once you are saved you are entitled to all the blessings of Heaven in spite of how one lives the Christian life on earth. This is a fallacy. What Jesus told James and John is a message to all believers. Commitment to Jesus Christ, taking up our Cross and following Jesus to death to the self-life, identifying with Christ's sufferings, surrender, a single eye, obedience, faith, faithfulness are necessary to qualify. It is identity with the Christ life that is required. Unfortunately, this message is rarely heard anymore. The Church today has mixed her priorities with the arm of the flesh and consequently, lost her way.

The Lord Jesus is depending on the Holy Spirit to bring Him a most beautiful Bride that is worthy of being His Bride, just as did Eliezer for Isaac. This work of the Spirit began on the Day of Pentecost in the upper room, when Jesus gave birth to a Spirit filled Church, and He is coming back for a Spirit filled Bride. The Holy Spirit is not going to be embarrassed at the Marriage of the Lamb and say to Jesus, "I'm sorry Jesus, but this was the best I could do." Oh, no! The Spirit will not fail! He will present to Christ a most beautiful Bride, without spot or wrinkle, just like Jesus. This tells us there is a connection between the Baptism of the Holy Spirit and qualifying to be in the Bride of Christ. Jesus was Spirit filled and so must His Bride be Spirit filled.

We will stop here and continue with part 3 of this message next month.

Remember—Maranatha! The Lord Cometh!

"THE SPIRIT AND THE BRIDE"
PART 3

In this article, we want to address the meaning of the Parable of the man without the wedding garment in *Matthew 22:1–14*, and how it relates to the Bride of Christ. This is a very important Parable with insights to help us understand the mysteries of the Bride and being part of the Bride.

The Parable is of the Marriage of the King's Son and identifies with the Kingdom of Heaven or the Marriage Supper of the Lamb in verse 2. The fact that the King, who is the Father, is the one who made the marriage for His Son, coincides in type with Abraham, who also prepared everything for the marriage of his son Isaac.

The next point deals with the invitation to the wedding, which was a great honor. To reject the King's invitation would be a great insult, yet the people invited made light of his invitation, by coming up with selfish excuses not to attend the wedding *(v. 5)*. To make matters worse, the disrespectful invited guests further insulted the King by persecuting his servants, and even killing some of them simply because they were the carriers of the invitation.

Today, the invitation to be part of the Marriage Supper of the Lamb is as real as it was when Jesus spoke this parable. ***Revelations 19:9 says, "Blessed are they which are called unto the Marriage Supper of the Lamb."*** The call is to the saints *(Rev. 19:8).* The common idea that the Bride is made up of all believers is not the case at all, as this parable will show. Here is where the servant's persecution appears, for if one dares to preach this message he can expect rejection. Truth is not always accepted because it goes contrary to opinion. Take note, the message of the Bride is hardly ever heard anymore. There are exceptions of course, but it is rare indeed to hear a sermon preached about the Bride. It's much easier and safer not to preach this subject than venture out and find disapproval for a lack of understanding the message of the Bride.

Others have interpreted the message in this parable, of Israel rejecting the invitation of the King and the Gentiles accepting it and are brought in from the highways and by-ways. While there is an element of truth here, the parable goes deeper. It is telling us of the need to be found *"worthy" (v. 8)* of an invitation to the Wedding.

Worthy (*axios* in Greek) means **"deserving, comparable or suitable; it is due reward."**[7] The serious minded believer will put the goal of being in the Bride above all the distractions of the world. He or she seeks to live a life of great anticipation of **this greatest of events-the Marriage Supper of the Lamb!** The believer will put aside anything and everything that would rob him or her from being part of the wedding feast. The greatest eternal reward we can ever have is to be part of the Bride who marries the Lord Jesus Christ. To be worthy will make us comparable and suitable to be part of Christ's Bride, as she will be a proper match for the Bridegroom.

The wedding is prepared and the appreciative guests, who responded favorably to the invitation, are seated. The king is pleased to see them *(v. 11)*, until he sees a man who does not have the proper dress. Consequently, he is ejected. Now the question is, how did he get in *(v. 12)?*

The message here is that one must qualify to be in the wedding. The Marriage Supper of the Lamb takes place in Heaven. So, this man is in Heaven and now is ejected from the feast. Was he thrown out of Heaven? No, absolutely not. The message is not that one can be ejected from Heaven once he gets there, for no one will ever be ejected from Heaven. The heart of the message of this parable is that one can make it to Heaven and not be part of the Bride. The parable has a two-fold message. First, it serves as a warning of missing out of God's best for us, and second, it serves as an encouragement to pursue the Bridegroom with all our heart, soul, mind and passion.

Paul references this when he said in **Philippians 3:14, *"I press toward the mark for the prize of the high calling of God in Christ Jesus."*** The high calling is our invitation to the Marriage Supper of the Lamb. This should be our goal in life; anything else is minor. To be in the Bride and in the Marriage Supper of the Lamb is major!

The man was thrown into *"outer darkness"* *(v. 13)*. This is not Hell. One cannot be in Heaven and then thrown into the outer darkness of Hell. The meaning of outer darkness is to be left outside of a revelation that is given by the Lord, in this case, to a group of people. When the Five foolish virgins neglected the additional oil, though saved, they were left outside of the marriage *(Matt. 25:10)*. As a result, they were not part of the revelation that followed behind the closed door. This was outer darkness to the Five foolish virgins.

Thus, this parable has a strong message for the Church and it behooves us to understand its message. The unfortunate point is that the man was so close and yet so far. Let us not just be close, but committed to press on and into God's very best for our lives, so we do not come short of the glory of God and His purpose for our eternity. In the next article, part 4, we will look at the message of the Ten Virgins.

Maranatha! The Lord, Our Bridegroom, Cometh!

"THE SPIRIT AND THE BRIDE"
PART 4

We now come to the parable of the Ten Virgins and their message *(Matt. 25:1–13)*. Many opinions have been expressed and preached about the five Foolish Virgins. Perhaps the strongest opinion is that they were back-sliders, but that isn't true for backsliders are not looking for the coming of the Lord nor are they waiting for Jesus' Return as did the Five Foolish Virgins. When the Rapture takes place the backsliders will not be awakened to meet the Bridegroom. Only those waiting and looking for Him will be awakened *(Heb. 9:28)*.

A scriptural definition, describing the nature of Virgins is given in **Revelation 14:3–5**, in reference to the 144,000 taken from the Twelve Tribes of Israel during the tribulation. They are *"redeemed"* or saved *(v. 3); "they were not defiled with women,"* were moral *(v. 4); "they which follow the Lamb whithersoever he goeth"*, they were faithful and obedient to the Lord *(v. 4);* they had *"no guile"* (were not defiled by their talk), and were *"without fault"* before God (pleased God) *(v. 5)*. Since the Ten Virgins were called virgins they **all** fit the above definition. The opinion that the Five Foolish Virgins were backsliders has to be rejected, as backsliders do not fit the description of virgins in **Revelation 14**. The Ten Virgins lived a separate life and were waiting for the Coming of the Bridegroom.

This brings us to the issue as to why the Five Foolish Virgins were not permitted to enter the marriage *(Matt. 25:10)*. The issue was oil. The Wise took oil in their vessels with their lamps, a double amount *(v. 4)*. The Foolish took their lamps, which had oil, but they didn't have oil in their vessels. Oil is a type of the Holy Spirit and oil in their lamps speaks of the indwelling of the Holy Spirit at salvation, and oil in their vessels, speaks of the Baptism of the Holy Ghost.

There is a two-fold experience with the Holy Spirit. He comes in us at salvation *(John 20:22)*, and upon us at the Baptism of the Holy Spirit *(Acts 2:1–4)*. When Jesus breathed on the Apostles that first Easter Sunday evening in the Upper Room, the Spirit came to indwell them. Then, fifty days later on the Day of Pentecost, the Spirit was sent by Jesus and came upon them *(Acts 2:1–4)* in the Upper Room and they were filled with the Holy Ghost and fire.

This is when the Lord Jesus gave birth to the Church, with the expectation that all believers, from the Day of Pentecost to the day of His coming, would be filled with the Holy Ghost and fire. He gave birth to a Spirit-filled Church, just as He was Spirit-filled *(Matt. 3:16)* and He is coming back for a Spirit-filled people.

Heaven will be filled with saved people who are part of the Church but were not Spirit-filled on earth. They are virgins, who also are waiting for the Bridegroom but have refused or neglected for some reason, to accept the Baptism with the Holy Ghost, with the evidence of speaking with tongues. Though they are saved and will be in Heaven, they are disqualified from the Bride because the Bride must be Spirit-filled to be equal to the Groom. The Baptism of the Holy Spirit is a major requisite to be part of the Bride of Christ. So, where does the Bride come from? She comes out of the Mystical Body of Christ, the Church, just as Eve came out of the body of Adam.

John the Baptist had a unique part with all of this, which is seen in his four-fold calling. 1) He is the voice heralding the coming of the Lord *(Matt. 3:3)* and calling the people to repentance; 2) He is to identify the Son of God, as the Lamb of God *(John 1:29, 34);* 3) He is to announce the Baptism with the Holy Ghost and fire by Jesus *(Matt. 3:11);* 4) He is the first to make reference to the Bride and Bridegroom *(John 3:29).* The point here is to see John, through his pronouncements, connecting these four messages as one, and in particular, the Baptism with the Holy Ghost and the Bride and Groom.

Now, how will the Lord deal with the saints of the Middle and Dark Ages when emphasis on the Baptism with the Holy Spirit was minimal? Will they be left out of the Bride? That must be left to God. **"Shall not the Judge of all the earth do right?"(Gen. 18:25).** But we today must not minimize the value and importance of the Baptism with the Holy Ghost. There are far too many Christians who believe they will get everything in Heaven as anyone else, with or without the Baptism and consequently, they do not see the value of the Baptism with the Holy Ghost.

The Baptism with the Holy Spirit is essential to receiving our inheritance because today we receive only an earnest of what awaits us there. ***Ephesians 1:13–14*** shows us the connections between the Holy Spirit of

Promise in verse *13* (Baptism of Holy Ghost), and the earnest of the Spirit in verse *14*. They are connected.

In many Pentecostal Churches today, the Baptism with the Holy Ghost is deliberately put aside to be accepted by other Churches. This should not be done. We are not to be ashamed of the Baptism with the Holy Ghost and must always keep this wonderful truth before our people. As Pastors, Ministers and Leaders, we must emphasis the importance of the Baptism with the Holy Spirit so our people do not miss out on God's wonderful blessings.

Maranatha! The Lord, Our Bridegroom, Cometh!

Especially For Pastors

THE WILL OF GOD AND THE MINISTRY

The importance of the will of God in our lives cannot be overstated nor underestimated. Especially is this true in the life of the minister. As ministers, we need to seek to know and follow His will. *(Col. 1: 9, 10)*.

Because of the day in which we live, with the over emphasis on intellectualism and rationale, it is easy for one to be misled into thinking that the will of God can be determined on that premise. The will of God must be determined by the **leading of the Holy Spirit** *(Rom. 8:14).* While outward circumstances may confirm the will of God, they must not be allowed to become the criteria in determining the will of God.

When we look at and focus on the will of God, it is very important to recognize several factors. One is that **relationship precedes profession**. Or simply stated, the minister and his relationship to the Lord and his eternal status are more important to the Lord than one's ministry. What we are, or being, means more to Him than our doing. It means that God is at work in us, using all available means to make us more than just part of the family of God *(Heb. 13:21).* His ultimate objective and purpose is to conform us into the Image and Likeness of His Son, the Lord Jesus Christ *(Rom. 8:28–29)*. Everything in our lives is directed towards that end.

Keeping that perspective before us will help in coping with adverse situations that tend to rise periodically in the ministry. One area especially where this will help and give direction is when one is called to pastor a Church. Often ministers have a tendency to see their call to a particular Church as the Church needing them. While that may play a part, the will and purpose of God goes beyond that. Often it is the minister needing that specific Church, at that particular time, for his own spiritual growth and development more than the Church needing him.

What the minister will receive in ministry from that Church body will be part of God's ultimate purpose in shaping and conforming that individual into the eternal Image and likeness of Christ. Each specific Church has something to add to the pastor that no other Church is able to give. Years later, as a pastor looks back at all the places where he has ministered, he will recognize the uniqueness of each Church and its contribution to his personal life and ministry. Of course, Churches also benefit.

Therefore, it is imperative to understand that where the Lord sends us now is extremely important because of timing, circumstances and the people involved. It takes time for the Lord to set up the exact conditions needed for our particular spiritual benefit at any given time. These conditions will not exist anywhere else, nor will they be permanent in that Church. In fact, they may only exist there for a year or two but just enough time for you to go and benefit from them. This is why it is so important to get the mind of God and move in His will.

At times His leading may appear odd, but He knows what we need at the moment and the stage of our spiritual development. He also knows how to providentially arrange the match of the minister to the right Church. Hence, timing, location and obedience are key factors for the working out of the will of God.

A danger that always looms at times of decision is choosing a particular Church solely for personal reasons. Either because it will put one nearer to relatives, or the prestige of pastoring a large Church and staff, or because of the financial and retirement benefits or even geographical reasons. These factors, standing alone, can hinder one from fulfilling God's plan for their lives and deter one from the will of God. The possibility of personal spiritual loss is existent when one chooses solely for any of these reasons.

Jesus addressed areas of concern in *Matthew 6:25–33*, where He tells us that the will of God must supersede all other concerns *(Matt. 6:33).* It is the natural man (the Gentiles *v. 32*) in us that looks at these things because the natural man is at a constant struggle against that which is spiritual *(1 Cor. 2:14)*. Because of this struggle, security, comfort and prestige compete with the Will of God.

Another area of concern is seeing ourselves as "successful" in the outward indicators such as numeric growth, giving, outreach programs, or building programs. In spite of these, one may still not be where God wants him.

How can this be? As we know, God's Word will not return void in spite of the vessel. Once the Lord calls to the ministry, He will not recall that gift and calling; *the gifts and callings of God are without repentance (Rom. 11:29)*. So, while the minister will not lose his gift in ministry and may see results in spite of himself (compare with *Matthew 7:21–23*), yet his personal spiritual growth will be temporarily halted until he realigns himself with God's perfect will.

The will of God is not predicated on results. Success before God is more than numbers and expansion; it is obedience. A classic example of such obedience is Philip who was sent from a great citywide revival in Samaria down to the desert to minister to one man. He never questioned nor wondered. He just obeyed. This is all the Lord desires of us *(Matt. 6:10)*.

Turning back to *Romans 8:26–27*, we see three components at work promoting the purpose of God in our lives. They are our **infirmities**. This reflects our spiritual need and where we are at the moment in reference to the development of the Image of Christ in us. **The ministry of the Holy Spirit** in intercession in our behalf, so that we will allow Him to work in us as He sees fit, and **the will of God**. These combined with God's Providence, all move towards one goal and purpose: the development of the Christ-like character and image in the life of a yielded and obedient vessel.

We must always keep in mind that all events, people and places in our lives contribute in some way to our spiritual life. They become part of the will of God that moves in one direction and that is towards the purpose of God, which is the revelation of Christ in our lives and our conformity to His Image. *"All things that work together for good" (Rom. 8:28)* encompasses all of this, and He is at work for our eternal benefit *(1 Cor. 15:49)*.

This all takes a lifetime. As one has said, "The longer we make Him wait, the less time He has to work in us." The will of God and the obedience of faith are both always relevant. They cannot be separated nor do they end at the retirement age of sixty-five. As servants of God, this is our calling and lifestyle till Jesus comes, we know no other way.

Maranatha! The Lord Cometh!

"THE ROLE OF THE PASTOR AS SHEPHERD"

The call of God is priceless and is a great honor to be chosen of God for the ministry. His call indicates that He saw something in you that moved Him to call you into the ministry. It's much like David, who risked his life to save a lamb from the mouth of the lion and the bear. When the Lord saw David kill the lion and bear, He knew He had found the right man with a shepherd's heart to care for His people. If David would risk his life for a lamb, how much more would he risk his life for God's people? God's heart has always been towards man, and in David He found a man after His own heart.

The heart of a faithful shepherd will always be after God's own heart, and the heart of a faithful shepherd will always be filled with the love of God for the people of God. Like the Lord Jesus, the Great Shepherd, the Pastor is to be a love slave to the Church because the Church is Christ's Body. In one of our Bible School classes one of our teachers said, **"when you become a Pastor, you also become a love slave for the Church you pastor."** You cannot separate Christ from His Body, the Church. They are inseparable. The Pastor who is called to a Church is expected to love and protect it at any cost.

Jesus brought the Church into existence by dying for her. As a man is willing to die for his wife, so Christ was willing to die for the Church. Paul's testimony to the Church of Colosse was, *I "rejoice in my sufferings for you, and fill up that which is behind* (lacking in the local Church) *of the afflictions of Christ in my flesh for His body's sake, which is the Church"(Col. 1:24).* Paul rejoiced in his sufferings for the Church at Colosse, and felt honored to be counted worthy to suffer for that Church. Paul's words express the true heart of a servant shepherd. Paul was also willing to be *"accursed from Christ"* for Israel's sake *(Rom. 9:3).*

Another example is Moses, who *"verily was faithful in all his house, as a servant" (Heb. 3:5).* As a servant, he was willing to have his name taken out of the Book of Life for his congregation, Israel. See Moses' unfinished sentence in ***Exodus 32:32***. Pastors must be willing to put aside their interests for the sake of the Church they pastor. They must be willing to die to self, especially when mistreated.

There is another area where the shepherd must protect his sheep. It has to do with the danger of new teachings and ideas that filter into the Church through Church members, who may be well meaning but are misled. These members may have gone to other meetings and think they have discovered something more "spiritual" than what they have at their Church. The danger is that it leads to division and trouble in the body.

Even now, there is a new concept that is popular and has crept into the Church that says, God is first, family second, and Church third. Of course, God is always first, but the second and third priorities are out of order. The words of Jesus in **Luke 14:26–27,** are very clear and direct as to priorities. Even the US Marines have their priorities correctly. Their motto says God first, country second, and family third, so the Church's motto should be "God first, Church second, and family third."

Obviously, nobody is anti-family, but the result of putting family before Church has been detrimental to the Church. Since congregations have heard this concept from pulpits, many Christians are using it as an excuse to stay home from Church services. This concept has led to another danger and that is the changing of the Lord's Day to family day, which says that family comes second and the Church comes third. There are Christians who now see Sunday as family day. Thus, the Lord's Day has been eclipsed by the family day. This says something about the state of the Church and shows how subtly, the enemy has used the family as a means of weakening the Church.

There is encouragement for the Pastors, who conscientiously care for their flock. As a Pastor, it is reassuring to know that as he watches over God's flock, the Lord watches over him and his family. We see this in **Mark 6:48,** when Jesus watched over the disciples, as they struggled in the storm, ***"And he saw them toiling in rowing; for the wind was contrary unto them; and about the fourth watch of the night he cometh unto them."*** As Jesus watched over them, so does He watch over us in our storms and will always come to our rescue.

Maranatha! The Lord Cometh!

THE NEED FOR PREACHERS

We are living in a time that has altered the call and ministry of preaching. The Church today needs once again to hear the proclaiming of true and pure preaching of the Word of God. Instead, we are witnessing the eclipsing of the message and the power of Pentecost by a new method of "teaching." We are aware of the bona-fide teaching ministry as given in *Ephesians 4:11*, but we are hearing a different teaching from the legacy of our forefathers. It is true that we have ministers, but we have few preachers.

As a result of this new shift, many Spirit-filled believers hear the new sermonizing from the pulpit, but aren't sure how to relate to the sermon because it does not have the **"ring" of the Spirit.** It does have a sprinkling of Scripture in sermons to make it sound spiritual but it's hollow. It is a sermon that may have results but is void of the witness of the Spirit. These Spirit-filled saints find themselves in a dilemma, as they don't want to leave their Churches and yet realize that something is amiss. Sermons not only reveal the spiritual level of the Minister but also reveal the spiritual level of the Church. A Church is only as spiritual as is its Pastor, and it is possible for one to be in a leadership role and still miss God because position is no guarantee of God's approval.

There are wonderful Pastors, who labor faithfully and will do whatever is necessary to see their Church grow. In their search of ideas for Church growth, they seek out articles and books describing how to grow a Church and then begin "copying" those Churches. They don't realize they are letting go of the paths that once took the Church to higher ground. In its place they go on a new and different highway, which leads into a different direction. Sadly, in many areas methods are replacing the place of faith. Consequently, many Pastors, especially young Pastors, are being drawn into a new wave of methodology on how to grow a Church, instead of focusing on being a fellow worker with the Spirit, who will add to the Church *(Acts 2:47, 5:14).* Technology cannot take the place of the Spirit.

We are witnessing the danger which the Apostle Paul warned of in *2 Timothy 4:3–4.* The time would come (and is here now), when people will not want to hear about the cost of discipleship nor a sermon on the topic of Hell or the conviction of the Spirit. Many Churchgoers want a pleasant emotional experience when attending Church such as favorable comments from the pulpit. They want their ears tickled, meaning "eager to hear" the new topics and sermons that make them feel good. Lecturing has taken the place of preaching, with topics of self-helps, psychology and motivational topics.

Preaching of the Gospel is being put aside for a new message of accommodation. The new emphasis is on making people feel good and thus win them to Christ with a gentle message. The Lord Jesus preached the Gospel *(Luke 20:1)* even though it cut across the prevailing culture. He said, *"that repentance and remission of sins should be preached in His name among all nations" (Luke 24:47).*

Jesus was a preacher, Jonah was a preacher, John the Baptist was a preacher and Paul was a preacher, In fact, Paul felt his mission was to preach the Gospel wherever he went. Paul embraced the Gospel in so much that he calls the Gospel *"my"* Gospel *(Rom. 16:25),* showing how deeply he felt about the Gospel *(Rom. 1:9).* Paul said he was *"separated unto the Gospel of God" (Rom. 1:1).* The Gospel was the basis of his ministry for preaching. The message of the Gospel is that of repentance and remission of sins, which the Church needs once again to hear from our pulpits.

Maranatha! The Lord Cometh!

GOD'S PRINCIPLE FOR PREPARATION — GAL. 4:1–5A

Solomon in *Ecclesiastes 3:1*, says, *"To every thing there is a season, and a time to every purpose under the heaven."* In this article we want to look at the value of time as related to the purposes of God. Time and Purpose go hand in hand. The Lord has a purpose for each of our lives that will require time to bring His purpose to fruition. In watching this process we see the way God works in lives.

This is seen in ***Galatians 4:1–5,*** where the Apostle Paul is writing about the law in relation to the child of God. Nestled away in this passage is a principle of God's working in the believer's life. The principle contains five important components to operate: (1) the heir *(v. 1)*; (2) the tutor *(v. 2)*; (3) the timing *(v. 4)*; (4) the Standard (His Son, *v. 4*); and (5) the purpose *(v. 5)*.

The first is the "heir," who is a young child of God, not necessarily young in age but in understanding the ways of God. At this stage, he may be unaware of the purposes of God and needs a tutor to guide and instruct him in the ways of God. Our tutor is the Holy Spirit *(1*

John 2:27), who faithfully teaches us by experience and revelation of the Word.

The experiences He uses to instruct us are both sweet and sour to temper us as steel is tempered. To temper steel hot water and cold water are both necessary to make it premium, so the Lord uses sweet and sour experiences to make us like steel. As our tutor, the Holy Spirit decides the timing and the experiences necessary to develop us in fulfilling God's purpose for our lives. Then there comes a day when the heir becomes aware of God's plan and call for his life. This comes by revelation, not education.

The value of experience is that it develops faith and character in us. Jacob's father-in-law, Laban, saw the value of experience and said, *"I have learned by experience" (Gen. 30:27).* Even Solomon, communing with his own heart, recognized experience, under God, brought him great wisdom and knowledge *(Eccl. 1:16).*

Second, you have the tutors that the heir must submit too, UNTIL the time appointed by the Father is fulfilled. The tutors are part of the experimental process the Lord brings into one's life. The heir must undergo testing to learn dependence on the Lord and not in himself. He must also pass the test of faithfulness in "the little things," before he can be trusted with "the greater things."

Third, is the *"fulness of time."* In *Galatians 4:4*, the promise of the coming of God's Son, the Messiah, is stated to come in the fullness of time. Timing and purpose go hand in hand. The time came for Jesus to appear on earth and His purpose was to *"redeem" (Gal. 4:5)* man from sin and legalism. Though He was promised to come in *Genesis 3:15*, yet Jesus had to wait four thousand years before it was the right time to come. Why this long? So the timing would be right. God always does the right thing at the right time. He does not do a good thing at the wrong time. He is exact and precise knowing exactly when to do things correctly and properly. His works are **"like apples of gold in pictures of silver" (Prov. 25:11).** This constitutes the **"fulness of time."**

Fourth, yet the most important of these components is that Jesus is God's "Standard or Model" for us. When we study the life of Jesus we'll see the Father working in Jesus with obedience **(Heb. 5:8)** and surrender **(Matt. 26:39).** God uses the same method in us. The fact that Jesus is our example and leader—**"the captain of their salvation" (Heb. 2:10)**—indicates He must go first and lead the way as does the **"husbandman . . . must be first partaker of the fruits" (2 Tim. 2:6).** All this is to show how the Father prepared Jesus the same way that He prepares us, so we can fulfill our destiny in life, as did Jesus. Every purpose of God for the heir centers on the Lord Jesus Christ.

Even in the lives of the Old Testament prophets we find these basic ways of God at work. The Father called and prepared the prophets, after the example of Jesus, even though Jesus was not yet born. This is why they are called "types and anti-types." God used men before The Example (The Lord Jesus) was physically born, because the ways of God are not bound by dispensations of time. To God, who is the Beginning and the End, time is always in "the present."

Fifth and lastly is God's "purpose" for one's life, which is a very serious matter as it deals with eternal issues. The process requires the Lord testing us in order to separate the **"vessels of honor,"** from the **"vessels of dishonor" (2 Tim. 2:20–21).** The vessel of honor puts great value on God's purpose for his life and strives to fulfill it, whereas the vessel of dishonor, even among ministers, disregards the value of God's purpose for his life and falls into the Esau class, who sold his purpose, "birthright," to satisfy the craving of the flesh.

Let's look at some of the examples in the Old Testament. Our first man, who is called of God for a specific purpose, which was to save Israel from famine and death so she would become a great nation, is Joseph. He is called of God, via his two dreams but is unprepared at this point in time to fulfill God's purpose in his life. In fact, God's purpose for his life is somewhat vague to Joseph due to his circumstances. He may have even questioned what God was doing in his life and may have felt stuck in Egypt.

Looking into his life we see the man, his call, and God's purpose for his life, all wrapped up in the man Joseph, but the timing had not reached its fulness. ***Psalm 105:17–19*** says that Joseph was sent by God and tested with fetters and iron, ***"Until the time that his word came."*** **In Joseph's fulness of time, meaning now he is ready, his word came from God to step into action now, as he was ready to fulfill God's purpose for his life.**

The preparation and training and maturing of Joseph took about fifteen years, after which the man, the call, and God's purpose and timing were finally united as one. God's process in the life of Joseph was fulfilled to man's amazement and to God's glory. **Man's amazement is always God's glory *(Acts 2:12)*.**

God made Joseph the savior of a nation (Israel) for God's long-range plan of the ages, which is the coming Redeemer. However, we must not overlook God's process in preparing Joseph for this awesome responsibility. The parallels between Joseph and Jesus are astounding. They show God's method of working with others is based on

His workings with His Son even though it's 1700 years before Jesus is born.

Moses is another example who also went through God's method of preparation so he could become what God called him to be, but it was all via a process. ***Exodus 2:23* says,** *"And it came to pass in process of time."*

This is to encourage us and teach us. God is never in a hurry when he sets Himself to prepare a man. He has His ways of preparing us and he keeps good time as well, so we will be properly prepared and thus be effective as we follow His leading.

Thus, dear fellow minister, do not be discouraged at your circumstances of the present, for you do not know what God is preparing you for in the near future. Just trust and obey for there is no other way.

Maranatha! The Lord Cometh!

"FROM COMMON TO HALLOWED"

It is a high calling of God to be called into the ministry. With the calling comes a process of breaking, molding, and being changed into another man. The process is not easy. It is challenging and necessary to prepare one for the work of God. It is also necessary to make him sensitive to the voice of God, who called him. The voice of God is known in scripture as **"the word of the Lord" (1 Sam. 3:7).** Samuel was called of God but now must have an ear to distinguish the voice of the Lord from other voices.

To see the change of the man called of God, we find a marvelous principle in the story of David, when he went to Ahimelech the priest for bread for himself and the men with him *(1 Sam. 21)*. The priest told David he had no *"common"* bread at the moment, but did have *"hallowed"* bread, which he gave to David. There is a parallel here with bread that is common and mankind. We were all born common until the Lord called us, at which time we became hallowed because of His call and hand on our lives.

In this story, we see the role of the priest and the hallowed bread (the Shewbread) that was brought into the presence of God in the Holy Place. The priest was to place the bread on the Table every Sabbath morning for one week. The bread was common, until the priest poured frankincense on it and it became sanctified and hallowed. The priest and his sons were the only ones permitted to eat the loaves of bread from the previous week, because it was hallowed bread and they were hallowed men *(Lev. 24: 5–9)*.

The frankincense became the anointing for the bread. Thus, we see a divine movement, **from** something it was, common, **to** something it wasn't before, hallowed. While the bread continues to maintain its physical composition, it will never be common again. So with us, when God calls us, we are the same outwardly in our physical bodies, but inwardly, we will never be the same. As the hallowed bread was separated from the other loaves of bread, it now can fulfill its divine purpose of standing in the Tabernacle (House of God). We, as *"servants of the Lord,"* are to *"stand in the house of the Lord, in the courts of the house of our God" (Ps. 135:1–2)*.

Thus, the principle seen by the common and hallowed bread carries over in how the Lord works in the lives of men whom He calls into the ministry. He takes them from their present, and guides them into their future. A good example of this is Aaron, who was living a very common life until the Lord moved and took him out of his comfort zone and surroundings and sent him to minister with his brother Moses *(Exod. 4:14)*.

Little did Aaron realize how drastically his life would change: from a common man to Israel's lifelong high priest. What made the difference? The blood of **the burnt offering, which was a type of Christ *(Exod. 29:21)*,** and *"the precious ointment upon the head ... that went down to the skirts of his garments,"* **which is a type**

of the Holy Spirit *(Ps. 133:2).* When does one change from common to hallowed? After the **blood** is applied (Salvation), followed by the **anointing,** (Baptism of the Holy Ghost). Everything changes gloriously when the Holy Spirit takes over.

There is always trauma in spiritual issues, going from one's present state to what God is calling him to do. The trauma is due to the inner struggle of making a decision of obedience. Some begin the new walk of faith in the ministry with joy and exhilaration, but after awhile become discouraged and fall aside being **choked with cares and riches and pleasures of this life.** Others struggle with hardships and then, over time, decide not to continue and miss out of God's best for their lives. In Bible school, one of the students began, and shortly thereafter decided to go back home and walked away from the call of God during the night. This doesn't mean he lost his salvation, not at all, but it does mean he lost God's best for his life. It's much like the young ruler who Jesus called to follow Him, but his possessions possessed him, causing him to walk away empty *(Luke 18:18).*

There are a couple of examples that show us how we are to respond when the Lord moves on us. Elisha is an excellent example. Before Elijah was translated to Heaven, he asked Elisha what he could do for him. Elisha put the spiritual above the earthly and asks for a double portion of Elijah's spirit. To receive that request, Elisha was required to see Elijah ascend to heaven. As Elijah ascended heavenward, his mantle fell at Elisha's feet. Elisha, as Elijah's servant, poured water on Elijah's hands for eight years *(2 Kings 3:11)* until he picked up Elijah's mantle. It was then that he experienced a radical change in his life. He tested the mantle and found power and authority, and went from water boy to the office of prophet. The mantle (Holy Spirit) separated him from the sons of the prophets, who recognized, by bowing before him, that he was no longer a common servant, but is now God's anointed before Israel.

There are times when the Lord calls a man with a dramatic experience. Such was the case with Moses. God met him at the burning bush and changed his life forever. Isaiah is another example of a life changing experience when he saw the Lord high and lifted up and heard Him say, *"Whom shall I send, and who will go for us?"* Isaiah responded and said, *"Here am I; send me"(Isa. 6:8).* Not all have such a dramatic experience, but all do have a very real experience because of the touch of God.

Amos' experience shows how the Lord **"takes a man,"** from the fields, who is unqualified by the religious standards of the day, to be a prophet. He was a shepherd and a caretaker of fruit by occupation, yet called of God to be His prophet and said to Amos, *"Go, prophesy unto my people"(Amos 7:15).* This was traumatic for Amos. Unexpectedly, and not feeling capable, he obeyed God and went from being a common man to being God's prophet, **from being a nobody to being somebody for God.**

God's call and obedience to His call is very serious. God honors the man who honors His call and stands by that servant with the words, *"Touch not Mine anointed" (Ps. 105:15).* God's anointed represents God, and His call to that man is a high call, with privilege and honor before the Lord and not to be taken for granted.

Maranatha! The Lord Cometh!

"TAUGHT OF GOD"

"And they shall be all taught of God"
(John 6:45)

There is no greater privilege of learning the ways and truths of God than through divine revelation. Revelation is truth imparted to one's mind by the Holy Spirit. God has chosen revelation as His manner of teaching His children the insights of the Word. Commentaries are fine and have their place in giving **explanations** of the Word. Preaching gives **illumination** and is wonderful in proclaiming the Word. Then there is **divine revelation** by which the Holy Ghost teaches us *(1 John 2:27)* and opens to our hearts and minds the **"hidden manna"** of the Word.

The personification of the Word and truth is the Lord Jesus who said, *"I am the way, the truth, and the life" (John 14:6).* Yet, in spite of the fact that He is the **fullness of truth** *(John 1:14),* He still took upon Himself the *"the form of a servant, and was made in the likeness of men" (Phil. 2:7)* to identify with man. Being a man now, He must empty Himself of His Deity, which included His omniscience and submit Himself to the training and teaching of the Father, where He would learn truths to impart to us.

The procedure of passing truth on to us is seen in the Book of Revelation, when the Father gave Jesus the Revelation of *"things which must shortly come to pass"* who in turn gave it to John *(Rev. 1:1)* to pass on to His servants. Following Jesus' pattern, we to must submit to the Father's teaching via the Holy Spirit if we desire insights in the Word *(John 6:45)*. Jesus said, *"As my Father hath taught Me, I speak these things" (John 8:28)*. As the Father teaches us we, too, must speak of the things He has taught us.

One may wonder how the Father taught Jesus spiritual truth in His humanity. Scripture doesn't leave us dangling on this point. The beauty of being taught of God is that the Father teaches us today, in the same manner He taught Jesus. The Word tells us the way the Father taught Him.

Isaiah tells us in *Isaiah 50:4: "he wakeneth morning by morning, he wakeneth mine ear to hear as the learned."* The Father, somewhere in time, began to awaken Jesus in the early morning hours to reveal truth to Him. This is evident from the fact that at twelve years of age Jesus already understood **"His Father's business."** From the first day that the Father awakened Him, the Father taught Jesus truth that astounded the doctors and religious leaders in the Temple *(Luke 2:46–47)*. If I may take a bit of literary freedom and say, the Father was proud of how Jesus represented Him and conducted Himself at the Temple. With all due respect, we can imagine Him saying, **"Now, That's My Son!"**

Without a doubt, the times of ministering to Jesus in the morning hours were very special for the Father. We can only speculate the Father calling Him **"My beloved Son"** in those morning hours. By faithfully responding to the Father's call, Jesus *"increased in wisdom and stature, and in favor with God" (Luke 2:52).*

We have a precedent in scripture of the Lord calling someone early in the morning. It is Samuel. The Lord awakened him by calling his name audibly. He gave Samuel a message for Eli, and thus revealed to Samuel, *"the word of the Lord."* At this time, Samuel *"did not yet know the Lord, neither was the word of the Lord yet revealed unto him" (1 Sam. 3:7).* It was Samuel's first experience in hearing both the voice of the Lord, and the word of the Lord. Since he could recognize the voice of Lord, the Lord would teach him the ways of God.

The Lord knows how to get our attention. **Revelation 3:20 says, "I stand at the door and knock."** This passage is often used as God knocking at one's heart for salvation. This is fine, but the word goes deeper. This passage is speaking about **"supping"** with the Lord. It is a call to go deeper in God. The Lord still uses this means to awaken us while asleep. It is His way of calling us to prayer and to seek His face in the morning hours when we are fresh and alert. He beckons us to come aside and *"sup,"* with Him in fellowship before we begin the duties of the day.

If we don't get alone with the Lord in the morning, it is highly unlikely that you will meet with Him the rest of the day. It is when we do meet with him in the morning that He will teach us and give us insights into His word. **Proverbs 8:17** says, *"those that seek Me early shall find Me."* It may difficult at first, but with discipline, and the Lord's help, you will get used to it and appreciate every moment. It will bless your life and ministry and impact the lives of your children when they know you get up early to seek the Lord.

Many of God's people, including ministers, have at times heard a gentle knock on the door while asleep. It awakened them, causing them to think someone knocked at their door. When they didn't hear the knock the second time, they thought it was a dream and fell back to sleep without realizing it was the Lord calling them to come aside and be with Him in those early morning hours. Over the years I have had people tell me this happened to them and never realized it was the Lord calling.

Another way He awakens us is by *"songs in the night" (Job 35:10).* You are asleep and then a song begins in your spirit while you are asleep that awakens you. You had nothing to do with it and found it going over and over in your spirit and wondered how it began. It was birthed by the Holy Spirit to awaken us, to come aside and fellowship with the Lord in the quiet hours of the morning. It is during this time the Lord not only fellowships with us but also shares insights and revelation of truth. Waiting on God during these morning hours also sharpens our discernment. God does many things in those morning hours.

There is a price to pay to have God's best for our lives and it begins with responding to His call. The key to being taught by God is to respond to His beckoning. The Lord gives an invitation to come into His presence so He can fellowship with you and reveal truth to your heart. Sensitivity to His call is critical and extremely important to receive God's best for one's life.

Maranatha! The Lord Cometh!

HONORING GOD

"For them that honour me I will honour"
1 Samuel 2:30

The story of Eli and his sons *(1 Sam. 2–4)* serves as a warning to ministers and to remind us of the seriousness of the ministry. God's call to be a minister is the greatest honor the Lord can bestow on a man, **"And no man taketh this honor unto himself, but he that is called of God, as was Aaron" (Heb. 5:4).** In God's eyes, the call into the ministry is not only an honor but also a treasure *(2 Cor. 4:7).* Like our Lord Jesus, let us not look for the honor of men but look for the honor of God *(John 5:41).*

The danger is that one can begin in the ministry with great promise, but with the passing of time, becomes lax and loses the vision that once burned in his soul. Such an event will change one's priority. As a father in ministry and wanting his sons to follow his footsteps, Eli was happy to have two sons in the ministry but his priorities shifted from honoring God to honoring his sons. Apparently, something happened when they were younger that showed up when they became priests and refused to listen to their father's voice *(1 Sam. 2:25).*

Both of Eli's sons, Hophni and Phinehas, were in the ministry but did not know God *(1 Sam. 2:12)*. How could this be? It happens more often than we realize. They occupied the office of the priesthood and knew how to fulfill the priest's responsibilities, but didn't have a heart for the things of God. They entered the ministry by inheriting the priesthood through their father, who was the High Priest, but they did not have a personal relationship with the Lord. Consequently, the priesthood was a **"profession"** and an occupation with social prestige. In fact, they disdained the ministry and lorded over God's people. These same dangers lurk in the Church today as in Eli's day.

In *Judges 17,* we read of an opportunist Levite (name is *Jonathan, Judges 18:30)*, who went looking for a place to serve as a priest *(17:8–9)*. A man named Micah saw him and hired him to be his and his family's personal priest. He accepted the offer and would receive food, money and lodging. It all sounded good but over a period of time men, from the tribe of Dan, came into the area and recognized the Levite whom they had known from back home. They made him a lucrative offer, which impressed him and without seeking the will of God, he accepted *(18:19–20)* their offer. Now remember, this young man is an opportunist, devoid of any sense of loyalty except to himself and his ambitions. He went from being a priest of one family to being a priest to an entire tribe. The prestige was too good to pass up.

Jonathan and his sons were priests to the Tribe of Dan until the day of captivity of the land, which took place when Israel lost the Ark to the Philistines *(Judg. 18:30–31)*. They had control of the priesthood, yet they did not have God's approval. The message here is that one can have an outwardly successful ministry without having God's best.

One must remember that what looks like green pastures outside of the will of God, will soon dry up. What the Levite did back then is still being done today by those looking for greener pastures. They will end up in disappointment for their pursuit of opportunities rather than the will of God. These see the ministry as a glamorous vocation and as a career rather than recognizing the ministry as the call of God and the pursuit of God's glory.

Now as we look back to Eli we see the consequences that followed the attitude and behavior of Eli's sons in not honoring God, which eventually did bring the judgment of God on both of them as well as on Israel. Decisions made in life not only affect the individual, but also those around him and those he serves. These two men, who, as priests, were to represent God, dishonored Him by their behavior and brought disgrace to the offerings of the Lord *(1 Sam. 2:17)*.

Hophni and Phinehas died, and with their death lost the most holy tangible object of the revelation of God to Israel, the Ark of the Covenant, which Israel had safeguarded from the days of Moses. Now, for the first time in Israel's history, the Ark of the Covenant fell into the hands of the heathen. More importantly was the loss of the glory of God. The message is a warning to the Church today that it can happen again when God's people and His servants do not honor the Lord. The consequences are the same, a great loss, great sorrow and great regret.

The most important act in honoring God is **obedience**. We honor God by honoring His call on our lives. We honor Him by our speech and demeanor. Once people know you are a minister, they expect more of you because you represent the Lord of Glory. Many people, Christian and non-Christians, respond to the things of God, either favorably or unfavorably, predicated by the behavior of ministers *(1 Sam. 2:17)*. If they see ministers honoring God, they will follow and also honor Him. If, however, they see the Pastor dishonor the Lord, they will lose all respect for the Pastor. Honoring the Lord is a very important matter in the eyes of the people and the Lord.

The components of honoring the Lord are made up by, **(1) loving the Lord (2) being obedient to Him (3) putting Him first in our lives.** *"And thou shalt love the Lord thy God with all thy heart, and with all thy soul, and with all thy mind, and with all thy strength: this is the first commandment."(Mark 12:30).*

Faith and obedience will take you on the path of righteousness that leads to the heart of God. It is far better to honor the Lord by putting Him first and living a life that pleases Him, than to gain the prestige of the world. The Lord honors those who honor Him and those who do not shall be lightly esteemed, *"They that despise me shall be lightly esteemed" (1 Sam. 2:30).* This verse warns that one can be saved and a minister and leader, but honors God with a partial commitment. He will go to heaven but will be lightly esteemed and will have great sorrow and remorse. Let us take heed of the lessons of Eli's life, and strive to be vessels of honor.

Remember the words and example of Jesus when He said, *"I honor my Father" (John 8:49).*

Maranatha! The Lord Cometh!

"THE SNARE OF THE FOWLER"

Psalm 91 is a wonderful Psalm of hope and promise and gives great comfort to the child of God. It also warns of the *"snare of the fowler"* that is set up to hinder the child of God, especially Pastors. The Christian life is filled with traps and snares set up by the evil one and has been going on since Eden.

It goes without saying that we are living in a dangerous world. Today's danger is two-fold and stalks everyone. There is the physical danger, and more importantly, there is the spiritual danger. In this article we want to look at the spiritual danger, especially how it can affect Pastors and Churches.

While the child of God goes about doing his daily business, the devil doesn't stop doing his business, which is to undo what God is doing in the lives of Pastors and the Churches they pastor. Peter warns Christians, especially Pastors and leaders to be *"vigilant" (1 Peter 5:8),* watchful, and spiritually alert because Satan takes no vacation. Peter describes the devil as a *"roaring lion,"* seeking prey to devour. He is cunning and patient, as he waits for an opening to mislead Pastors in order to damage their ministry. All the enemy needs is just a small opening in one's life, and then, lies still for awhile and then slowly, he moves further and further into the life of a Pastor.

Hosea makes reference as how the enemy of our soul finds an opening to do damage to God's people. He tells how Israel **"committed falsehood,"** that opened the door to the thief *(Hosea 7:1)*. Satan is the unrelenting thief, who comes *"to steal, and to kill and to destroy" (John 10:10)*. The danger is not to be taken for granted. Peter, as an Elder *(1 Peter 5:1),* warned us, and we in turn as Pastors must alert our congregations to the spiritual dangers in this world. Satan's goal is to **"neutralize"** the power of God in a Pastor's life and ministry and thus make him and his Church ineffective. A Pastor, with a genuine call of God, can gradually go astray if he is using the ministry to gain position and prestige.

One of the great dangers and snares for Pastors today is to forget our roots, learned at the feet of Spirit-filled men of God. Remember the words of Solomon, so wise and yet caught in a snare said, *"How have I hated instruction, . . . And have not obeyed the voice of my teachers, nor inclined mine ear to them that instructed me!" (Prov. 5:12, 13)* The voice of our teachers of old, who taught us the ways of God, now calls us back via their memory with the words, *"This is the way, walk ye in it" (Isa.30:21)*.

Another area of concern, that seems so innocent and yet leads into a snare, has to do with Pastors, who do not take time on a daily basis to wait on the Lord in prayer. Then when Sunday comes, he is unprepared to give his people a fresh word from the Lord. He wasted precious time for the trivial things of life. In time, this leads to discouragement, which can easily bring the Pastor to look elsewhere for sermons, such as Sermon Books that can be bought. The snare now becomes apparent when a Pastor, in this state, wants to be "successful," and turns to copying other minister's style of preaching and life styles, so he to, like them, can be successful.

It is important for Pastors to understand that when they copy others, they are denying the Holy Spirit the opportunity to develop the style God has only for him and a style that flows with one's calling and personality. People respond to reality in the Pastor's message, which lives in his life. The people can tell if one is real or not. They have discernment as well as do Pastors. To be "real" one must be true to himself, and when the Lord sees reality in the heart of a Pastor, He will use him in such a way that will bring true glory to God and fulfillment for the Pastor.

David is a classic example of being real and not using man's technique, as did Saul. Saul only knew man's way, but David, a young man with a heart after God's own heart, was real and understood God's way of doing things. Indeed today, such understanding is mentioned but rarely seen. Like David, we are all given a spiritual armor that best fits us, but when we try to fit in someone else's armor we become frustrated and hindered. David tried to fit into Saul's armor to face Goliath, but could not move. The armor of Saul speaks of the natural, man-made war provision, but David was a man of the Spirit and could not operate in any other way. Had he faced Goliath in Saul's armor, it would have been a snare that would have neutralized him and cause him to fail and be killed. He realized Saul's way was not God's way for him, and immediately David took it off and ran to fight Goliath in *"the name of the Lord" (1 Sam. 17:45)*. David's confidence was in God. David's victory is a lesson for all God's servants. **Put on the armor of the Lord, not the armor of men.**

Maranatha! The Lord Cometh!

CORRUPT WHAT CANNOT BE CURSED

The messages of the Seven Churches (***Rev. 2–3***) are both prophetic and literal, as seen in Church History. Every one of the Seven Churches (except Smyrna) gives a warning, a call to repentance, ***"he that hath an ear, let him hear what the Spirit is saying to the Churches" (Rev. 2:29),*** and hope if obeyed.

The Seven messages were given by the Lord Jesus Himself to alert the Church through the ages of impending dangers. The Lord gave the Apostles an earlier warning with the Parable of the Mustard Seed in ***Matthew 13:32*** and the ***"birds of the air."*** The tree is the Church and the birds are Satan's emissaries who want to lodge under the tree to get in the Church stealthily, and slowly, and create havoc and trouble.

The danger to the Church is so great and severe that Paul uses the term ***"perilous times" (2 Tim. 3:1)*** to describe how terrible things will be in the last days. The word perilous (*chalepos* in Greek) means **fierce and furious**[8]**, with the intent of weakening the Church's strength in the battle of** *"contending for the Faith once delivered to the saints" (Jude 3).*

THE PASTOR'S PEN

While all of the Seven Churches have a message, there is one particular Church whose message shows the subtlety of the enemy in contriving a plan to circumvent God's word. It is the third Church the Lord speaks to which is the Church of Pergamos *(Rev. 2:12)*.

"Pergamos," symbolizes the uniting of the world and the Church in an ungodly union in the last days. It is a marriage that brings **MIXTURE** into an unsuspecting Church. Daniel prophesied of this mixture *(Dan. 2:41–43)* of the last days when He interprets Nebuchadnezzar's dream of the statue. Today we are seeing a mixture that is froth with subtle danger. It is everywhere we turn: in the Church and in the world's culture.

The message of separation for the believer needs to be heard once again *(2 Cor.6:14–17)*, *"come out from among them, and be ye separate, saith the Lord."* Separation is from the world, and where the division occurs is at the Cross. Separation separates us from death unto life and causes people, who were joined together or mixed, to no longer be joined of mixed. Spiritual separation forms a boundary of withdrawal from what was (a life of sin) to what God now wants (a life of holiness). Jesus said, *"Suppose ye that I am come to give peace on earth? I tell you, Nay; but rather division" (Luke 12:51).* The Church has no common ground with a world that hates our Lord and crucified Him *(John 15:18; 1 Cor.2:8)*.

Mixture is dangerous as seen in the Church of Pergamos, who so enraged the Lord Jesus, that He calls them to repent or He will judge them with a two-edged sword *(Rev. 2:16)*. He is especially angry at the Pergamos Church for allowing and tolerating two false doctrines in their midst. The doctrine of Balaam *(v. 14)*, and the doctrine of the Nicolaitanes *(v. 15)*, which Jesus hated.

In this article we will deal with one of them, the doctrine of Balaam.

The story is in Numbers, chapters 22–25. As ministers we are all aware of the story of Balaam, the soothsayer *(Josh. 13:22),* and Balak, the king of Moab, who hired Balaam to curse Israel. But the Lord intervened and would not allow Balaam to curse Israel because Israel was blessed of God and **no one can curse what God has blessed.**

Being a covetous man *(Jude 11),* Balaam fretted over the loss of the silver and gold Balak was going to give him. In a short time after arriving home, Balaam came up with a very sinister plan of **corrupting the children of Israel, since he could not curse them,** so that Lord would bring judgment on Israel. The plan pleased Balak and Balaam would get his "rewards of divination."

The plan was to invite the young men of Israel to come to an evening party and "MIX" with the young girls of Moab *(Num. 25:1–15, 31:16).* This led to debauchery and Israel committing idolatry by worshipping their gods *(25:2).* Without realizing it, *"Israel joined himself unto Baal-peor: and the anger of the Lord was kindled against Israel" (25:3).* This brought the judgment of God on Israel causing twenty-four thousand to die *(25:9).*

The devil is using the same tactic of **mixture** today in the Church, and without realizing it, the Church is copying the ways and techniques of the world. We do not operate by the ingenuity and methods of the world but *"by My Spirit saith the Lord" (Zech. 4:6).* The world has nothing to offer us. It is spiritually dead and the Church is spiritually alive with the power of God. There is no place for a mixture of the world with the Church.

Sadly, the Church is being deceived into believing that using the ways of the world will fill our pews. While many Churches have increased their attendance, where is Jesus in all of this? We have a message the world does not want. It is the message of His Cross, which is the power of God *(1 Cor. 1:18)*. The Cross is rejected by the world as it points to dying to self, of which the world wants no part.

In many circles, Churches are justifying the means by the end results, which will lead to mixing with the world and ending up in corruption. While Satan cannot curse the Christian or the Church, he can corrupt the Church and keep her from fulfilling her destiny and receiving God's best. **Pergamos is a warning to Pentecost.**

Maranatha! The Lord Cometh!

FROM DECEPTION TO CORRUPTION

The Apostle Paul warns the Church of a tactic the enemy uses against the Church, which is to first beguile (deceive) the Church then corrupt it *(2 Cor. 11:3).* This is the method he used in Eden and continues to use because of its effectiveness. This article will focus on the following three paradigms that ultimately will lead to the state of the end time Church.

The first example is the Garden of Eden, which was created for man to live happily on the earth. The Lord's first command was given to Adam *(Gen. 2:16, 17)* not to eat of the Tree of the Knowledge of Good and Evil. Adam disobeyed and fell. From Adam's Fall to Moses, men lived by conscience, until the Ten Commandments, which were given for the purpose of protecting Israel from the world's corruption. To help us understand Satan's methods, we go to the Word that shows how Satan works **gradually** to deceive and corrupt.

It all **begins with something good from God** as with the Garden of Eden. It was good and beautiful and created for man's enjoyment. However, Satan enters Eden and deceives Eve *(1 Tim. 2:14),* which led to corrupting her and Adam, knowing the end result would be the removal from the Garden. This is Satan's pattern. Wait for God to give His people something good, and then corrupt it so the Lord will have to destroy it.

The second example is **the Law**, which the Lord gave to Israel. The Law *"is holy . . . and good" (Rom. 7:12)*. It contained truth and was meant to develop a national relationship with His people. Eventually, Israel turned to idolatry and lost God's glory *(Ezek. 11:23),* leading to the Seventy Years of Captivity. After returning from the Captivity, the Israelites decided to avoid repeating the sins of their fathers, so not to come under judgment again. This was a meaningful step for Israel, but gradually, over the years, Satan took advantage of Israel's zeal and deceived them through their religious leaders, which would lead to **legalism.**

When Jesus began His ministry of the Kingdom of God and spiritual freedom *(Luke 4:18),* He was brought in direct confrontation with the religious leaders who promoted legalism *(Matt. 23).* Jesus constantly clashed with the leaders over legalism because He saw how they used legalism to lord over God's people and bring them into spiritual bondage. Legalism became the corruption of the Law, which Jesus had to abolish *(Eph. 2:15).* In place of legalism, Jesus gave His followers a New Covenant that would never be corrupted, for it is founded on the Blood of Jesus and *"The gates of Hell shall not prevail"* against the Spirit-filled Church to corrupt her *(Matt. 16:18).* Since Satan corrupted the Law via legalism, he and legalism had to be destroyed.

Satan is not omniscient, but he knew that one day he would have to confront Jesus, *"And I will put enmity between thee and the woman, and between thy seed and her seed; it shall bruise they head and thou shalt bruise His heel" (Genesis 3:15).* Several translations use the word **"crush"** instead of bruise Satan's head. Satan tried to kill Jesus beginning when Jesus was an infant. Had Satan known that the cross would destroy him, he would never have used the Cross as the instrument to kill Jesus.

Jesus was brought to judgment in Pilate's hall *(John 18:28)* and Satan would also be brought to judgment *(John 16:11).* The following are two translations that show this in ***John 16:11: "About judgment, because the ruler (prince) of this world (Satan) is judged and condemned and sentence already is passed upon him"*** (AMP). *"and in regard to judgment, because the prince of this world now stands condemned"* (NIV).

Jesus fulfilled that sentence at the Cross, where He crushed Satan's head and destroyed him. When Jesus cried on the Cross, *"It is finished" (John 19:30),* it included the *"end of sins" (Dan. 9:24),* and the end of the author of sin-Satan who was judged, condemned, and sentenced to be destroyed at the Cross. The crushing of Satan's head *(Gen. 3:15)* **"was fulfilled in the first instance at the cross, but will culminate when the triumphant Christ casts Satan into the Lake of Fire"** *(Rev. 20:10)* *(New Defender's Study Bible).*[9]

How would Jesus destroy Satan? *Hebrews 2:14* says*, "through death he* (Jesus) *might destroy him* (Satan) *that had the power of death, that is, the devil." Colossians 2:14–15* says that **Jesus nailed the handwriting of ordinances that was against us to His Cross. At the same time by His crucifixion, Jesus, in the Spirit, nailed Satan to the Cross when He spoiled the evil principalities and powers, and made a shew of them openly, triumphing over them in it (the Cross).** Jesus nailed all the things that were against us to the Cross including sin, Satan, disease, corrupt ordinances, legalism, and He abolished death *(2 Tim. 1:10).* Then on the Day of Pentecost, Jesus gave birth to the Church, His Body, with a New Covenant. Hence, Satan hates the Cross, because it is where Jesus destroyed him. **Hallelujah!**

The third and last example is the New Testament Church. Jesus warned the Disciples in the Parable of the Mustard Seed *(Matt. 13:31, 32),* of the *"birds,"* which represents Satan, and who will lodge under the branches of the Kingdom of Heaven, which is the Church. In this parable, we again see Satan's regular method of deception and corruption of the Church.

This corruption has led to the deception of numerous denominations becoming one in a universal Church. This universal Church will eventually identify with the false prophet *(Rev. 13:11–16),* having been corrupted by Satan to abandon the *"Faith . . . once delivered to the saints" (Jude 3).* Sadly, the universal Church has no place for the Lord of Glory and His Church.

The Word of God shows the abominable state of the universal Church. It *"has a name that it lives but is dead" (Rev. 3:1)* and has become *"the habitation of devils,"* and it is *"a cage of every unclean and hateful bird" (Rev. 18:2).*

The question now is how did the Church of today arrive to such a state? The answer is that the Church has been deceived and corrupted by the wiles of Satan, in forsaking the foundation laid by the Lord Jesus Christ and the Apostles *(Eph. 2:20–22; 1 Cor. 3:11).* However, the Lord always has a remnant. They are the Pentecostal and Evangelical Church, whose power and influence Satan still seeks to **neutralize.** However, we must understand that in the midst of the spiritual battle we are fighting, **Pentecost is the last hope for the Church of today.** At any cost, we must remain faithful to the message and the power of Pentecost, as we are commanded to hold fast to what God has entrusted to us *(Rev. 3:11).*

Maranatha! The Lord Cometh!

"THE TWO CONTRASTS IN THE CHURCH"

There are many believers today, who find themselves bewildered at what they see happening in the Church, especially the Pentecostal Church. A silent struggle has developed between those whose spiritual foundation was built on the Second Generation of Pentecost, which is the **first contrast**. Then we have the **second contrast,** which is the Third Generation, who are zealous in wanting change in the Church. The First Generation is not considered a contrast; **it is the pattern** for the other two generations.

The three generations of Pentecost are: (1) the First Generation, which refers to the days of Azusa; (2) the Second Generation, which refers to the children of the First Generation; (3) and the Third Generation, the present younger Pentecostals.

The First Contrast has to do with the Second Generation of Pentecostals, who are today's seniors, and trying to find direction and a sense of belonging with the changing events in the Church. Then, you have the second contrast made up of the new Third Generation of Pentecostals, whose motive is honorable and sincere, yet removed from the spiritual needs of the seniors. While it is true the Church provides programs for the seniors, as outings, gatherings and other activities, it doesn't satisfy the longing of their heart to once again experience Pentecost, as they once knew it.

The Third Generation really doesn't want to be a problem, nor cause problems within the Church. They only desire change to be more contemporary, with the hope of being relevant to today's culture in reaching the lost. However, the changes they aspire to, run contrary to the heart of the Second Generation, who experienced the power and glory of the First Generation.

The First Generation of Pentecostals experienced the outpouring of the Spirit at the Azusa Street revival in 1906–1909. The Second Generation, obviously are the children of the First Generation, is today made up of Senior Pentecostals. Now we have entered the Third Generation of Pentecostals *(Judg. 2:10),* with the new contemporary emphasis, which is leading the way in penetrating the world's culture. This all sounds good until you look at the dissension it has created within the Church. This brings us to the question, **"How are we to reconcile the zeal of today's youth, with the severe changes they are introducing in our Churches?"** The strain has brought on concerns as to the direction of the Church, and the feeling that we are losing the Pentecostal message and experience. Sadly, many in the Pentecostal Churches have become frustrated and feel they are not being heard with their concerns. Many also feel that the young leaders of today operate on a corporate level, more as CEO's (Chief Executive Officer) than as Pastors, and want their Churches basically to be filled with young families.

Consequently, many seniors feel the young leaders don't care if the older people leave the Church. The sad part is that some of the young Pastors, caught up in this new trend, have told the older saints that if they can't handle the new changes, they should consider finding another Church to attend. Sadly, many of the Second Generation have scattered and no longer attend a Pentecostal Church. They left brokenhearted, as they were the ones who paid the price with fasting and prayer to keep the faith and message of Pentecost for the next generation. Their hope was to pass on the Pentecostal torch that was given to them to the Third Generation. As a result, some of the older saints chose to leave, while others stayed, as painful as it is in their thinking, and are willing to tolerate the new trend because they don't know where to go.

A concern of the Second Generation is that the Church is increasingly moving further and further from Pentecost to Evangelicalism, with less emphasis on Pentecost. It seems that the emphasis on evangelism has over taken Pentecost. Of course, we are not anti-evangelism, but evangelism is secondary, not primary. Thus, the strain between the Two Contrasts becomes increasingly more obvious.

The priorities in ***Mark 3:14*** show where we are to keep our focus, ***"And He ordained twelve, that they should be with Him*** (first of importance), ***and*** (second of importance) ***that he might send them forth to preach."*** First and foremost comes our personal relationship with the Lord Jesus Christ, by spending time with Him, and waiting on Him in prayer and worship daily. After this comes the second directive when He sent them forth to preach.

Jesus is always to have the ***"pre-eminence" (Col. 1:18)***, which means to have first place. The Church of Ephesus ***(Rev. 2:2–7)*** teaches that evangelism, good works, and sound doctrine are all good, but not first. Works have their place, but not at the expense of losing our first love for Christ.

There are a number of issues that have become complex and distressing in the Church. Among the issues is the **change of music** in the services. Recently, a Pastor told his congregation to get used to contemporary music because it is staying. As a result, many left that Church with heavy hearts.

The **casual dress** has become another issue that has offended many, especially when they see Church leaders serving communion with shirttails hanging out of their back trousers. When Joseph was called to Pharaoh's court, he was first taken to the baths from prison, and then properly dressed for his presentation before Pharaoh *(Gen. 41:14).* Aaron also serves as another example with proper dress when in the presence of God. He was directed by God how to dress when entering the Holy of Holies *(Exod. 28:1–5).*

Ezekiel 42:13–14 further shows that during the Millennium, the priests are to wear garments specifically set aside when ministering to the Lord. The priests were not permitted to wear street clothes, when going into the holy place and God's presence to minister to the Lord. Worship clothes and street clothes were to be separated. After ministering to the Lord, then the priests were permitted to wear *"those things which are for the people,"* or street clothes. These examples tell us that **our personal dress code reflects how much we respect the person we are visiting.**

Another issue, which is unbelievable, has to do with **entertainment** in the House of God. There are Pentecostal Churches that invite comedians and jugglers to entertain the congregation in the sanctuary during a Sunday morning service. These are a couple of issues, but there are more that show why many have left their Churches.

What is the answer? Genuine repentance and a return to the altar. *Jeremiah 6:16,* is a verse that stands between the two contrasts, *"Thus saith the LORD, Stand ye in the ways, and see, and ask for the old paths, where is the good way, and walk therein, and ye shall find rest for your souls"* or a negative response, *"But they said, We will not walk therein."*

Maranatha! The Lord Cometh!

"THE BURDEN OF THE LORD"

We have noticed that many words with meaning for the spiritual life are becoming increasingly absent. Consequently, we are losing expressions that once helped us to understand spiritual meanings. We have allowed the world to limit and change our vocabulary in their effort to have us be part of the one world mentality.

The one word the Church has lost is the word *"burden,"* in relation to *"the burden of the Lord."* There are six references for the word *"burden"* in the Old Testament, which are all located in the Book of Jeremiah *(Jer. 23:33–40).* There are seven references to *"burden"* in the New Testament, of which one relates to a spiritual burden. The words of Jesus, *"My yoke is easy and my burden is light" (Matt. 11:30),* has reference to discipleship in daily living, and deals with the challenges of life that believers experience in an evil world.

The words, the *"burden of the Lord,"* was greatly misused and ridiculed by the false prophets scoffing Jeremiah. The true prophets used the words, *"the Burden of the Lord,"* as a means of identifying with the burden of God for His people. It also expressed the weight and responsibility of God's Word that was constantly on the hearts of the true prophets. The misuse of the words *"burden of the*

Lord," by the false prophets, was their way of mocking the true worship of God and the sacred things instituted by Moses. The words, *"the burden of the Lord,"* in themselves, are fine, but the sacrilegious attitude of the false prophets and the people was blasphemous before God as seen by the scoffers who mocked Jeremiah by asking, *"What is the Burden of the Lord?" (Jer. 23:33)*.

The believers today can expect the scorn of the world as Jeremiah experienced. Peter warned the Church when he said, *"Knowing this first, that there shall come in the last days scoffers, walking after their own lusts, And saying, Where is the promise of His coming?" (2 Peter 3:3,4)*. In Jeremiah's day they mocked with the words, *"What is the burden of the Lord?"* Today, the scoffers mock with the words, *"Where is the promise of His coming?"* Judgment did come as prophesied by Jeremiah, and so will the Lord come as He promised and as the Church proclaims.

What is the burden of the Lord? **It is the very heartbeat of God and His concern for the spiritual state of His people and in particular, the Church**. Seldom do we ever hear the words, **"the heartbeat of God."** Why is that? It is because many believers are now taken up with the affairs of this life and have lost their sensitivity to the voice of the Spirit of God.

When we speak of the heartbeat of God, it takes us to John, the Beloved Apostle, who **leaned on the breast of Jesus** *(John 13:23).* John is the first of whom it says he leaned on the breast of Jesus and there he could feel and hear the heartbeat of the Lord. Though we cannot lean on Jesus in the physical, as did John, we can lean on Jesus in the Spirit by faith. The privilege of leaning on Jesus is still real to anyone willing to wait on the Lord and stay in His presence.

An interesting point is when John leaned on Jesus at the Last Supper, the Lord gave him the insight of identifying the traitor. The heartbeat of God opens insights of truth to those who lean on Him.

The **burden bearer** will be a man of prayer, who has his ear open to the voice of the Spirit. God is always searching for burden bearers, especially Pastors and Leaders, who are willing to identify with the burden of the Lord, in behalf of His people. *"For the eyes of the Lord run to and fro throughout the whole earth, to show himself strong in the behalf of them whose heart is perfect towards Him" (2 Chron. 16:9).* **Our concern in this life is to be concerned with what concerns God, His business, just as Jesus said,** *"Wist ye not that I must be about My Father's business?" (Luke 2:49)*

An example of carrying *"the burden of the Lord"* is the High Priest Aaron, whose duty it was to daily carry the Breast Plate on his chest, which had the twelve names of the Tribes of Israel inscribed on it. Aaron carried the burden of Israel in prayer as High Priest.

If ever the Church needed intercessory prayer, it is today. The Church needs ministers to carry the burden of the Lord in light of the last days, and the spiritual trauma the Church is experiencing. While it is true God's heart is grieved over the state of the world, His burden is not the world, it is the Church. Jesus said, *"I pray not for the world, but for them which thou hast given me; for they are thine" (John 17:9).* The condition of the Church today is the result of becoming neutralized by forces, within and without the Church. As Pastors and Leaders, we are to discern erroneous teachings and teach our people to stand on the Word, and to test what they hear by the Word of God as did the Bereans *(Acts 17:11).*

*"**The Burden of the Lord**"* is the mind of the Spirit *(Rom. 8:26–27).* Joel was a Burden Bearer of the Lord, and calls us to *"Blow the trumpet, . . . assemble the elders. Let the priests* (Pastors), *the ministers of the LORD, weep between the porch and the altar, and let them say, Spare Thy people, O LORD" (Joel 2:15–18).*

The Church needs Pastors and Ministers, who are willing to put aside the temporal things for the eternal things and are willing to stand in the gap for their congregation, by carrying *"the Burden of the Lord."* **It is a privilege to carry** *"the Burden of the Lord!"* **In that day He will say to you,** *"Well done, thou good and faithful servant! (Matt. 25:21)*

Maranatha! The Lord Cometh!

"THE JOB PRINCIPLE"

We are all familiar with the story of Job and his trials, for it is written in the oldest book in the Bible, the Book of Job. The Lord had blessed Job greatly with a wonderful family of ten children, a great household, and herds of livestock, making him the richest man among all the men of the east *(Job 1:3).* He was highly esteemed and served as the senior councilor of the city as well as being a member of the governing body. He had a positive influence far and wide *(Job: 29:7–10, 21, 25)* and was recognized as a role model.

Job was a righteous man with a vibrant relationship with the Lord *(Job 29:5).* In gratitude for God's blessings, Job ministered to the less fortunate, by sharing his abundance with the needy *(Job 29:12–17).* Job deeply feared God but was concerned for the future *(Job 3:25)* because of his blessings. What he feared came upon him. Job's experience is a lesson to us not to fear, *"God hath not given us the spirit of fear; but of power, and of love, and of a sound mind" (2 Tim. 1:7).*

Job had no idea the adverse events that would come upon him suddenly and change his entire life. He didn't know nor understand the reason for these terrible events until he came to the end of the Book. He had no way of knowing he was the central figure in a challenge by Satan to God, and he was written in God's Word to encourage God's people through the centuries.

We can learn of the Lord's workings from Job's personal experience. One of the points is that the Lord doesn't always tell us our future in advance, only that we are to live by faith. What we do know is the Lord has all in control and whatever He brings our way is always in our best interests.

What makes Job's handling the test so outstanding is the fact that he didn't have a Bible for comfort, nor someone to encourage him. He went through it all alone on faith and hope, as seen in his statement, *"I know that my Redeemer liveth" (Job. 19:25),* meaning, **the Lord has been true to me all these years, and now that I am tested, I will not blame Him nor fault Him, but will confess Him as my Redeemer who lives forever.**

The scripture says, *"In all this Job sinned not, nor charged God foolishly" (Job 1:22).* These words are **Job's Principle,** though he never entitled it as such. Job's principle is to praise the Lord in spite of circumstances, and to trust the **"integrity of God"** to bring you through whatever trial you are in. All God's servants go through difficult times but must learn to stand on God's Word to bring them out victoriously.

If you find yourself in darkness and not sensing God's presence, remember Job's words, *"Behold, I go forward, but He is not there; and backward, but I cannot perceive Him: On the left hand, where He doeth work, but I cannot behold him: he hideth Himself on the right hand, that I cannot see him: BUT He knoweth the way that I take: when He hath tried me, I shall come forth as gold" (Job 23:8–10).*

Like Job, hold steady and wait for the Lord to come to your rescue. Light will come for the Lord said, *"Unto the upright there ariseth light in darkness" (Ps. 112:4).* Job further said, *"when by his light I walked through darkness" (Job 29:3).*

We have an instrument Job did not have-**the written Word of God** and in Isaiah we have a word from the Lord to help us overcome any trial. Apparently, Isaiah also experienced abandonment and the silence of God and wrote, *"Who is among you . . . that walketh in darkness and hath no light? let him trust in the Name of the LORD, and stay upon his God" (Isa. 50:10).* To stay on God means to believe God and stay or stand in faith on the faithfulness of God, that He will not forsake us. He will come and say to you, *"behold, it is I" (Isa. 52:6).* Meaning, this test is from Me. *"It is I,"* who is behind this trial for a reason. These are the same words Jesus spoke to the Disciples when they thought they would drown, *"Be of good cheer; IT IS I; be not afraid" (Matt. 14:27).*

While Job did not understand why these things happened, he did come into a deeper understanding of God at the end of his test and said, *"I have heard of thee by the hearing of the ear: but now mine eye seeth thee" (Job 42:5).* If we remain faithful to the Lord, He will reward us with a revelation of Himself we never had before. Let us learn from Job's Principle, to continue in faith and praise to the Lord and not find fault with His ways.

Maranatha! The Lord Cometh!

"LOSING JESUS"

It is difficult to think a believer could ever lose Jesus. This statement has nothing to do with backsliding, but only with the reality that believers, and even Pastors, can lose Jesus for various reasons.

It all begins with the fact that by virtue of our new birth in Christ, we are related to Jesus. As our Savior, He has made us sons and daughters of God. Since we are the sons and daughters of God *(2 Cor. 6:18),* it means that Jesus, also the Son of God, has made us His brothers and sisters in Christ.

As we look in scripture, we discover it is possible to know and love Jesus, as did Mary and Joseph, and yet loose Him temporarily *(Luke 2: 41–49),* as they did for three days. Today we can lose Him for a longer period of time without realizing it. The message here is that we are related to Jesus and yet for various reasons can lose Him. As Christians, we are **the most unlikely people** to lose Him and yet we do. Pastors and Ministers especially, must be aware of this threat, because it will show up in one's preaching and demeanor. People, like sheep, are sensitive to their shepherd-Pastor, and can discern if something is different with the Pastor.

Mary and Joseph lost Jesus at the **most unlikely time**, during the annual Passover, which is really all about Jesus, the Lamb of God. Christmas is an example of an unlikely time to lose Jesus, but many Christians have become so taken up with the fanfare of Christmas that they have forgotten Jesus, who is Christmas.

Mary and Joseph also lost Jesus at the **most unlikely place,** Jerusalem, the City of God, where God's people came to worship the Lord. It was easy to be taken up with *"kinsfolk and acquaintance" (v. 44)* during the great Feast of Passover. In our daily living, **busyness is a threat and a thief.** It is a kleptomaniac that robs us of God's blessing. In many of our conferences, it is easy to be taken up with so many activities that we lose the true meaning of why we have gathered together. All our meetings should center on Jesus, who is *"preeminent" (Col. 1:18).* Not only is He the central figure of the Seven Churches *(Rev. 1:13)* but must always be the center of all our meetings.

Mary and Joseph took Jesus for granted by *"supposing Him to have been in the company" (Luke 2:44).* This shows how they lost Him; they assumed Jesus was with them. In life and especially the spiritual life, we must not assume anything but always be diligent, alert and thankful and not take the Lord for granted.

Joseph and Mary were unaware they had lost Jesus until the next day. Up to that point, everything seemed normal but Jesus was missing! Finally, they realized their loss. Ministers especially, must pause and ask themselves, **"Have I lost God's touch on my life? Am I were Jesus wants me to be? Have I lost the vision? Are my priorities in place?" These are important questions as we face the most challenging times today.** When one loses Jesus, what is he to do? Follow Mary and Joseph's example and go back to where they began.

Billy Graham's secret was that he never wavered from where he began. He stayed on the same course and calling of God that God gave him from the very beginning of his ministry. He had no aspirations in expanding his ministry to draw attention to himself. Paul speaks of this truth with Titus *(2 Cor. 8:6)* who remained faithful to God's call and didn't alter from it.

Mary and Joseph sought Jesus among their kinsfolk and acquaintances. When one loses Jesus, people turn to programs and works to find Jesus, which have their place, but are not the answer. Mary and Joseph did not find Jesus among the kinfolk and acquaintance (programs etc.). They retraced their steps and went back to where they lost Him, which was at Jerusalem and the Temple. They now are seeking Him in Jerusalem and are closer to where they will find Him, in the House of God, the Temple.

It took three days to find Jesus. It is easier to keep what you have, than to lose it and try to regain it. People don't realize the value of what they have until they lose it. Where will you find Jesus? In Church, where Mary and Joseph found Him, and that is where you will find Him.

Maranatha! The Lord Cometh!

THE CURSE OF THE THORNS AND THE FIR TREE

"Instead of the thorn shall come up the fir tree"
Isaiah 55:13

Once again we find ourselves commemorating Christmas in what has become the most wonderful time of the year. At this joyful time, we as ministers are always challenged to seek the Lord for a fresh word of truth and insight into the miracle of Christ's Virgin Birth.

While we all know Jesus was not born on December 25th, yet we rejoice that He was born, and that the world still takes time to remember His birth. Yes, there are abuses of Christmas, but for the believer it affords a wonderful opportunity to share the message of ***"good tidings" (Luke 2:10),*** as did the angels to the Shepherds. The ***"good tidings,"*** spoken by the angel were in reference to the long wait for the Redeemer who finally arrived after four thousand years of waiting for the fulfilling of God's promise to Adam and Eve *(Gen. 3:15).*

Adam and Eve's fall brought severe consequences to mankind. Yet, it is noteworthy to read the Lord's words to Adam after his fall. The Lord told him in ***Genesis 3:18,***

THE PASTOR'S PEN

"Thorns also and thistles shall it bring forth to thee." The curse of the thorn has been with man ever since that day.

As a result of man's Fall, a redeemer and a remedy must be found for man or he will spend eternity in Hell. In the heart and mind of God, the answer was the Cross. But because crucifixion was not yet used widely by any nation, the Lord waited for the fullness of time for the birth of His Son and also the development of crucifixion under the Roman Empire.

Crucifixion requires a tree, and as we look into the Word of God, there are many trees mentioned, but the one mentioned with prophetic significance is the fir tree. It is a member of the pine family and the only tree the Lord speaks to on a number of occasions in the Old Testament. From the Historic and Poetic books, to the Major and Minor prophets, we find it has a meaningful purpose in prophecy.

The characteristics of the Fir Tree fit the requirement for crucifixion. It is strong enough to hold a man without it breaking and also soft enough to prevent nails from bending when hammered into the hands and feet of the victim. Thus, it is most likely Jesus was crucified on a Fir Tree, which has great spiritual significance for the Church that has been overlooked.

The Fir Tree is a type of the cross. This is the message of ***Isaiah 55:13*** when he prophesied, ***"Instead of the thorn shall come up the fir tree."*** In other words, instead of the curse of the thorn of ***Genesis 3:18,*** condemning and accusing man, the Cross shall come up and stand between redeemed man and the curse of the thorn. The Cross will remove all condemnation to the child of God! It will also free man from the bondage of living under the thorn's curse. The Cross took away forever the curse of the thorn!

As we look back at Eden, God's perfect Garden, with its array of beautiful trees and flowers beyond human imagination, we notice there aren't any thorns in Eden. The thorns appeared as judgment after Adam's Fall, which not only brought judgment on Adam and his posterity but also on all creation, including animals, trees, and vegetation *(Rom. 8:22–23)*. Everything on earth went into a condemned state. Sin destroyed Eden.

Now, to restore what sin did to God's creation and man, it required someone strong enough to confront the perpetrator of sin and evil, namely Satan. But who qualifies to take on such an enormous challenge since all mankind is condemned under sin and in bondage to Satan as a result of the Fall?

This is the predicament facing man and is addressed in *Revelations 5:1–7,* with the answer for man, *"The Lion of the Tribe of Juda, the Root of David, hath prevailed!"* who is this One who qualifies? He is the slain Lamb in the midst of the throne of God *(Rev. 5:8)*. Out of all creation, He alone qualifies to go in man's behalf. But how will the Lamb defeat the Serpent? By the secret weapon of the Cross, made of the Fir Tree. He will come into the world as a Babe, grow up into manhood, and then aggressively attack the kingdom of the devil.

What will it cost Him? His life, for He must die to win, which is true for all of us as ministers of the Gospel. To identify with Christ, we must also be willing to go the way of the Calvary Road, which is self-denial and dying to self. He must increase in our lives and we must decrease. The ego is our worst enemy. This principle is seen in

Hebrews 2:14, "That through death He might destroy him that had the power of death, that is the devil."

In this deadly battle with sin, the Lord Jesus dismantles the kingdom of darkness by His death. References to the Fir Tree in scripture show the tearing down Satan's dominion one by one by the death of Christ. This article shows just one of a number of strongholds Jesus dismantled by His death on the Cross. It is the removing of the thorn curse of ***Genesis 3:18.***

The tearing down of the thorn curse begins with the Roman soldiers platting a crown of thorns and putting in on the head of Jesus. Little did they realize the impact their act would have on the kingdom of darkness. This act said, "We now put man's curse on Christ, the Redeemer, who will carry it to the Fir Tree which is the Cross, where it will die with Him."

At the Cross He will remove the curse of Adam forever. Man brought this curse on all mankind and man (soldiers), laid it on the head of the Redeemer to have it removed forever. Notice Isaiah's prophecy of the role of the Fir Tree, ***"Instead of the thorn shall come up the Fir Tree" (Isa. 55:13).***

As we must look into the Old Testament we find a man, who, out of his death triumphed victoriously and thus is a type of Christ's death and victory. This man didn't know he was a type of Christ's death and victory, but God did! From man's perspective, this particular individual appeared to be a failure just as Jesus also appeared to be a failure in the eyes of the people of Jerusalem. **How wrong man is in his rationalizations and misses God!** It will be through this man's death that we discover how Jesus dismantled Satan's throne. **Hallelujah!**

Who is this mysterious man serving as a type of Christ? It is none other than Samson, who is the type of Christ's death and victory *(Judg. 16).* Through Samson we see Jesus destroying Satan. Samson is like Jesus in that Samson gave his life to destroy the Philistines and Jesus gave His life to destroy Satan and his kingdom of darkness. This may be why Samson is in God's Hall of Fame in *Hebrews 11*.

Let us look at the type being fulfilled. The emphasis leading to the destruction of Satan begins with the Cross, Satan's enemy, because it was the Cross that destroyed Satan. It was the Cross that dismantled the house of Satan and brought its pillars down.

Just as the Lord has pillars in His kingdom as wisdom and her seven pillars *(Prov. 9:1),* so Satan copied the Lord and built pillars on which he built his throne. His pillars are man's fear of death *(Heb. 2:14, 15);* the hopelessness of an afterlife *(1 Cor. 15:19);* the bondage of sin *(Rom. 6:22);* and Satan's guile and deception *(2 Cor. 11:3,14).* These pillars held up Satan's throne.

The house where the Philistines made sport, had pillars where the lords of the Philistines sat among the best seats *(Jud. 16:27).* Satan sat on his throne with pillars in Hell. As the Philistines gave praise to their god Dagon *(v. 23)* for Samson's captivity, and proclaimed Dagon stronger than Jehovah, even so, when Jesus was crucified and in Hell for three days, the demons of Hell praised Satan in thinking he was stronger than Jesus. How wrong they were!

Samson's right hand and his left hand, pressing against the pillars holding up the house of the Philistines speaks of Christ's right hand and left hand stretched out on the Cross. Samson pushed with his two hands on those pillars holding up the house, causing the house to come crashing down and killing three thousand Philistines. So, with Jesus, by His death and outstretched out hands on the Cross brought down the house of Satan and destroyed it forever *(Heb. 2:14).* Samson, by his death destroyed the house of Dagon; Jesus by His death destroyed the house of Satan!

The house fell on Samson and killed him, but not so with Jesus. Satan could not destroy Jesus for Jesus was sinless. All Satan could do to Jesus was *"bruise"* His heel with death, but Jesus, the stronger man, crushed Satan's head! *"He will crush your head, and you will strike his heel" (Gen. 3:15, NIV).* The Resurrection completed the finished work of Redemption! The Cross brought down the kingdom of darkness.

Revelations 22:3 says, "And there shall be no more curse" because Jesus died for us and overcame the devil. In the place of the curse will be the memory of the power of the Cross and its victory. Now, the Cross is seen as the Fir Tree in *(Isa. 55:13)* and will be with us throughout eternity as a reminder of Christ's battle with Satan and the victory of the Cross.

This is the message of *Isaiah 55:13,* for the Cross removed the curse and we will forever and everlastingly glory in the Cross! So, now when one looks at a Christmas Tree, we can understand its message of the Cross dismantling Satan's kingdom. **To God be all the glory for He is worthy!**

Maranatha! The Lord Cometh!

AN UNFORGETTABLE CHRISTMAS SEASON SERVICE

At one of our monthly Church Board Meetings prior to Christmas, we discussed if we should still have our regular Wednesday evening service since Christmas Eve would be on Thursday, the very next day. We always have a Christmas Eve Service. The Board asked what I thought about it, as many if not all of our local Churches, canceled their regular mid-week service since Christmas Eve was the next day and they were planning a Christmas Eve service. My reply was that I felt we should go on with the Wednesday service and whoever came, came. The men felt the same so we went on with the Wednesday evening service as scheduled.

On Wednesday, as the people were gathering for the service, I wondered how many would attend the service since we were coming back on Thursday for the Christmas Eve service. To my joy, we had a wonderful turn out.

The service began with our Music Director leading our singing and worship with Christmas carols. Suddenly, as we were singing and worshipping, we became aware of a strong sense of the Presence of the Lord that entered the sanctuary. It was so strong, it caused me to sit up in my chair and look at the congregation from the pulpit to see if they sensed what I sensed. They did, for I could tell by their faces that they were serious and alert and looking around as if it were to try and see this invisible Presence.

The music director was done and about to sit down when I intercepted him, and told him to continue singing as I felt this is what the Lord wanted, so we continue to worship and sing. Shortly thereafter, he again turned the service to me and I went to the lectern to minister on the Book of Revelation, which we had been studying for several weeks. But I was unable to proceed more than just about three minutes. I had to stop and say to the people, "This is not the time to speak on Revelation, I can't continue. Let me speak to you on the Christmas message." I spoke for about twenty minutes and stopped.

Still under the influence of the Presence of God, I asked the people to stand and join hands across the aisles. To this day, I do not know what they heard, or whether the Lord caused them to hear something other than what I said, I just don't know. All I know is that instead of joining hands, the entire congregation, 100 percent, in unison moved forward to the altar. I said to myself, "What are they doing, I didn't tell them to come to the altar, I told them to join hands across the aisle. But their coming to the altar is better." Though puzzled, I was thrilled for what was happening.

The Presence of the Lord was so strong that all we could do was to stand still and silent at the altar in awe of His Presence. Some stood and others kneeled with up raised hands. Then suddenly, the Spirit fell on the organist in a mighty way. She stood up, and under the anointing of the Holy Spirit began to sing Mary's "Magnificat" without notes. It was beautiful and real.

As we were in this state, the children in the Royal Rangers and Missionettes, had concluded their services and were coming for their parents in the sanctuary which brought the service to a close, but not without favorable comments as to how wonderful the service was to the Lord's glory.

Upon arriving home we received a phone call from our daughter and her husband, who lived seven hundred miles away. We told her about the service and how the Lord met us. She said, "O, Mom and Dad, I wish we were there as we didn't have service tonight. It was canceled because of service tomorrow evening." As I turned the phone to my wife so she could continue speaking with her, the Lord spoke to me and said, **"Tonight, I wanted to attend Church and saw your Church lights on and your doors open, so *I CAME AND HONORED YOU WITH MY PRESENCE!"***

From that day on, we always kept our Church doors open and our lights on for service. We didn't know when Jesus would return for another visit, but we were determined not to miss Him, nor did we want Him to find the Church doors closed and the lights out.

Friends, the Lord makes periodic visits to Churches. He comes to be among His people to see what is going on in their Church. He wants to see if the Church is still maintaining *"the faith which was once delivered to the saints" (Jude 3).* This is the faith He left to the Church through the Apostles.

How many times, the Lord has come down to visit a Church and the doors were closed and the lights were out and He had to pass it by. When services are unnecessarily canceled there is a danger of missing God. The day you chose to close a service could have been the very day He planned to visit your Church. How sad and tragic and what a loss. O, dear friends, how the Lord Jesus loves to join us in Church and worship to sing praises to the Father, *"I will declare thy name unto my brethren, in the midst of the Church will I sing praise unto thee" (Heb. 2:12).*

But if the doors are closed and the lights are out, He won't sit there and wait. He will move on to the next Church whose doors are open and lights are on. Only Heaven knows how many Churches have missed the Lord through negligence, when He wanted to visit them with His Presence.

Without realizing it, we honored Him by keeping the Church open, and He in turn honored us, by coming to our service and manifesting His Presence.

I close with these words,

"Tonight, I wanted to attend Church and saw your Church lights on and your doors open, so *I CAME AND HONORED YOU WITH MY PRESENCE!"*

Maranatha! The Lord Cometh!

"MINISTERING TO THE LORD"

We are living in the last days. Consequently, we find ourselves very busy in caring for our families, and also with Church demands. Among the areas of ministry in the Church demanding time is the emphasis today in Christendom to provide for the poor. The history of the Church has always been charitable; however, we must not view giving to the poor as dominant. Giving to the poor is noble and wonderful, but scripturally there is an issue that precedes giving to the poor. The lesson is similar to the message of the Church of Ephesus. They did everything right except they lost their first love for the Lord. We can also do all goods deeds, including giving to the poor, but have lost ministering to the Lord. Christ must have the pre-eminence over all of us and over all our lives *(Col. 1:18)*.

Mary of Bethany: Mary, the sister of Martha, knew the importance of ministering first to the Lord. When Mary took the costly pound of ointment of spikenard and proceeded to anoint the feet of Jesus, Judas criticized her and used the poor as an excuse for his greed. Jesus in turn rebuked him and said, *"Let her alone . . . For the poor always ye have with you; but me ye have not always" (John 12:3–8).* The message is clear, that while it is good to minister to the poor, who are always with us, it is far more important to minister first to Jesus. Then after we have ministered to Him, we can minister to the poor and others. As ministers and leaders of the Church, called of the Lord, we must stay focused on our priorities and relationship with Christ.

Without realizing it, Mary is a lesson in showing us what it means to go beyond daily living for the Lord. She did something out of her heart that wasn't required, and her act of love in anointing the Lord deeply touched the heart of the Lord. The people in the house saw what she did, but they did not understand **why** she did it. But Jesus understood why, and was moved by it. Her love was motivated deep within her heart, not knowing the Lord would soon die. ***"She hath done what she could" (Mark 14:8)*** for the Lord, who in turn showed His gratitude in saying, ***"Wheresoever this Gospel shall be preached in the whole world, there shall also this, that this woman hath done, be told for a memorial of her" (Matt. 26:13).*** When we do something for the Lord from our heart, beyond what is expected and without a hidden agenda other than honoring and ministering to the Lord, it will bring His favor into your life.

Walter Beuttler: God always looks for and finds men and women who desire to do something extraordinary for Him, *" For the eyes of the Lord run to and fro throughout the whole earth, to show Himself strong in behalf of them whose heart is perfect toward Him" (2 Chron. 16:9).* One such man was Walter Beuttler, a man of the Spirit. He taught at our Assembly of God Bible School many things of the Spirit that he learned by his own experience of waiting on God. He told us the story of how he felt moved to set the clock at 3 a.m. so he would get up early to wait before the Lord. He told the Lord, **"Lord, You are up, but everyone here is asleep and I did not want you to be alone in the middle of the night so I have come to sit with you for awhile,"** which he did often. What an effect his early rising had on his life and ministry! It is seen by the tremendous anointing the Lord put on him in teaching and preaching. His anointing was so strong that he was sought after all over the world. **When you do for God, God will do for you!**

David: This principle of wanting to do for God is also seen in David, who one day, while sitting in his house, felt a desire in his heart *(2 Sam. 7:2, 3)* to build God a house for the Ark of the Covenant. He shared his thoughts with Nathan, the prophet. God was so touched by David's concern for the Ark, that He sent Nathan that night to tell David, He would build David a house that will be forever *(2 Sam. 7:13).* This is another example of the Lord returning greater to us than we do for Him. It all began with one man, David, who wanted to do something for God because of His love for the Lord. David's act was ministry to the Lord. We minister to the Lord regularly, without realizing it, but there will always be an opportunity to do something special for the Lord.

The early Church Ministering to the Lord: In *Acts 13:1–2,* the Church leaders gathered together to minister to the Lord. Their gathering was an example of what ministry means to the Lord. He longs to see His people gather together with the purpose of seeking His face. The Lord especially looks, when His people gather in His house, the Church, for prayer and fasting. God always responds to His people when they earnestly seek Him. This is when the supernatural happens. It is very important for God's people to learn how to wait and tarry in the presence of the Lord, as did the early believers in the Upper Room *(Acts 1:13–14)*.

Ministering to the Lord begins with worship and waiting on God. Many Christians find themselves wondering, what is waiting on God? **Waiting on God is to be silent and still in His presence**—*"Be still, and know that I Am God" (Ps. 46:10)*—**and just wait.** When Adam walked with God, they spoke with each other but did not speak continually, as God taught Adam to spend time waiting in God's Presence. It's much like Moses, who silently gazed on God while on the Mount for forty days and when he came down the Mount was filled with the glory of God on his face. That was the effect of being still in the Lord's Presence.

An example is a good restaurant "waiter" who rarely talks to the guests. He waits on them to see if they are in need of something. As a good waiter waits, we should give God time in His Presence. To minister is to be still before the Lord. When Aaron went into the Holy of Holies, he was silent and stood before the Lord reverently. Let us learn the value of ministering to the Lord in the Spirit.

Maranatha! The Lord Cometh!

"FAITHFUL TO THE VISION"
PART 1

The Church is a prophetic body with a vision of the reality and purposes of God. As the Body of Christ, the Church is to see what the world can't see, and her mission is to proclaim what she sees to a world steeped in darkness and deception. The Church is the only Light the world sees and we are their only hope of truth and warning for future events. But if the Church has lost her vision, not only is the world in jeopardy, but so is the Church.

In such times as we are living in these last days, it is imperative for the Church to be alert to the conniving works of the enemy. The Apostle Paul was keenly aware of the subtle activity of the devil, whose intent is to divert the Church from her calling and her heavenly vision. When Paul boldly gave his confession of faith to King Aprippa, he told him, *"I was not disobedient unto the heavenly vision" (Acts 26:19).* As a minister of God, the fire of Paul's vision burned in his soul. As a result, Paul constantly warned the Church of the dangers of questionable men, whom Paul called grievous wolves *(Acts 20:28–31).* These men spoke of perverse things that were not of God and they themselves were perverse, whose objective was to dominate the Church. These dangers began with the birth of the Church and will continue to exist until Jesus comes.

Paul gives further warning of the subtleness of the enemy, ***"But I fear, lest by any means, as the serpent beguiled Eve through his subtlity, so your minds should be corrupted from the simplicity that is in Christ"(2 Cor. 11:3).*** As we move closer to the coming of the Lord, the Church finds herself under spiritual conflict. Like Paul, we must cherish our ***"vision"*** of truth, so we can ***"earnestly contend for the faith which was once delivered unto the saints" (Jude 3).***

Moses cherished his "vision," from the time of the Burning Bush throughout his entire life ***(Heb. 11:23–29).*** Moses may have thought he lost everything when he killed the Egyptian and fled from Pharaoh. He felt as though he failed God and his people. Later in life it is said of him that, ***"he endured, as seeing Him who is invisible" (Heb. 11:27).*** The word ***"seeing"*** in this phrase means to gaze and to look on God. Moses gazed on God when he was alone with God in His glory and presence. Moses never lost his vision for he ***"verily was faithful in all His house, as a servant" (Heb. 3:5).***

Whatever would draw away from God's best for ministry must be rid of. As Ministers, with the call of God on our lives, we must not exchange vision in place of being drawn to the things of this world in order to achieve a better life style. Our vision is too important to be in involved with things of the world that will blur our vision.

Vision not only affects individuals but also Churches. The state of many Churches indicates the Church has unknowingly lost its vision and direction. Sadly, they have turned their ear to the influence of the world instead of being a light led by their vision. In many areas the Church is allowing our culture to neutralize the Church and ultimately steal our vision.

Another area of concern has to do with "goals." We cannot operate on the premise of goals, as does the world. Goals are fine in the business sector but not in the spirit realm. Businesses operate with their own technique tested over time and it works well for them. However, the Church operates differently. The Church is a living organism, led by the inspiration of the Holy Spirit, whom we can't see, but depend upon for His directions by *"a still small voice" (1 Kings 19:12).* On the other hand, the business world operates on a lifeless organizational system. The danger of goals in the Church is when well-meaning Church members infiltrate the Church with ideas not of God, and will cause the Church to lose her vision.

It behooves us to cherish our vision, as there are signs indicating **the Church in general has lost her vision that has led to losing the passion for Her Soon Coming Bridegroom.** The Spirit will find a people, who have not forsaken the vision of the early Church and are waiting for the Bridegroom.

"And the Spirit and the Bride say, Come" (Rev. 22:17).

And Jesus replies, *"Surely I come quickly!" (Rev. 22:20)*

Maranatha! The Lord Cometh!

"FAITHFUL TO THE VISION"
PART 2

The incredible story of the birth of Samuel brought hope to Israel, at a time when the people of God had fallen into lethargy since the days of the Judges. The events surrounding the life of Samuel and his family have the markings of God that would unfold in time. God found in the child Samuel the future makings of a man, whose destiny was carved by the hands of God. In time he would be needed for the purposes of God, and would bring back the voice of God to the people of God. Samuel would be God's faithful instrument to penetrate the spiritual darkness hovering over his people and to restore Israel.

The times of Samuel are noted in **1 Samuel 3:1, "there was no open vision."** In those days it meant, there was no voice of God, no oracle or prophet for revelation, who would have a quickened word for God's people in those times. Contact with Jehovah was scarce in those days until the Lord raised up Samuel. Ever since the passing away of Joshua and his generation with the elders, **"there arose another generation after them, which knew not the LORD, nor yet the works which He had done for Israel" (Judg. 2:10).** The results were the loss of vision for the next generation following Joshua, until years later when Samuel came on the scene and became the voice of God.

Why was there no open vision in Israel, in light of their great miracles and deliverance's from Egypt, and the conquering of the Land of Promise? It goes to show how an individual, a people, or a denomination can have an illustrious history but in time lose their way by negligence and carelessness. There was no open vision in Israel because of their failure as seen in the book of Judges until 1 Samuel 3. Throughout the time of the Judges *"there was no king in Israel, but every man did that which was right in his own eyes" (Judg. 17:6).*

Apparently, the people neglected the Word of God given by Moses, which is the Pentateuch. Those who continue to neglect God's Word will find themselves in great loss. His Word is still *"a lamp unto my feet, and a light unto my path" (Ps. 119:105).* The path of God will faithfully lead the child of God into the ways of God.

There are two very important points to consider. First, *"there was no king in Israel,"* indicating the people forgot the Lord and took Him for granted. However, the Lord remained faithful as their King, and never left them, although they put the Lord aside.

Secondly, *"every man did that which was right in his own eyes."* They were brazen and defiant. Thus, individualism set in, causing them to be self-assertive. Consequently, Israel's spiritual state declined gradually and worsened to the point that, *"the word of the LORD was precious in those days; there was no open vision" (1 Sam. 3:1).*

Spiritual vision is necessary and important in the realm of faith and truth. Vision is more than seeing with the natural eye. We are born with two sets of eyes, one for our earthly affairs, and the other for our spiritual life.

Spiritual vision is inspired by the Holy Spirit, who gives us insight into the things of God so we can understand the ways of God *(1 Cor. 2:9–16)*.

Paul said he was not disobedient to the heavenly vision, for he was faithful to the reality of his salvation experience. It affected him throughout his entire life, for the vision of Christ quickens us by the Spirit.

To understand the vision of Christ, we must go to the following scriptures:

(1) ***Isaiah 61:1–3 and Luke 4:18,*** the vision of Christ became a reality when He entered the Synagogue and spoke the words of ***Luke 4:18.*** (2) The words Jesus spoke at the Synagogue are similar to those spoken by Jesus at Paul's conversion *(Acts 26:18).* (3) The words of Christ when He commissioned the Church to fulfill the Great Commission *(Matt. 28:16–20).* These scriptures define to us the meaning of **the vision and burden of Christ.**

The Lord gives visions for many purposes and uses His people as His vessels to convey His message. The Lord will give visions to our sons and daughters, who in turn will minister to the Body of Christ, with visions and prophecies *(Acts 2:17–18).* The Lord uses visions as He deems necessary to touch lives.

The above examples contain the foundation for vision in Christ. All vision must originate in the Spirit of Christ, who sends revelation of truth as needed. Vision is the revelation of Christ, in order to minister to a need in the Body of Christ or for a blessing to the Church. ***Jude 3*** prophesied his vision to the Church today when he wrote, ***"It was needful for me to write unto you, and exhort you that ye should earnestly contend for the faith which was once delivered unto the saints."*** The Body of Christ desperately needs vision and prophecy today in order to maintain the burden of the Lord, as part of our heritage and ministry.

The Old Testament version of "vision" served its purpose via the prophets until Jesus came. Then, when Jesus came, He gave the Body of Christ a new understanding of "vision," founded on His words and beyond the Old Testament vision, which served in its time. When Jesus came, He made all things new, including the vision of His heart in ***Hebrews 1:1–2: "God, who at sundry times and in divers manners spake in time past unto the fathers by the prophets, Hath in these last days spoken unto us by His Son."***

The Spirit of Jesus is the Spirit of prophecy so that vision and prophecy go together for, ***"The testimony of Jesus is the Spirit of prophecy" (Rev. 19:10).*** As one with Christ and as a child of God, we all have His Spirit of prophecy, which includes His "VISION."

So important is the understanding of the burden and vision of Christ, that Jesus spent forty days after His Resurrection with the Apostles, teaching them, ***"the things pertaining to the Kingdom of God" (Acts 1:1–3).*** The teachings of Christ during those forty days became known as "the Apostle's doctrine" *(Acts 2:42).*

The vision of Christ includes, **Salvation by faith in Christ; Water Baptism by immersion; Baptism of the Holy Ghost with speaking in tongues; Praying over the sick and anointing them with oil in the Name of the Lord; and the Great Commission of teaching all nations to observe all things Jesus commanded the Apostles and the Church.**

Maranatha! The Lord Cometh!

"THE SEVENTH CHURCH"

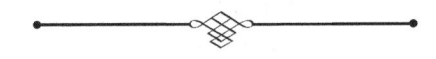

It is important to see and identify the transition from one Church era to another. Each contributes to the others, with the hope that each Church over the years would bring blessings into the Church. Sadly, it did not transpire as was hoped. The error occurred after the Apostles and the Early Fathers of the faith passed away. It was then that ambitious men began to put their hands to the "Ark," instead of letting God fulfill His plan and purpose. Consequently, man's hand pulled the Church down from what God wanted the Church to be, as recorded in Church History. The Church was always meant to be a perpetual Glorious Body, with a Glorious Message of hope, life and light, for a hopeless world in darkness.

The hope was built on the Lord Jesus Christ, the Chief corner stone *(Eph. 2:20)* and began with the Resurrection, followed by the Ascension of Jesus. Then there followed the forty days in which the Lord was alone with the Apostles, teaching them ***"of the things pertaining to the Kingdom of God" (Acts 1:3).*** Then Pentecost followed and the Church was immediately born, when they were all filled with the Holy Ghost and spoke in tongues (glossolalia) as the Spirit gave them utterance, and the three thousand souls were immediately baptized in one day ***(Acts***

2:41). In the beginning, there was only one Church under the auspices of the Apostles, located in Jerusalem. Form, direction and order were necessary to protect the Church in its infant state.

As we look at the history of the Seven Churches, we discover their individual messages were meant for the good of all the Seven Churches, then and now. Other than the Church of Smyrna, the Church of Philadelphia, which is the Sixth Church, was the only Church that fulfilled its role. The first worldwide revival was birthed on the Day of Pentecost *(Acts 2)*. Thereafter, the Church declined gradually, until the worldwide Pentecostal revival came under the Church of Philadelphia in the twentieth century. We still see wonderful pockets of revival around the world, but we also see decline in the Church. However, the Lord still has a faithful remnant in spite of the decline of the Church.

The Church of Laodicea has now taken the place of the Church of Philadelphia as seen in **Revelations 3:14–22**, which indicates the state of the Laodicean Church today. Based on **Revelations 3:17**, the Church's emphasis appeared to be one of materialism and financial riches. The Church of Laodicea was increased with goods and did not have need of anything. Today's Church is in the same state. The Laodicean Church is the last Church.

The Church's emphasis today should be the urgency of the Coming of the Lord and the need to awaken the Church to its realization. We are at the end of time and it behooves the Church and Ministers, to focus on the Coming of the Lord as it was during the days of the Church of Philadelphia. The emphasis should be on preparing God's people for the Lord's Return.

The Pastor's Pen

The Seven Messages given to the Seven Churches by Christ are relevant for our times. The Seven messages constitute warnings and blessings for our benefit. If we will heed His messages and accept His warnings, there will be hope and restoration. If not, there will be spiritual loss.

The importance of the Seventh Church is its significant message for today's Churches. The warnings remain valid and foreboding. The outward condition of the Laodicean Church appeared healthy but in truth, its condition was the worst of the Seven Churches.

The Lord's concern for the Laodicean Church was their spiritual state *(Rev. 3:15–17),* as they were neither cold nor hot, but were lukewarm. This necessitated the Lord to deal severely with them and to *"spue"* them out of His mouth.

The Lord's further concern was their blindness *(Rev. 3:17),* though they thought otherwise. Their prosperity failed to reveal their true state. Here, the Laodiceans lost their way and their eyes became blurred. As a result of mingling with the world, they were in a perilous predicament. The Church did not realize her danger, as she had a divided heart between the world and the Church. Now, confronted by the very words of Christ, they were brought to a place of decision. The message for the Church today is to alert God's people to the times in which we live, lest we also will fall into a snare, as did the Laodiceans. The Church has been called since its birth to separate from the world. In fact, throughout Scripture, both in the Old and the New Testament, God's people have constantly been warned by the Lord and the prophets to live a separate life from that of the world.

We are to use the world but not abuse it *(1 Cor. 7:31)*. This means that as humans, living in a cursed world that is under the judgment of God, we must learn to use the world for our physical needs, but we are to remember that while we are in the world, we are not of the world. **"Whosoever therefore will be a friend of the world is the enemy of God" (James 4:4).**

As a result, we must remove ourselves as much as possible from the influences of the world that cater to the urges of the flesh, and place our emphasis on the spiritual *(1 Cor. 2:12–14),* especially in light of the Soon Return of Christ. **"For all that is in the world, the lust of the flesh, and the lust of the eyes, and the pride of life, is not of the Father, but is of the world" (1 John 2:16).** If we do not remove ourselves from the world's system, the world will corrupt the Church.

As Believers we must now deal with attitude and begin to strip ourselves, by God's help, of self-righteousness, pride, arrogance, haughtiness, conceit, pompousness, which come gradually as a result of success in ministry or business. Riches and prosperity have their place, but they are not our emphasis, as they can lead to the danger of materialism.

While there may be worldwide troubles ahead, yet, as God's people and the last Church, let us **"look up, and lift up your heads; for your redemption draweth nigh" (Luke 21:28).** For the present day Church has never been as close to the Return of Christ as it is today. The Church of Philadelphia fulfilled its role, now the Laodicean Church must do the same. The Church's emphasis is for God's people to be ready for the Coming of the Lord, **"and unto them that look for him shall He appear the**

second time without sin unto salvation" (Heb. 9:28). That's how close we are to His Return!
"Even so, come, Lord Jesus" (Rev. 22:20).

Maranatha! The Lord Cometh!

"PERILOUS TIMES"

The present time speaks to us of the Perilous times and the scripture unveils what is taking place today and shows the secrets of the difficult times in which we are living. The attitudes of our time are now an open door for the evil one in our country, to destroy our present generation, namely the youth. Today's generation is described by the Bible story of the demoniac of the Gadarenes *(Luke 8:26–39)*. Unclean spirits can possess an individual and a generation as seen in *Matthew 12:43–45*, where Jesus describes *"this wicked generation."* We must also know that the evil one feeds on people via their habits. This shows why children must be taught the truths of the Word of the Lord.

In 1963, the Supreme Court removed Bible reading from public schools, which opened the door for unclean spirits to enter the school system. The Lord was no longer welcomed in our schools and when the Lord left, the unclean spirits entered more wicked than before. The school system was *"empty, swept, and garnished" (Matt. 12:43–45)*. The seeds of rebellion had been sown and began to appear with the Hippie Movement and Woodstock. The youth of today do not realize the serious state of this generation.

It took forty years for the evil to work through one generation into the present generation, whom the enemy has conditioned to accept the anti-Christ. Consequently, our youth are paying a price in their lives. In the last days, demonic activity is out to destroy our youth, for a generation can be demon possessed. To better understand what is happening, we must go to *2 Timothy 3:1-4,* where Paul describes what to expect in the last days. In the story of the demoniac of Gadara *(Matt. 8:28),* the word *"fierce"* is connected with Paul's word *"perilous" in 2 Timothy 3:1*.

In the Greek, the word *chalepos* means **"FIERCE"**[10]. Daniel also referred to the anti-Christ *(Dan. 8:23)* and called it *"fierce."* The passage in Timothy is also to show the results of the devil who infects our present generation.

2 Timothy 3:2: the emphasis on Self-Love and self-image.

2 Timothy 3:3: corrupt society and dishonesty.

2 Timothy 3:4: hedonism, *"Traitors, heady, high minded, lovers of pleasures more than lovers of God."*

2 Timothy 3:5 "Having a form of godliness, but denying the power thereof (the Holy Ghost): *from such turn away."* Form of religion and formal religion.

2 Timothy 3:7: deception of new doctrines and spiritual blindness.

2 Timothy 3:8: rebellion and the resistance in God's house.

2 Timothy 3:11-12: persecution of Church *(Mark 13:9-10).*

We also must recognize the serious State of the Churches. In the last days the evil one has infiltrated our Churches. The increase of demoniac activity is to destroy the Church, for the enemy works to possess Churches *(1 Tim. 4:1)*. The enemy said, *"Let us take to ourselves the houses of God in possession" (Ps. 83:12)* and the entire passage speaks of the oppression by the enemies of the Church *(Ps. 83:1–18)*. *Matthew 12:39* refers to the **present generation**. *Matthew 12:41* refers to the **past generations**. *Matthew 12:43–45* speaks of any generation forsaking God's laws.

The enemies said, *"Come and let us cut them off from being a nation* (the Church*); that the name of Israel* (the Church*) may be no more in remembrance. For they have consulted together with one consent: they are confederate against thee* (us*)" (Ps. 83:4–5)*. The Church must be alert at all times, because the enemy constantly attacks the Church. The enemy wants to control the Christian Churches. The Church is in spiritual warfare with constant hostilities. The challenge for the Church is as Jesus said, *"When the Son of man cometh, shall he find faith on the earth?" (Luke 18:8; Jude 3)* This is where the Church is today, and it needs Jesus as the answer, for only Christ can break every fetter and bondage existing today.

"Truth is fallen in the street"
Isaiah 59:14

Maranatha! The Lord Cometh!

"SPEECH, THOUGHT, AND MOTIVE"

Christians in general struggle to know the most important qualities for a child of God. With the many voices on Christian television emphasizing various aspects of truth, it becomes very perplexing to say the least. In the pursuit of sorting things out, the Christian finds himself confronted by spiritual forces seeking to steer him away from truth in order to confuse him. The enemy's goal is to steal, kill and ultimately to destroy a child of God any way possible. The conflict is in the mind where the enemy attacks to influence one's **speech, thoughts, and motives.** These three words are very important for it is in these three areas where the child of God struggles.

The first area we want to look at is the area of speech. Jesus warned of the danger of misused speech in *Matthew 15:18*, when He said, *"those things which proceed out of the mouth . . . defile the man." James 3:2* connects the character of a man with his speech, *"If any man offend not in word, the same is a perfect man."* Speech exposes one's demeanor as well as one's character.

Carelessness in one's speech often happens when someone speaks negatively about another person. Even if what is said is true, that does not grant license to repeat it. Solomon said, *"It is the glory of God to conceal a thing" (Prov. 25:2),* not propagate it. The danger of propagating information is that it is more hurtful to the one who propagates it than to the one who is being discussed. Misguided speech is fertile ground for the devil to defile a child of God and hinder his spiritual life. A godly man once said, **"Others may — you cannot."**

Then there is the issue of **complaining speech**. The Israelites were notorious for complaining. *1 Corinthians 10:10* warns of the danger of murmuring. Repeatedly in the wilderness, Israel angered the Lord with their complaints *(Exod. 15:24, 16:2, 7; Num. 11:1)*. They didn't understand that the tests in the wilderness were to teach them principles of faith *(Heb. 3:15–19, 4:2)*. Instead, they gave themselves to complaining, which resulted in severe judgment. **They did not realize that finding fault with God and His ways constitutes judging God.**

As Christians and ministers, we face a great danger in the area of complaining because of the influence of the world's spirit of complaining infiltrating the Church and defiling many *(Heb. 12:15)*. We live in a day when personal rights are first and foremost in place of *"in honor preferring one another" (Rom. 12:10)*. The enemy knows the damage that can be done by negative speech and how it can stir great trouble among believers. He is also aware that negative speech can defile a whole body, and is a fire from hell *(James 3:6)*.

The next area of concern is in the mind, where the **battle of thoughts** occurs. The enemy goes from negative speech, which is spoken out, to thoughts that are kept hidden within one's mind until spoken. In these last days, on the very heels of the Lord's Return, with the goal of beating up on God's children, it appears the enemy is increasing his strategy of using blasphemy against the Lord in the mind of the believer.

He seeks to bring condemnation to the believer in making him feel he is guilty of initiating terrible thoughts about God. The devil is a liar and the child of God did not initiate such blasphemous thoughts. They originated in hell, not in the mind of the believer. The enemy uses blasphemous thoughts to incapacitate the child of God, and bind him in the lie of thinking he has now committed the unpardonable sin and is unworthy of God's favor. These are lies from hell.

Let us take Paul's admonition in *2 Corinthians 10:4–6, "For the weapons of our warfare are not carnal, but mighty through God to the pulling down of strong holds; Casting down imaginations, and every high thing that exalteth itself against the knowledge of God, and bringing into captivity every thought to the obedience of Christ."* He continues in *Phil. 4:7–8, "And the peace of God, which passeth all understanding, shall keep your hearts and minds through Jesus Christ. Finally, brethren, whatsoever things are true . . . honest . . . just . . . pure . . . lovely . . . of good report; if there be virtue, and if there be any praise, think on these things."*

We have a powerful weapon, *"the Blood of the Lamb and the Word of their* **(our)** *testimony."* It is the Blood of Jesus, or as our forefathers would say the pleading of the Blood of Jesus and our confession of our faith in Jesus that overcomes the devil *(Rev. 12:11)*.

Now the third area of concern is the matter of **motives**. Pure motive is where the real you lives and is the seat of honest attitude and behavior. Jesus addressed motives in the Sermon of the Mount *(Matt. 6)*. He said to do alms in secret; when you pray, pray in secret; when you fast, do it in secret. Obedience to these words will protect motives and intentions. The religious leaders did nothing in secret because their motives were to impress people and draw attention to themselves.

Motive can be used either way, for good or for bad. One honors God and the other honors man. There's nothing in between. Motive is where the split occurs between character and personality. There are ministers who have a charismatic personality but their character is questionable. Sadly, their objective is prominence and position. The call of God is second to them while promotion is first. To them servanthood is a means to an end and not the end in itself, which is to follow the Great Servant, Jesus Christ.

Matthew 7:21–23 shows that on Judgment Day, doing the will of God, along with truth and character, will be the criteria for eternal reward. Personality will be revealed as vanity. Many ministers will be exposed because they assumed the blessing of God as an indication of His approval instead of recognizing *"that the goodness of God leadeth thee to repentance?" (Rom. 2:4)* God blesses and uses a ministry because He called a man and gifted him, but then this man went astray. However, he continued ministering with results. One will say, "How can this be?" It is because the Lord honors His gifts in spite of an individual's failure. Paul said, *"the gifts and calling of God are without repentance" (Rom. 11:29).*

Saul is a good example. He was anointed of God to be king but disobeyed the Lord, yet the Lord still used him in prophecy *(1 Sam. 19:23–24)*. The Lord did not take away his anointing as king. The Lord does not take back what He gives. He deals with it in other ways. Then someone will ask, "Why does God still use such a man?" For His people's sake *"who are beloved for the fathers' sakes" (Rom. 11:28).*

Everything is governed by motive. The foundation of pure motive is the love of God. Paul said, *"For the love of Christ constraineth us" (2 Cor. 5:14).* Constrain means to arrest like a prisoner. His love is the dynamic that will keep us near to the heart of God, and it is this power of God's love that will help us grow in pure motive.

1 Corinthians 13 shows that love must always be our motive. One can have great works, as listed in verses 1–3, but they are meaningless unless the love for God is our motive. When Love is the motive, the end result is *"the glory of God" (1 Cor. 10:31).* Our works will be judged strictly on motive.

This is seen in the parable of the Widow's Mite *(Mark 12:41–44).* Her love for the Lord constrained her to give her utmost while the motive of the others was to receive recognition.

"And now abideth faith, hope, charity (love), these three; but the greatest of these is charity (love)" *(1 Cor. 13:13).* **Love is the greatest of the Three because** *"God is love" (1 John 4:8).*

Maranatha! The Lord Cometh!

PREPARING THE LAMB TO BE THE SHEPHERD

*G*od has a great desire for His people to know Him and not just be acquainted with Him. Since man is finite and limited, and the Lord who fills the universe is great and mighty, He endeavors to reveal His nature and character to His people through His many names. Each name has a meaning that reveals an aspect of His person, character and infiniteness.

So, God's Son, the Lord Jesus Christ, also wants us to know Him in a personal way as we know the Father. To accomplish this, He, too, has names that reveal His person and nature. However, since He is the Son of Man, He wants to identify with man in everyday life and to do this He has earthly occupations of men as carpenter, physician, and shepherd. By using these terms His intent is to help us to understand Him.

The one name we want to look at in this article is Jesus' role as Shepherd, which has its roots in the Old Testament. The Old Testament is all about Jesus. He is seen and referred to from Genesis to Malachi in prophecies, types, and metaphors that are fulfilled in the New Testament. The Old Testament is the shadow of these types and the

New Testament is the fulfillment of the types, which is called substance. The term substance refers to reality and by Jesus coming to earth in a tangible human body *(1 John 1:1),* we see reality.

The Father's plan is to exalt His Son by showing the many roles of Christ in His Word, which is comparable to Himself. The Father's love for Jesus is far greater than humans could ever imagine. Their relationship is boundless. So great is the Father's love for Jesus that His heart revolves around His Son. There isn't anything the Father would not do for Jesus *(John 16:23).* In fact, if we were to open the heart of God, we would find Jesus in its very center. In ***Revelations 5:6,*** John saw the center of God's Throne and in its midst he saw the Lamb. God's throne speaks of God's heart and in its center is Christ, the Lamb of God, slain from the foundation of the earth.

In the Old Testament, the Father is seen as the Shepherd *(Ps. 80:1)* of Israel in His love and care for them. Even so Jesus, whose heart is after the heart of His Father, wants to also be a shepherd just like His Father, and becomes our shepherd *(John 10).* **This helps identify the meaning of *"a man after God's own heart"* (Acts 13:22). This is one who loves the peoples of God as does the Father and the Lord Jesus, and as did David.**

Every boy wants to be like his father when he grows up, so Jesus wants to be just like His Father in every way and emulates the Father in everything the Father does. And the Father takes great delight in seeing Jesus following Him in all His ways. Jesus said, *"What He seeth the Father do . . . these also doeth the Son likewise" (John 5:19).* Like Father, like Son.

Because he wanted man to understand Him, God made man in His own image. Man, through his experience with his children, can understand how God feels about His only Begotten Son. The Father wants us to see how we interact with our children, how He interacts with His Son. We must keep in mind that simply because the Father and Son are perfect does not make their relationship bland. He treats His Son like earthly fathers treat their sons. This puts joy and purpose into their relationship, which is reflected in Jesus' many roles, but especially as shepherd.

In ***Psalm 80:1***, the Father is seen as the Shepherd, but in verse 17, reference is made to Jesus: ***"Let thy hand be upon the man of thy right hand (Jesus), upon the son of man whom thou madest strong for thyself."*** Now, the words, *"whom thou madest strong for thyself,"* have great significance.

This is telling us that even though Jesus is the Son of God and perfect, yet the Father is going develop His perfection by experience. The word "madest" in ***Psalm 80:17*** means, "to **prepare or shape.**"[11] Thus, the Father is going to arrange experiences throughout the Old Testament for Jesus that will facilitate His development. The Father is carefully observing and instructing Jesus in every detail of His life. If we may use the term, the Father did not spoil His Son. He trained and prepared Him in the presence of the angels. ***"The Lord God hath given me the tongue of the learned, that I should know how" (Isa. 50:4).*** The Father is teaching Him to *"know how."* Since Jesus is the Son of God and knows all things, then why did the Father have Jesus go through all of this? It was for our benefit, so **Jesus can identify with us**, because God is also working in us and preparing us for eternity.

Hebrews 12:6–11 speaks of God working in the lives of His children by chastening. The word "chastening" speaks of training up a child by instructing and nurturing,

THE PASTOR'S PEN

as well as disciplining when necessary. As earthly fathers train their children, so our heavenly Father trains and instructs us. To identify with us, Jesus submits to His Father's training, and though He never needs discipline, yet He understands by experience our training. As a result of His training He is one with us. The Lamb is being prepared by experience to be our shepherd

Even the children of kings and rulers must be trained for their roles in life, so the Father diligently prepared Jesus in the Old Testament for His role in the New Testament, which leads ultimately to His eternal role as *"KING OF KINGS and LORD OF LORDS!" (Rev. 19:16)*

Hebrews 5:8 says, "Though he were a Son, YET learned he obedience by the things which he suffered." **Even though He is God's Son and perfect with the nature of God, He still had to learn obedience and submission. Perfection does not exempt one from experience. It is experience that develops us to make us complete in Christ.**

In looking in the Old Testament we see the involvement of Jesus. The Son is going to be trained by experience, in preparation for His role as shepherd to the Church. *Isaiah 63:11–14* shows Jesus' involvement in the crossing of the Red Sea. The reference of *"the greatness of his strength" (Isa. 63:1)* corresponds to *Psalm 80:17: "whom thou madest strong for thyself."* These two verses show His training has made Him strong and ready.

In *Isaiah 63:11–14*, reference is made to Moses and the crossing of the Red Sea. *"He that brought them up out of the sea with the shepherd of his flock."* Though the inference of shepherd appears to be Moses, who is a type of Christ, it is really Jesus who is called shepherd here.

Jesus was there at the Red Sea when Israel crossed it and He led them through it *"by the right hand of Moses with his (Jesus') glorious arm, dividing the water before them, to make Himself an everlasting name?"* *(Isa. 63:12)* Moses was not making an everlasting name for himself.

This is the Lord Jesus who is all-glorious and comes in His glorious name *(Matt. 21:9).* This is all preparation for His role as shepherd for His New Testament people, His Church. The Church will experience spiritually the power and glory of the Lord as Israel experienced it physically.

There are several other experiences Jesus was involved with. One was when Jesus appeared with the three Hebrew children in the feiry furnace. Nebuchadnezzar threw three men into the furnace but when He looked in, he saw four men, and the Fourth looked like the Son of God

Another is when we read of Melchisedec, *"made like unto the Son of God,"* to whom Abraham paid tithes *(Heb. 7:3).* Melchisedec blessed Abraham *(Heb. 7:6)* the less. *"Abraham rejoiced to see my day: and he saw it, and was glad" (John 8:56).* Melchisedec was a manifestation of the Son of God to Abraham.

Another is in *Exodus 23:20,21* when God said, *"I will send an Angel before thee."* Angels are not addressed with capital letters, as seen here. This *"Angel"* is given power to forgive or not forgive transgressions: *"for my name is in Him".* The Father's name is the name of authority and This Angel is Jesus for He has His Father's name just like we have our earthly father's name. In *Matthew 9:6,* when Jesus healed the man of palsy, He exercised His right from the Father to forgive sin as He was given all judgment *(John 5:22).* Jesus forgave this man as the Son of God, and forgives as the Angel in *Exodus 23*, who is the Lord Jesus Christ.

These examples are all experiences of preparation for Jesus. As the Son of God, He went through this preparation in order to identify with us, showing how deeply He loves man. Even before Jesus came to earth, He identified with man in the Old Testament. God, the Father, prepared Him as He is preparing us to be a part of God's eternal plan for the ages to come. Our Great Shepherd, Jesus, is leading us through Red Seas and Fiery furnaces to bring us to our glorious Land of Promise. What a wonderful Savior is Jesus!

Maranatha! The Lord Cometh!

THE PASTOR'S JERUSALEM

Of the five Administrative Gifts in *Ephesians 4:11*, that of the Pastor has a special place in the Kingdom of God. The Pastor is the only one of the five administrative gifts called a shepherd. This makes the Pastoral call special because it identifies with the Good Shepherd, the Lord Jesus Christ.

Being a Pastor is a great privilege. The privilege of knowing that the Lord is working in your life as a Pastor (Shepherd) so you will follow the steps of the Good Shepherd, whom you represent. Many miss this truth. Often a Pastor goes through difficult times and becomes very discouraged in the ministry. His people may turn on him and criticize his preaching and everything he does or doesn't do. But if you study the life of Jesus, you will find an identity of your experiences aligning with Jesus' experiences.

As the Lord Jesus' trials began in Jerusalem, even so the Church you pastor is your Jerusalem. While the name Jerusalem means peace, it is also a city of controversy, as any Pastor will tell you by his experiences.

A study of the Apostles is certain to reveal a stereotype of people every Pastor has in his Church. In a local Church, there will always be a Peter, the outspoken and

THE PASTOR'S PEN

rambunctious type of person; a John and his brother James, who love the Pastor and will defend him (thunderous type) against unkind comments; a Thomas, who questions everything the Pastor says; a Philip, who encourages support for the Pastor; an Andrew, a man who loves prophecy; a Nathanael (Bartholomew) who is wary in his approach but willing to try things the Pastor says; Judas (not Iscariot), who appreciates the revelations of the Lord *(John 14:22);* Matthew (Levi), who joins and strongly supports the Pastor; James (son of Alphaeus), a quiet natured man who presents his ideas in a subtle way, either for or against the Pastor; Simon, a good listener who says little, but supports the Pastor. These character types and varied personalities among the Apostles are not dangerous though they may be trying for the Pastor, as they were for Jesus. These character types are found in every Church.

Often, there is the man who is the first to welcome you as the new Pastor. He will invite you to his home for dinner and seeks to become your close friend. He pretends to care for you and your family, but behind all his efforts to embrace you he has an agenda. His agenda is to have prominence in the Church by having an influential position or office. He is a man that over a few years you came to trust and with whom you may have shared your personal matters.

So it happens with Pastors; the man who raved over you when you came to the Church as pastor is now the man who is going to turn people against you to get you out. *Psalm 41:9 says, "Yea, mine own familiar friend, in whom I trusted, which did eat of my bread, hath lifted up his heel against me."*

Where does this all take place? It takes place within your local Jerusalem Church, where prophets are killed. The world did not crucify Jesus. His own people, the religious leaders of Judaism in Jerusalem, killed Him. The world will not crucify you. Your people will do it. For Pastors it may not be physical death, but it is a spiritual crucifixion in identifying with the Crucifixion of our Lord.

The ministry is God's way of doing a great work in the lives of His chosen Pastor servants. Pastors are especially blessed, as their Church becomes their personal Jerusalem, where they will experience in a small way what the Lord Jesus went through. **There is no better setting for a shepherd than that of a Church, to accomplish God's purpose in identifying with Christ, the Great Shepherd, in the fellowship of His sufferings.**

It is a great honor for a man, chosen by God, to be a Pastor. Do not seek a different calling, but be the shepherd He has called you to be in the place where He has put you. **If you will truly be a faithful servant of the Lord, your eternal reward will exceed your expectations.** Pastor, be thankful the Lord has called you to be one of His Pastors. Pastoring is a great calling to cherish and not despise. God does not seek results in your life because He is the One who gives results. He seeks faithfulness on your part.

God bless you dear Pastor, and remain true to the high calling you have received from the ***KING OF KINGS and LORD OF LORDS!***

Maranatha! The Lord Cometh!

Bibliography

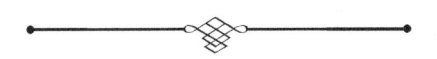

Cayne, Bernard S., and Lechner, Doris E.,eds. *The New Lexicon Webster's Dictionary of the English Language*. New York: Lexicon Publications, 1989, 1987.

Guralnik, David B., ed. *Webster's New World Dictionary*. New York: Simon and Schuster, 1984, 1970, 1972, 1974, 1976, 1978, 1979, 1980, 1982.

Morris, Dr. Henry M. *The New Defender's Study Bible, King James Version*. Nashville: World Publishing. 1995, 2006

Strong, James, LL.D., S.T.D. *The New Strong's Exhaustive Concordance of the Bible*. Nashville: Thomas Nelson Publishers, 1995, 1996.

Young, Robert. *Young's Analytical Concordance to the Bible*. Peabody: Hendrickson Publishers

End Notes

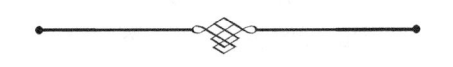

[1] Robert Young. *Young's Analytical Concordance to the Bible* (Peabody: Hendrickson Publishers). 1064

[2] James Strong, *The New Strong's Exhaustive Concordance of the Bible* (Nashville: Thomas Neslson Publisher, 1995, 1996), Greek Dictionary 50.

[3] James Strong, *The New Strong's Exhaustive Concordance of the Bible* (Nashville: Thomas Neslson Publisher, 1995, 1996), Greek Dictionary 59.

[4] Bernard S. Cayne and Doris E. Lechner, eds. *The New Lexicon Webster's Dictionary of the English Language*. (New York: Lexicon Publications 1989, 1987). 833

[5] James Strong, *The New Strong's Exhaustive Concordance of the Bible* (Nashville: Thomas Neslson Publisher, 1995, 1996), Hebrew and Aramaic Dictionary of the Old Testament 60.

[6] Bernard S. Cayne and Doris E. Lechner, eds. *The New Lexicon Webster's Dictionary of the English Language*. (New York: Lexicon Publications 1989, 1987). 604

[7] James Strong, *The New Strong's Exhaustive Concordance of the Bible* (Nashville: Thomas Neslson Publisher, 1995, 1996), Greek Dictionary 9.

[8] James Strong, *The New Strong's Exhaustive Concordance of the Bible* (Nashville: Thomas Neslson Publisher, 1995, 1996), Greek Dictionary 98.

[9] Dr. Henry M. Morris, *The New Defender's Study Bible* (Nashville: Word Publishing, 1995, 2006), Notes 21, 22.

[10] James Strong, *The New Strong's Exhaustive Concordance of the Bible* (Nashville: Thomas Neslson Publisher, 1995, 1996), Greek Dictionary 98.

[11] David B. Guralnik, ed. *Webster's New World Dictionary of the American Language.* (New York: Simon and Schuster, 1984, 1970, 1972, 1974, 1976, 1978, 1979, 1980, 1982). 849

CPSIA information can be obtained
at www.ICGtesting.com
Printed in the USA
BVHW04s0539190718
521989BV00007B/24/P

9 781545 632994